The Business of Death

LIBRARY OF INTERNATIONAL RELATIONS

The Business of Death:
Britain's arms trade at home and abroad

NEIL COOPER

Tauris Academic Studies
I.B.Tauris Publishers
LONDON · NEW YORK

Published in 1997 by Tauris Academic Studies
an imprint of I.B.Tauris & Co Ltd, Victoria House,
Bloomsbury Square, London WC1B 4DZ

175 Fifth Avenue, New York NY 10010

In the United States of America and in Canada distributed by
St Martin's Press, 175 Fifth Avenue, New York NY 10010

A full CIP record for this book is available from the British Library

A full CIP record for this book is available from the Library of
Congress

ISBN 1 85043 953 2

Library of Congress catalog card number: available

Set in Monotype Ehrhardt by Ewan Smith, London

Printed and bound in Great Britain by WBC Ltd, Bridgend,
Mid-Glamorgan

Contents

Tables

Figures

Acknowledgements

This book has had a long gestation period and there are many people who have contributed to its final delivery. These include John Groom, Dan Hiester and Stephen Chan, who helped guide it to its first manifestation as a PhD thesis. I also owe a debt to Lester Crook at I.B.Tauris, who commissioned the version published here and who has remained committed to it throughout the trials and tribulations of its birth. I would also like to thank all those who consented to be interviewed and gave not only their time but also their knowledge and insight.

The chapter on defence exports is an updated version of an article that originally appeared in *Contemporary Security Policy*. Both the editor, Stuart Croft, and the publishers, Frank Cass, have kindly given permission to use the article here. I would also like to express my gratitude to a variety of colleagues who have commented on the whole or parts of the book at various stages of its development. In particular, I would like to thank Alex Cunliffe, Phil Gummett, Mike Pugh, Ron Smith, Joanna Spear and Sue Willett. As ever, however, responsibility for any errors or misjudgements rests solely with the author.

Finally, I would like to thank my mother and father for the guidance and assistance I have received over the years and above all my partner, Ratna, for her patience and support – both practical and moral – during the development of this book.

Introduction

The aim of this book is to examine government policy towards the British arms trade from the accession of the first Thatcher administration in 1979 to the present day, especially the reform of the weapons acquisition process undertaken by successive Conservative administrations. In particular it focuses on the impact of the Ministry of Defence (MOD) competition policy, the approach adopted towards collaborative procurement, the restructuring of the European defence industrial base, and the expansion of support for defence exports that has occurred over the same period.

The essentials of the new approach to weapons procurement were outlined in 1983 in a paper entitled *Value for Money in Defence Equipment Procurement*.[1] Consequently, the reform of procurement is often dated from around the period 1983–5 and associated in particular with the former secretary of state for defence, Michael Heseltine, and the then chief of defence procurement (CDP), Sir Peter Levene, although it is suggested here that the genesis of the new approach occurred prior to the arrival of either at the MOD. As a consequence of the 1983 paper, the various initiatives introduced to reform procurement practice have come to be known as the 'value for money' policies and are referred to as such throughout the text.

The declared aim of the reforms has been to make the process of weapons acquisition more efficient, and a variety of initiatives have been introduced to this effect. These include reorganisation of the MOD, relocation of staff, initiatives to improve project management and the expression of weapons requirements in terms of performance criteria. However, the *core* reforms have been concerned largely with introducing market mechanisms into the procurement process, the aim being to replace the corporatism of the 1970s with the supposed efficiencies of the free market. At the heart of these core reforms has been the commitment to increase competition in the allocation of contracts. The reforms also include the virtual elimination of what are known as cost-plus contracts and the greater use of incentive contracts, a declared willingness to abandon the traditional protectionist approach to weapons procurement, privatisation, and a greater stress on the through-life cost of weapons. It is with the impact of these core reforms that this book is primarily concerned.

Chapter 1 attempts to place the value for money reforms in context by outlining the procurement philosophy of the 1970s and the waste and inefficiency that the reforms of the 1980s were intended to eliminate. Chapter 2 details the influences – both economic and political – that led to the reform of procurement policy in the early 1980s. It is argued that a combination of several factors acted to place the defence budget under strain in the early 1980s. These included the introduction of cash limits and the rising cost of weapons development which were partly responsible for a number of overspends against budget, of which that of 1980–1, and the consequent moratorium on the procurement of new equipment, was the most traumatic. This further increased the pressure to effect a change in procurement practice, pressure which persisted from the mid-1980s onwards as the budget for procurement expenditure was persistently reduced. However, it is also argued that the move to 'value for money' can only be properly understood if account is taken of the way in which the philosophy (albeit contradictory) of Thatcherism influenced the evolution of policy towards the British arms trade. Here it is suggested that the contradictions inherent in Thatcherism have been reflected in policy towards the arms trade. On the one hand, the commitment to the free market in Thatcherism implied an attack on the defence establishment with the introduction of competition and the adoption of a *laissez-faire* approach to the defence industrial base. On the other hand, the commitment to strong defence implied a continuation of the military-security bias that has been the hallmark of British foreign and defence policy. Thus, far from attacking the defence establishment, successive Conservative governments since 1979 maintained relatively high rates of defence expenditure, continued a broadly protectionist approach to weapons procurement (despite their rhetoric to the contrary) and actually intensified the support given to arms exports.

Chapters 3 to 7 concentrate on particular aspects of government policy towards the arms trade and the extent to which declared policy has actually been implemented. Whether the MOD's current approach to the arms trade has succeeded in making weapons procurement more efficient is also considered. Chapter 3 presents an analysis of the MOD's success in introducing competition. Here it is argued that while there has been a substantial rise in the proportion of new contracts let by competition, for a variety of reasons, the ministry's statistics exaggerate the actual level of competition in the procurement system as a whole. It is also noted that the UK defence industrial base (DIB) is characterised by an absence of competition in a number of key equipment sectors and that the competition initiative has been pursued in tandem with a protectionist procurement policy which has effectively diluted its impact.

Chapter 4 considers the effectiveness of the competition initiative, arguing that the substantial savings claimed as a result of competition are not only based on dubious methodology but also fail to take into account the costs of competition – both to the nation and to the MOD. It is also argued that there are various fraudulent or corrupt practices by which contractors can, and do, subvert the intended effects of competition – indeed, that the ministry's system of fraud prevention, detection and punishment is seriously flawed.

Chapter 5 considers the MOD's policy towards collaborative weapons procurement and the restructuring of the European defence industrial base. With respect to the former it will be noted that the logic of rising costs and finite budgets has led the ministry to increase its commitment to collaboration. On the question of the latter, it is argued that, like much of its approach to procurement, MOD policy is contradictory. On the one hand, it has declared its preference for an open European market in which procurement decisions are made on the basis of value for money; on the other hand, its current notion of such a market is heavily circumscribed by domestic industrial concerns. Even the UK's apparently principled rejection of a 'fortress Europe' approach to defence procurement has, in reality, more to do with the importance of the US market for British arms exporters. In addition, the Eurosceptic thrust of wider British policy towards Europe has meant the government has been consistently reluctant to contemplate the kind of institutional reforms that might presage the development of an open European defence market.

Chapter 6 examines policy towards defence exports. The expansion of defence exports may not immediately seem to have any link with the attempt to make domestic weapons procurement more efficient. However, whilst not central to the value for money reforms, the concern to maximise UK arms sales has been a consistent element of the new approach. Indeed, the original 1983 paper on value for money noted the need to take into account the marketability of equipment when determining their technical specifications. It also emphasised the fact that the longer production runs made possible by overseas orders can benefit the MOD through reductions in the unit cost of domestic equipment purchases.[2] In addition, ministers were always clear that one of the subsidiary benefits of the competition initiative would be the creation of a leaner and fitter defence sector, better able to compete in the global defence market. Indeed, the UK's apparent success in the world arms market is now cited by ministers and officials as evidence that the value for money reforms have indeed made the British defence industry (and by extension domestic procurement) more efficient.[3] However, Chapter 6 goes on to argue that the success of British defence exporters in raising their market share has more to do with the structure of decline in the global arms market than with the inherent efficiency of the British DIB. In addition, it is argued that the economic, military and political security benefits that the government claims arise from arms exports are questionable, to say the least. This is particularly the case when account is taken of the extent to which defence exports are subsidised by the State, and the unhealthy leverage over domestic and foreign policy issues increasingly exercised by Britain's major arms customers.

Chapter 7 considers the extent to which the MOD's value for money policies as a whole have produced greater efficiency in the weapons acquisition process. It suggests that, despite the government's claims to the contrary, inefficiency in procurement remains rife and on a conservative estimate is currently costing the MOD over £5 billion. In addition, the flaws in the procurement process mean that equipment often arrives chronically late and with its performance scaled down from that originally planned, commensurately reducing the effectiveness of the UK's military forces.

Finally, Chapter 8 summarises the arguments outlined in the previous chapters, and also notes that many of the problems in current acquisition policy stem either from a simple failure to apply long-recognised principles of procurement, or the MOD's reluctance to abandon costly procurement strategies such as its preference for protectionism. In addition, it is argued that the worst form of inefficiency in the weapons procurement process arises not from flaws in the way the MOD buys its weapons, but from the military security bias in UK foreign and defence policy. This continues to mandate relatively high levels of defence expenditure, protection for the defence industry and the maintenance of prestigious weapons programmes of dubious utility in a post-cold war security environment. Moreover, such policies have resulted in an imbalance between expenditure on defence and other forms of security promotion both at home and abroad which, it is argued, can generate greater returns both for the UK and for global security.

To my parents

The cost-plus, bottomless bucket gravy train

The Procurement Executive

The birth of the PE In October 1970 the government announced its intention to rationalise defence procurement[1] and a project team was formed under the leadership of Mr (now Lord) Derek Rayner (although most of its research was undertaken by Lawrence Wilson, an under-secretary in the Ministry of Defence). The project team was asked to consider 'how best to organise the integration of all defence research and development and procurement activities, under the responsibility of the Secretary of State for Defence'. It was also asked to 'pay particular regard to the need to meet essential defence and civil requirements in the most economical and efficient way'.[2]

In April 1971 a White Paper was published which contained the results of the team's deliberations; it recommended there should be a single organisation entitled the 'Procurement Executive' (PE) which would take over responsibility for the procurement of all war-like stores (this had previously been the domain of either the services or the Ministry of Technology/Aviation Supply). The new organisation was also required to undertake the management of civil aerospace projects, although policy responsibility for them rested with the Department of Trade and Industry.

The head of the PE was to be a chief executive responsible to the secretary of state for defence, and underneath him or her were to be three controllers for sea, land and air systems, a controller for guided weapons and electronic systems, a controller for research and development establishments and four controllers each responsible for one of the following: policy, finance, personnel or sales. The chief executive and the four systems controllers were to be the accounting officers for their Votes. This was 'intended as an important innovation, as the accounting officer traditionally tended to be the permanent secretary of the department, and to be more concerned with the propriety of expenditure than with obtaining value for money'.[3]

The new organisation was generally welcomed by all sides: the services, the MOD centre and even the opposition parties.[4] Such support was due in no small way to a general dissatisfaction with the long delays, spiralling costs, and programme cancellations that seemed to have become a feature of weapons procurement. For instance, writing in 1970, Michael Howard could recall

> the £500 million spent on thirty-two major projects cancelled during the 1950s and 1960s; the increase in cost of Army equipment during this period by a factor of between two and four; the doubling of the cost of naval frigates; the ten-fold increase in the cost of aircraft, research and development accounting for up to a third of the total cost of sophisticated items of equipment of which only short runs are required unless substantial markets can be found for them overseas; a national growth rate entirely failing to keep up with this escalation of costs, so that defence expenditure is always tending to absorb an increasing proportion of the budget at a time when the political decision has been taken to progressively decrease.[5]

In just the seven years from 1964 to 1971 there were 19 cancellations at a cost of £235 million.[6] This included the ill-fated TSR2, of which Harold Wilson told the Commons in February 1965:

> the original estimate of R&D of this aircraft was £90 million. It has now risen to the region of £300 million, and the most authoritative estimate which I can get today for research, design and production is £750 million, which on an order for 150 would cost £5 million a plane, or twenty five times the cost of the Canberra which it was designed to replace.[7]

As Geoffrey Williams et al. wrote in 1969:

> the aircraft [TSR2] symbolised a fast-growing realisation that all was not right in the field of defence procurement ... Could defence expenditure be made more productive became a question no government dare ignore.[8]

Indeed, it was a question that had become increasingly difficult to ignore as the 1960s had progressed. The decade had opened with a directive from the permanent secretary at the Ministry of Supply stating that 'cost control must be accorded equal importance with technical control',[9] and proceeded with the Gibb–Zuckerman Report of 1961 which made recommendations aimed at improving procurement practice.[10] But with ever-rising equipment costs, the Ferranti and Bristol Siddeley scandals, the TSR2 crisis and the defence cuts of the Labour government, the problem refused to go away. By 1968 the MOD had committed itself to the introduction of post-costing, a revision of the profit formula and the establishment of a review board to oversee the latter's operation. The second half of the decade saw more reports, with attendant recommendations, that of the Downey Steering Group being of particular note.[11] Thus, the Rayner Report of 1971 represented the latest in a series of attempts to control a procurement system which had resulted in 'too many instances of defence projects costing multiples of the first official estimates for development, being late in completion and suffering severe escalations in unit production cost'.[12] Indeed, it is probably fair to say that the Procurement Executive was welcomed as much on the basis of 'better the devil you do *not* know' as anything else.

This is not to deny that the new organisation had some intrinsic attractions. Under the old system, responsibility for the procurement of guided weapons, the bulk of electronics instruments and aircraft for all three services rested with the Ministry of Technology which, because of the indivisibility of aerospace technology, also had responsibility for the civil aircraft industry. Many in the MOD, and particularly in the RAF, were unhappy with this situation. Thus there was pressure from the services to bring procurement totally under the auspices of the MOD.[13] This aim gained a good degree of justification as a result of the perennial problem of rising equipment costs and slippage, as well as a series of aircraft cancellations – HS681, P1154, the C5 aircraft and TSR2.

Thus, the new Procurement Executive was welcomed by the services largely because it was considered to be a price worth paying in order to ensure defence procurement was totally under the auspices of the MOD.[14]

The new organisation The concept of the PE was that of a self-contained organisation dealing with all other parts of the MOD on a customer–supplier basis (the services being the customers and the PE the supplier). Moreover, procurement of equipment was now to be organised along functional lines. Previously the services (with the exception of the RAF) had been responsible for the procurement of their own equipment, leading to duplication and an emphasis on performance at the expense of cost. In this respect then it is probably true to suggest, as Michael Hobkirk has done, that the PE was designed to be independent and to free the procurement process from single-service blinkers.

However, the new organisation was not intended to erode the influence of the services. For instance the Rayner Report had concluded that 'a defence procurement organisation is not its own master and must not become so since it only exists to meet user needs ... [and that an] arms length relationship between customer and supplier will, in fact be disastrous.'[15] Moreover, in practice the onset of functional controllerates did not imply any radical diminution of a single-service outlook. This was for a number of reasons. First, the changes took place at a time when the gradual move towards centralisation and functionalisation in the MOD was at least slowing, if not entering a period of reversal. For instance, the Heath Government of 1970–4 restored the post of parliamentary under-secretary for each of the three services, which meant they were better able to represent their separate interests.[16]

Second, after much lobbying by the services, and against the express preference of the Rayner project team, the heads of the sea, land and air systems controllerates within the newly formed PE were made members of their respective service boards (Admiralty, Army and Air Force). The effect was to ensure that each systems controller identified with his or her arm of the services. As Hastie-Smith has noted:

> it quickly became clear that the concession in the White Paper whereby the Sea, Land and Air Systems Controllers retained seats on the Admiralty, Army and Air Force Boards was leading not so much to a clash of loyalties as to a total re-direction of them. In the case of the ... Sea and Land Systems Controllers the concession represented a licence to continue with the arrangements which had existed before the Procurement Executive had been set up.[17]

This effect was underlined when the post of controller of guided weapons and electronic systems was abolished in 1973. The power and independence of the PE was further undermined in other ways; for example, the posts of controller of personnel and secretary were abolished and responsibility for personnel and financial services was assumed by the main MOD organisation.[18]

The PE, born out of dissatisfaction with the vagaries of a procurement system which had seen an endless stream of cost overruns and delays in weapons production, thus represented the latest and probably the most significant in a long line of attempts to reform that system. Coming as it did in the early 1970s it probably symbolised the high tide of a period of functionalisation and centralisation which the MOD had been experiencing for a number of years. However, caught in the (albeit temporary) ebb of this tide and the active concern of the military to preserve their influence over the procurement system, it found that it was neither as independent nor as free from single-service blinkers as some of its supporters had hoped it might be. The PE, then, did not represent a radical change in the procurement system but the kind of conservative evolution born out of compromise with vested interests that so typifies the history of procurement policy.

The procurement philosophy of the PE and the MOD   As has already been shown, the services and the established MOD organisation retained a good deal of influence in the new procurement organisation, but what of the defence industry? How did it fare under the new organisation and what was the policy adopted towards it? The Rayner procurement philosophy is perhaps best summed up in the following quote from the Report:

> Competition is an essential ingredient of good purchasing but the design, development and manufacture of defence weapon systems is quite different from normal commercial operations. Yet in many areas government purchasing is conducted against a background of trying to exploit the economic forces of the market place. There are, naturally, areas where these forces can operate effectively and achieve value for money, but they are relatively few and must be carefully chosen.[19]

In its practical application it meant the PE had favourite or preferred contractors to which it would turn to supply a particular piece of equipment. Competition, then, was at a minimum. For instance, in 1979–80 some 70 per cent (by value) of contracts placed by the MOD were non-competitive.[20] Moreover, once a company won a contract for the design of a particular piece of equipment it was virtually assured of obtaining the contract for the subsequent development and production. Thus the MOD's method of procurement can be characterised as one in which it gave preference to certain favoured contractors who were then likely to end up with projects which would be theirs from 'cradle to grave' – a kind of welfare state for defence firms. Other firms, even if they were British, found it exceptionally difficult to enter the market.[21]

To a certain extent the adoption of such an approach was an inevitable consequence of the defence industry's progressive rationalisation. There were now markedly fewer contractors available with the necessary skills to undertake the design and development of what were, and indeed are, highly complex and advanced pieces of equipment. As Sir Michael Carey, then head of the PE, told the Royal United Services Institute for Defence Studies (RUSI) in 1973, the MOD was 'in some areas already down to a single source'.[22] However, this situation was in part at least a consequence of government efforts from the late-1950s onwards to encourage the formation of large 'national champion' companies in the belief that such firms, although holding a monopoly in the UK, could best survive in the global marketplace.[23] Thus, for instance, the amalgamation of the British Aircraft Corporation and Hawker Siddeley to form British Aerospace in 1977 was merely the latest chapter in the rationalisation of the aircraft industry which had seen it shrink from 23 major firms in 1955 to four (BAe, Westland, Short Brothers and Harland with Rolls-Royce providing the engines) in 1977.[24]

However, it would be a mistake to characterise the 'preferred contractor' approach as wholly driven by the exigencies of the marketplace. There was also a definite belief in the advantages of this method of purchasing. The main benefit was that it allowed the MOD to choose contractors it trusted to supply a quality product that would be reliable, and also to build up a long-term relationship in which both the company and the ministry would come better to understand the other's needs and requirements.[25] The Rayner procurement philosophy was termed by Sir Frank Cooper 'the Marks and Spencer procurement philosophy'[26] – the belief that you should choose your suppliers very carefully, and that you should have a close but not soft relationship with them.

It would certainly seem there were benefits to this approach. To quote one member of the PE:

> given the relationship we had, if odd problems came up or whatever, you would find that the company would finance something. If our bureaucracy left a gap the company would keep things going, knowing it was going to be alright, and so forth. And you would find them

spending money on things, or not charging for certain things, because it was all a matter of give and take.[27]

However, there are obvious drawbacks to the preferred contractor approach. Clearly, where a company is fairly certain it will get a contract it is unlikely to offer as low a price as may be possible, and indeed it would appear there was a cost to be paid for this sort of relationship. To quote another member of the PE:

> I can understand that perhaps we have been charged too much by the designer of those aeroplanes, but I have accepted that as a premium which we need to pay over the years for instant advice as soon as we get a wing falling off an aeroplane. I can go to somebody, I know that he understands that aeroplane backwards, I know that he's going to react to my requirements because I play golf with him, I talk to him, I know him as a friend almost, and I need that contact, and my staff do.[28]

It is, of course, difficult to quantify the exact extent of this extra cost. However, the MOD currently claims that its more recent emphasis on competition has saved it £1 billion a year.

The pertinent question that needs to be answered here is not only whether, or how much, extra cost the preferred contractor approach resulted in for the MOD but also whether the advantages of this approach were actually worth any extra outlay that arose as a result of pursuing it. The Marks and Spencer approach to procurement may have been more costly but there are no doubt plenty of suburban shoppers who are prepared to testify to the fact that value for money is also constituted by such factors as quality of service and standard of product.

This question of whether competition policy or a preferred contractor approach represents better long-term value for money is one that will be addressed in more detail later, but it is perhaps relevant to point out here that, whether one opts for competition or for a preferred contractor approach, there are disadvantages associated with both methods. To quote a member of the PE:

> if you've only got one prime concern [company] he will tend to push the price up as high as he dare to be sure that he's producing the right performance. If you've got two primes competing against each other, they will tend to cut costs as much as they possibly can, at the peril of performance, and you have to try and spot that.[29]

In a sense then, whatever approach is adopted, the job of the PE is to 'spot' the problem and to ensure that it does not occur. As will be noted further on in this chapter, the PE's failure to do this was at least one factor among a number that led to unacceptable levels of slippage and cost increases in the development of weapons. Consequently, the cost overruns and delays that characterised the procurement system in the 1970s and early 1980s did not necessarily imply a failure of the preferred contractor approach *per se*, but a failure of the MOD adequately to police it.

It seems clear at this point that in the past the immediate cost of equipment was afforded less priority than has been the case recently because it was believed the extra outlay represented a good long-term investment.[30] To quote the Rayner Report once again: 'one must also be wary of treating second rate suppliers as cost-effective simply because they quote lower prices.'[31]

If it was felt in the PE, the MOD and successive governments that it was often necessary to forgo the possibility of cheaper equipment because of the long-term benefits that might accrue as a result of maintaining close relations with particular defence contractors, this appears to have been even more the case when it came to the vexed question of cost versus the need to maintain the (defence industrial base) DIB. As one MOD representative noted in a 1972 lecture:

> the rigid attitude that defence money must only be used for defence purposes and that the forces of the free market and competitive tendering should operate unchecked cannot be blindly applied to these issues. For a number of long-term considerations, there is a defence interest in maintaining in industry a certain basic level of capacity. This level may be affected by a number of factors – strategy and development of collaborative policies for example – but it will have a major effect on the investment pattern and the size of the industries concerned.[32]

What did such a policy mean in practice though? First, it meant the aim was to procure British designed and British manufactured equipment unless there was a foreign alternative which offered a significant and substantial advantage in terms of performance, time or cost.[33] Indeed, as Sir Frank Cooper has noted,

> [in the sixties] a figure of between sixteen and twenty per cent [below UK prices] was regarded as the norm if you were going to purchase

overseas, [in the seventies] it probably went up to twenty per cent, something like that. But it's a notional figure, it's not a law ... it would only apply at times of a really major buy; if you were going to buy something that was very costly.[34]

This policy meant that imports constituted a very small proportion of defence expenditure ranging from some 13–14 per cent in the late 1960s and early 1970s, to about 10 per cent in the late 1970s, down to a low of 4 per cent in 1982–3.[35] In comparison, 31 per cent of domestic demand for manufactured goods in general was met from imports in 1983, up from a figure of 16 per cent in 1970.[36]

Whatever the advantages or disadvantages of a buy-British approach in terms of preserving the DIB, in strict financial terms the result was often a failure to obtain value for money on equipment purchased. For example, when the development project for the Sting Ray torpedo ran into problems in 1976, the MOD had the opportunity to purchase an improved version of the American Mark 46 torpedo which, to quote the Committee of Public Accounts, 'offered a number of Sting Ray's characteristics for about half the cost and with an earlier in-service date.'[37] However, the ministry decided, 'in view of the Sting Ray's potentially superior performance and the *industrial advantages of retaining an independent UK capability* [my italics] that the programme should continue'.[38] By 1979 the predicted cost had risen to £920 million compared with £200 million for the purchase of the American torpedo (plus estimated cancellation costs of £161 million for the Sting Ray project). Moreover, the employment consequences of cancellation were estimated to be negligible.[39] Despite this, the development of Sting Ray proceeded apace. As the Committee of Public Accounts noted:

> We feel bound to say on the evidence available to us, we were not convinced by the MOD's case for spending an additional £720 million rather than purchasing the US torpedo [but] without a balanced technical assessment it is impossible to come to a final judgement about the value being obtained from the money spent and committed to Sting Ray.[40]

DIB considerations did not come into the reckoning solely on questions of domestic versus overseas procurement of equipment; they often played a significant role in determining the allocation of contracts *per se*. To quote Dr John Gilbert on his own experiences in the 1970s:

The minister can be faced with a situation where British industry has developed a product and he is told he has to buy it because if he does not buy it a plant will have to close and the design team's capability will be lost and he is therefore subject to, in a sense, blackmail to procure a weapons system. I am not saying it is typical by any means but these circumstances can arise and I speak from personal knowledge of one such case where the decision was made to procure a piece of equipment in this country which in my judgement at the time was clearly unsuitable for British defence purposes, purely on the grounds that not to do so would involve a critical loss of loading on a ... company.[41]

In the case of Rolls-Royce, concern to maintain the DIB not only had an influence on the distribution of contracts but even moulded wider government policy as Rolls-Royce's potential bankruptcy in 1971 caused the Heath Government to perform an embarrassing political volte-face and nationalise the company's defence interests.[42]

Of course, given the large sums involved in major defence contracts in addition to their high political profile, DIB considerations were (and still are) often interwoven with wider employment considerations (frequently weighed at cabinet level). To once again quote Dr John Gilbert:

I frequently was faced with decisions as to where to place orders for warships, as between Cammell Laird and Vosper Thorneycroft for example, and when the bids came in, the Cammell Laird bid was regularly two million to three million above the bid from Vosper Thorneycroft. There was considerable pressure put on me to spend defence money on procuring from Cammell Laird because the Cammell Laird shipyard was in an area of high unemployment and of course this was a consideration which any humane Minister is bound to take into account.[43]

Indeed, some procurement decisions were taken purely as a result of employment considerations. For instance, the government's decision in 1971 to re-phase the ship construction programme was taken to provide additional employment in development areas.[44] This involved the early construction of two Sheffield-class destroyers (from Swan Hunter on the Tyne) and four Amazon-class frigates (from Yarrow on the Clyde) at an additional cost of £31 million in 1972–3 and £32 million in 1973–4.[45] Another example would be the decision to procure an additional Nimrod squadron, of which the Expenditure Committee complained: 'It is hard to accept that projects of this type, which were not of military necessity but of the exigencies of the employment situation, should be sustained at the expense of programmes of greater military priority.'[46]

The environment in which defence procurement operated in the 1970s was also shaped by the fact that many of the principal defence companies were wholly or partly state owned. Financial crises brought about the nationalisation of the defence interests of Rolls-Royce and also a large government stake in Ferranti (rescued in 1974).[47] State control was further extended in 1977 when the then Labour government nationalised both aerospace and shipbuilding – two major defence industries.[48] By this point, other state-owned companies with significant defence interests included Royal Ordnance Factories, British Leyland, and Cable Wireless.[49] Indeed by 1978–9, of the ten companies awarded contracts of over £50 million, seven were wholly or partly in public ownership.[50]

Clearly considerations other than military necessity and value for money came into play in decisions to procure weapons for the services. How much of an extra burden upon the defence budget this represented is obviously difficult if not impossible to define. Apart from anything else, the purchase of any weapon can, no doubt, be justified as a military necessity, while production of the most strategically important equipment has beneficial effects on the employment figures. However, in 1974 Keith Hartley suggested that by not buying from the least-cost source of supply (i.e. USA), government support for the domestic aircraft industry exceeded £100 million a year, of which over £80 million was for British military aircraft.[51]

Thus, both employment and DIB considerations consistently influenced defence procurement decisions and the extra cost of such decisions was generally financed out of the defence budget. Other influences on the procurement process related to successive governments' attitude to the defence industry were the MOD's buy-British policy and its adoption of a preferred contractor approach to procurement. As has been shown, these policies often resulted in extra cost to the MOD. Whether such policies represented value for money in the longer term or whether they represented a waste of taxpayer's money is, of course, another question and one that is outside the scope of this chapter. However, these are not the only areas of the procurement process where the ministry's practices resulted in extra cost to the taxpayer.

Cost increases, slippage and their causes

Before beginning this section it is necessary briefly to describe the process that a weapon or equipment has to go through before it enters into service. The production of equipment is subject to what have become known as the 'Downey procedures' which were set out in the 1960s. The procedures require that a weapon goes through a number of different stages to ascertain such things as its likely cost, and the risk of it encountering developmental problems as it makes its way through the different phases and eventually into production.

The first stage of weapons development is the devising of an operational requirement (OR). An OR may arise as a result of new intelligence of an enemy's capability, a breakthrough in defence research, the fact that old equipment needs replacing, or a combination of these factors. The OR is then laid down as a staff target, which 'expresses in broad terms the functions and desired performance of a new weapon or equipment.'[52] This used to be examined by one, if not two central equipment committees – the Operational Requirements Committee (ORC) and the Defence Equipment Policy Committee (DEPC), although these have since been superseded by the Equipment Policy Committee (EPC) created in the mid-1980s.

If passed at committee stage the next step is a feasibility study (FS) which is carried out either in the government's research establishments – now the Defence Research Agency (DRA) – or in industry. This results in the production of a staff requirement (SR) which 'provides a detailed statement of the function and performance of the new equipment.'[53] This once more undergoes central committee assessment and, if it is again passed, the weapon or equipment then undergoes project definition (PD). The PD stage identifies and investigates potential high-risk areas and problems to be overcome if the staff requirement is to be met, and results in the production of 'comprehensive technical, time, cost and resource and management plans for full development.'[54] For a large project, PD may be separated into two stages. At the end of each stage the project is yet again submitted for central committee review. If the verdict is favourable the weapon or equipment may then enter into full development (FD). The prime objective of this phase is to 'establish the design, prove its suitability for meeting the service requirements (as amplified in the specifications) usually by developing, engineering and testing prototypes – and to establish full production specifications.'[55]

Only when this is completed does a weapon or equipment enter production.

Cost increases Despite the creation of the PE, cost increases and weapons cancellations remained a recurring feature of UK procurement (as indeed it was in other countries[56]). The most infamous example is the Nimrod AEW which was eventually cancelled after the expenditure of some £1 billion – its replacement, the American AWACS system, costing a further £860 million.[57] Nimrod was not an isolated case, however. The Type 21 frigate was not only two and a half years late, but its first of class costs rose from an estimated £1.3 million to £6.7 million (both at July 1974 prices). Another example is the case of the GWS 25/Sea Wolf. The unit production costs of the single-headed GWS 25 rose from £3.3 million to £6.8 million, and the double-headed rose from £4.8 million to £10.7 million. The original in-service date for the Sea Wolf was 1972, but it entered service in May 1981 – nine years late.[58]

On a more general level, the National Audit Office (NAO) examined all submissions (apart from those concerned with torpedoes and warships) to the Defence Equipment Policy Committee (DEPC) and its 1985 successor, the Equipment Policy Committee (EPC), between January 1979 and March 1985. Of the 101 submissions involving 67 different programmes there were 37 increased cost estimates involving 30 of the programmes. These included 24 estimates (involving 21 programmes) with real cost increases since the previous submission of 20 per cent or more. Twelve projects selected for more detailed study had shown real cost increases totalling £938 million since the staff requirement (SR) was approved. This represented an average increase of 91 per cent, with individual increases ranging up to 232 per cent. Even after the commencement of full development these projects had cost increases totalling £630 million, which represented an average increase of 47 per cent with individual increases ranging up to 166 per cent.[59]

The MOD's own report, *Learning from Experience*, from its assessment of 14 projects which had an average cost increase of 66 per cent from their earliest estimates and 29 per cent after full development, concluded:

> This implies £3–4 billion of 'unplanned' expenditure in the equipment budget each year, or £1–2 billion if only cost increases after the

start of Full Development are regarded as unplanned ... (t)he true
position may be even worse, since the figures quoted make no allowance for performance shortfalls. The history of the Nimrod AEW
project and others suggests that overruns on time and cost are
contained to some extent by cutting back on the original planned
performance.[60]

The causes The aim of this section is to examine those aspects of the
pre-value for money procurement process which contributed to the
various problems experienced in weapons development. This is important as an awareness of the flaws in procurement practice was influential
in informing the formulation of the current 'value for money' approach.

For the sake of clarity, the factors contributing to procurement problems of the 1970s will be examined individually under their respective
headings. However, it is important to emphasise that, generally, many or
all of these factors could be found at work in the same programme, and
that frequently the presence of one (i.e. cost-plus contracts) encouraged
the development of another (i.e. underestimation/gold-plating). In other
words, there was often an interaction between a number of factors which
tended to compound their effects.

The Downey procedures The reasoning behind the Downey procedures
was (and is) that by progressively defining equipment in ever more
detail and by providing break points at which the progress of a project
can be reviewed, problems in a weapon's development can be spotted at
an early stage, before too much money has been committed, and action,
including cancellation, can be taken to rectify the situation.

However, while the theory may seem straightforward, the practice
was often another matter. For instance, although each project was formally submitted for review by the central equipment committees at
least three times during its lifetime, the record of the committees in
actually cancelling programmes was not good. One 1976 management
review concluded that 'the committees questioned and delayed but
almost invariably ended up by agreeing',[61] and the Fisher Report noted
'how seldom the committees withhold such approval (as opposed to
requesting further studies/reports): over the period 1978–81 (April)
only twice within the service departments and not at all within the
centre.'[62]

This, however, was not the only deficiency in the application of the
Downey procedures. The aim of the procedures is to provide a step-by-

step development process, with permission to pass on to the next stage dependent on the success of the last. Despite this, overlap between the stages was not uncommon and in some cases stages were either missed out altogether or compressed, either to save funds or to speed development.[63] For example, the MOD itself informed the Committee of Public Accounts in 1986 that of 80 projects it had examined, roughly half had suffered from an overlap of development and production, with overlap contributing to increases in production costs in one-tenth of the projects examined.[64]

A further aspect of the MOD's failure to adhere to the Downey procedures was its persistent unwillingness to spend the necessary money on a project during the phases prior to full development. The MOD itself emphasises the importance of these stages in ensuring the final cost of a project is kept within reason[65] and the Downey Report found that the investigation required to provide an adequate basis on which to proceed to full development might involve expenditure of up to 15 per cent of the estimated development cost of a project (the Rayner Report actually recommended a figure of between 15 and 25 per cent).[66] However, in *Learning from Experience* it was found that, typically, only 8 per cent of development costs were committed before proceeding to full development[67] and the NAO concluded that in five out of the twelve projects it examined (Sonar 2026, CACS 1, SP 70, Javelin and Nimrod MSA) 'costs incurred before development were significantly less than 15% of the costs as then estimated.'[68]

The consequences of the MOD's failure to follow the Downey procedures were often unexpected technological problems, delays and large cost increases on programmes. As *Learning from Experience* noted:

> if realism emerges in FD (Full Development) the consequences can be extremely serious. Even the typical project ... has only discovered two-thirds of its cost escalation by the time it starts FD. Some projects encounter far more. The disruption caused by re-consideration, re-planning and re-approval of the project can last many months and be extremely expensive. Furthermore, because of the large degree of commitment by this point the potential risk of continuing will inevitably seem less unattractive than the certain misery of cancellation, leading to continued optimism, compromises on the development plan and a philosophy of 'planning for success'.[69]

Underestimation of costs   Another factor which resulted in equipment both arriving late and/or costing significantly more than originally planned was a tendency on the part of all concerned in the procurement process to underestimate the cost of a weapon in the first place, or as one MOD report put it: 'in the very early stages of a project "requirement" pressure pushes capability estimates up, while "programme" pressure pushes cost and time estimates down.'[70] Once again this was a problem that had prevailed for some time,[71] yet by 1979 the then CDP could still note that the 'MOD have under-estimated both time and cost'.[72] The problem was, of course, that all concerned with procurement – the industrialists, the military, the politicians and the civil servants – had an interest in making sure that a project came to fruition. To quote Sir Frank Cooper:

> There has been a tendency ... for the advocates of a new project to see that costs were as low as possible because that greatly enhanced the likelihood of it getting accepted, so there was a kind of conspiracy if you like to put it in that sense. Not an active conspiracy, a natural conspiracy between scientists and engineers, the Services who wanted the kit and the industrialists who wanted to get a piece of the action and get involved in making it, all of which tends initially to have a depressed effect on the cost.[73]

One reason for the prevalence of underestimation, on the part of contractors at least, was the ministry's use of cost-plus contracts. This, however, has not been the only problem related to the contracts.

Cost-plus The cost-plus contract is just what its name suggests – a contract in which the ministry agrees to pay the contractor all the costs of development, whatever they turn out to be, plus a set percentage of profit on top. The alternative contracts used (either firm, fixed or target price) all involve some degree of risk for the contractor in that a level of price is set, above which any extra cost is taken on board by the company.

The use of cost-plus contracts was motivated by a number of factors. First, the technologically ambitious, and, therefore, high risk nature of many weapons development projects meant that the cost-plus route was sometimes the only sensible option open to the MOD. There was certainly evidence to support such a view in the early 1970s as the new Procurement Executive was being created. In the case of both TSR2 and Rolls-Royce's development of the RB 211 engine for Lockheed, fixed price and incentive contracts had not prevented cost escalation. In the former case this led to the trauma of cancellation, in the latter case it resulted in the Heath government nationalising Rolls-Royce's defence interests in order to rescue it from bankruptcy. Such cataclysmic events, if nothing else, probably confirmed the MOD in its use of cost-plus contracts – after all, they appeared to show that incentive contracts were just as liable to price escalation as cost-plus contracts. As Sir Richard Clarke told the Commons Select Committee on the question of TSR2: 'we were too optimistic in the Department about what one could do with the incentive contracts'.[74]

Of course, the practice noted above of either failing to spend time and money defining specifications before development or, alternatively, totally missing out stages in the Downey procurement cycle does compound the problem of accurately defining specifications to the degree necessary to predict costs with the certainty required in incentive contracts. Furthermore, it may be argued that if contractors do go bankrupt as a result of taking on a risk contract, then that is their look out and should not be a consideration of the MOD. However, the ministry's procurement philosophy, with its commitment to preserving the defence industrial base and its emphasis on utilising preferred contractors, tended to preclude it from taking such a stance.[75]

The cost-plus contract also has the advantage that it allows greater oversight of both equipment programmes and corporate profit. In the context of a series of procurement scandals in the 1960s, and a succession of official reports bemoaning the lack of success in controlling and monitoring the activities of industry, this was an advantage not to be disregarded lightly.[76]

To some extent the use of the cost-plus approach also probably owed something to the tendency of large organisations, such as the MOD, to develop standard operating procedures which then become entrenched practice. In other words, the cost-plus approach was also pursued in the 1970s because it was 'the way it had always been done' as much as for any other reason.

Whatever the motivation, the fact is that a significant number of contracts for the development of equipment were let by the MOD on a cost-plus basis. Moreover, because cost-plus contracts tended to be used where it was thought there was a risk of development problems and excessive price overruns, they were most often applied to the more expensive projects – precisely because these tended to be the most technologically ambitious and, therefore, the ones most likely to encounter difficulties. For instance, while cost-plus contracts accounted for only 9 per cent of contracts let in 1979–80, expressed in value terms they represented 22 per cent.[77] Even this tended to underestimate the prevalence of cost-plus *practices*. For example, the Committee of Public Accounts recorded in a 1979 report that a quarter of supposedly risk contracts had not been priced by the time 75 per cent of the work had been completed (and at one point in the 1970s it had actually been a third).[78] Indeed, it was not unknown for some contracts to be completed and still not priced.[79] Even where risk contracts were in place, if the costs of a project began to rise to a larger extent than a company had budgeted for, because of the MOD's commitment to the defence in-dustrial base and its preferred contractors policy, it sometimes felt bound to alter the contract in order to allow for the cost increase.[80] Changing the contract did not necessarily involve altering the price. As *Learning from Experience* has noted, overruns of time and cost were sometimes controlled by cutting back on the planned performance of equipment.[81]

Thus, cost-plus contracts or cost-plus practices were the norm for a significant number of MOD programmes. Moreover, this was especially the case for precisely those high risk, technologically ambitious projects for which it was particularly important to give companies an incentive to keep costs to a minimum. However, the cost-plus contract – or what one representative of the services has termed 'the cost-plus, bottomless bucket, gravy train'[82] – manifestly failed to provide such an incentive. As has already been noted, the 'whatever it costs' guarantee of financing provided under cost-plus probably encouraged, or at the very least did nothing to discourage, the practice of underestimation on the part of firms eager to obtain the next contract.[83] Moreover, once a project was under way, as the Defence Committee have recorded, 'expenditure was allowed to escalate under cost-plus contracts.'[84] The contract failed to provide any real incentive to the manufacturer to control costs since the firm was guaranteed its set rate of profit whatever the outcome.[85]

Gold-plating A further factor which resulted in excessive costs was the practice of 'gold-plating' weapons. This was the tendency of the MOD to ensure that equipment was built to operate at the very highest standards when a reduction of, say, 10 per cent in performance might lead to significant cost savings. Clearly, the decision to sacrifice per-formance for costs is one that has to be weighed very carefully. In the military sphere a difference of 10 per cent in performance could well mean the difference between life and death for the soldier in the field, and perhaps even the difference between winning and losing a war. Moreover, the pace of technological change is such that it may often be necessary to alter an equipment requirement merely to ensure that it is not obsolescent before it rolls out of the factory. However, in practice there was a tendency to err too much on the side of performance at (literally) the expense of cost.[86] The services' wish for equipment which incorporated the very latest technology, combined with the scientists' eagerness to provide it and the centre's willingness to compromise, resulted in highly ambitious projects that foundered on complex technological problems and produced consequential cost increases and late delivery.

Reliability and maintainability One final aspect of MOD procurement which requires examination is its failure to pay sufficient attention to an equipment's eventual (reliability and maintainability) R&M during its design and development. The benefits of ensuring that a modern weapon is both reliable and easily maintainable can be quite significant. To quote the Defence Committee:

> the cost of supporting modern military equipment during its in-service life can exceed the acquisition cost by a factor of two or more. The potential savings from improved R&M are therefore extremely significant. Experience in the US suggests that investment/savings ratios of around 1:10 can be achieved.[87]

It is perhaps not surprising, therefore, that in 1979 the Committee of Public Accounts considered that an improvement in R&M was potentially the most cost-effective measure open to the department in the equipment field.[88]

Despite this, however, concern was still being voiced in the 1980s over the ministry's failure to obtain reasonable levels of R&M. For example, the RAF noted in one review that the cost of the Jaguar aircraft failing to achieve its specified R&M requirement amounted to £496 million (13 per cent of the aircraft's whole-life cost). It also estimated that in-service reliability modifications cost at least 70 per cent of the total cost of acquisition and that, in certain cases, this could be reduced to as little as 7 per cent if provided for in the original design. Difficulty in achieving R&M requirements even contributed to the cancellation of some projects – for example the SP 70 self-propelled howitzer and the Nimrod Mission

System Avionics, both cancelled, at a cost of £88 million and £880 million respectively.[89] Indeed, studies by the Air Force Department and the Procurement Executive estimated that unreliability added £1 billion a year to support costs.[90] The NAO also pointed out that during peacetime, between a third and a half of the front-line fast jet fleet of the RAF was unavailable because of scheduled maintenance, modification action and inspection of unscheduled rectification. This led it to conclude that the services' operational capability would be enhanced by improved R&M.[91] Thus, the potential financial and operational benefits accruing from a high level of R&M were lost because the MOD had not given it the priority it deserved.

This was due to a number of factors. Part of the problem was the difficulty of translating statements of reliability criteria into unambiguous and enforceable contracts.[92] This problem may have been further exacerbated by the MOD's preferred contractor approach. For example, the Defence Committee noted contractors' reluctance to accept the risks involved in agreeing reliability penalties/incentives in a contract, and pointed out that contractors would be more willing to accept such conditions where they were competing for a contract against other companies.[93]

A further factor inhibiting the attainment of reasonable R&M levels was the annual pressure on defence budgets which often resulted in short-term savings being made at the expense of long-term cost-effectiveness. This tendency to take the short-term view was further reinforced by the MOD's own practices. For example, the Defence Committee have noted that the use of discounted cash flow (DCF) investment appraisal techniques to assess projects placed an emphasis upon the reduction of 'up-front' spending, thus devaluing the importance of future savings.[94] Furthermore, despite the fact that the design and development of a modern weapon is a process that often takes well over a decade, project managers (who were described as 'fundamental' to the procurement process by the Rayner Report)[95] only had an average tour length of three to four years,[96] thus institutionalising a short-term view of what constituted success in the management of a project.[97] Much the same point can also be made with regard to the politicians ultimately in charge of the equipment programme – the knowledge that they were likely to face re-election in four or five years' time inhibited their willingness to sacrifice short-term economies for long-term cost-effectiveness.[98] This institutionalisation of the short-term view was compounded by the fact that, while the financial consequences of poor R&M fell on the services support budget, investment in R&M was met by the Procurement Executive's equipment budget.[99] In addition the Committee for Defence Equipment Reliability and Maintainability (CODERM), the main committee concerned with R&M (formed in 1976), proved to be ineffective. Indeed, by 1981 the Air Force Department had concluded that 'ignorance of CODERM's existence was universal.'[100] Finally, the lack of emphasis given to R&M meant that while most R&M programmes contained provision for reliability growth work, contractors were often permitted to exclude, curtail or cancel planned activities at the development stage.[101] In other words, as the NAO noted, R&M was consistently 'sacrificed to performance, initial purchase cost and time.'[102]

Summary

It seems clear that, despite a number of initiatives in the 1960s and the creation of the Procurement Executive in the 1970s, at the beginning of the 1980s the management of MOD weapons procurement was still far from being an unparalleled success.

To some extent this might have been expected. The design, development and production of modern weapons is neither a simple nor a cheap endeavour. Mistakes and failures are probably inevitable to some degree. Moreover, while it is easy to criticise the MOD for incurring extra costs by pursuing a preferred contractor approach or in attempting to maintain the DIB, ultimately, any judgement as to whether its policies in these areas represented prudent long-term investment or financial profligacy rests upon the weight one attaches to factors such as the importance of a good relationship between customer and supplier, and the question of how much (if any) of the DIB it is necessary to maintain for reasons of strategy and security of supply. Such questions are complex and have not been examined here as they are outside the remit of this chapter.

In other areas the ministry's record in the 1970s and early 1980s is less open to justification. Particularly depressing is the fact that the causes of cost increases and delays were neither new nor necessarily insoluble; they had been identified by a number of reports throughout the 1960s, 1970s and early 1980s which had often included detailed recommendations for their solution. Despite this, the MOD persistently failed to implement effective remedies. No doubt Sir Frank Cooper's 'natural conspiracy' of interests – the scientists, the services, and the defence industries – must take a fair share of the blame for the problems of defence procurement in this period. Ultimately though the responsibility rests with the Ministry of Defence, as the government body charged with ensuring that the influence of these natural interests did not subvert efficient and economical procurement. As one industrialist has stated, 'I don't ever accuse the defence contractors of malpractice, what I accuse the MOD of is of being a thoroughly unsophisticated and undemanding customer.'[103]

Worse still perhaps, as a result of its bureaucratic tendency to compromise and its own place in the roll call of natural interests, the MOD often demonstrated a marked lack of commitment to the application of its own principles of equipment procurement – principles specifically aimed at securing value for money. As *Learning from Experience* noted: 'the MOD has no shortage of procedures; what it lacks is the corporate ability to follow them. And procedures alone are not enough.'[104] Thus, it is difficult to resist the conclusion that the short-sightedness, over-ambition in equipment requirements and the simple failure to follow established procedures which characterised UK procurement resulted in not one, but a succession of very expensive 'bad deals' for the British taxpayer, many of which could have been avoided.

The MOD's record on procurement during this period is less than impressive, to say the least: cost-plus contracts, gold-plating, short-term 'savings' which resulted in equipment unreliability costing £1 billion a year, cost increases of up to 232 per cent, and £3–4 billion a year of taxpayers' money devoted to 'unplanned' expenditure. Of course, under the new approach to procurement promulgated by the ministry, competition and 'value for money' are now espoused, gold-plating and cost-plus contracts are disavowed in favour of 'Cardinal Points' and fixed price contracts, and officials even express a greater willingness to purchase from abroad.

It may seem that the numerous problems procurement produced in the past would be reason enough to search for an alternative approach. However, there were a number of other factors at work in the decision to adopt the more commercial approach now promulgated by the MOD. It is to an examination of these pressures that Chapter 2 turns.

2

Rising costs and finite
budgets

Chapter 1 outlined past procurement practices and the problems inherent in those practices which the present 'value for money' approach
is attempting to eliminate or alter. This chapter delineates the factors
that have led to that change in approach. It is suggested that the reform
of procurement can only be fully understood if account is taken of the
influence of Thatcherism on the procurement process. However, procurement also experienced severe budgetary pressures throughout the
1980s which created an incentive for reform over and above that which
came from the government's ideological commitment to competition
and the free market.

It is suggested that a number of factors combined to place the
defence budget under constant strain, thereby creating an incentive to
effect greater efficiency in the procurement process. These include the
introduction of cash limits in the late 1970s and the increasing cost of
weapons development. Such factors, in turn, were partly responsible for
a succession of overspends which culminated in the budget problems of
1980–1 and the imposition of a moratorium on the procurement of new
equipment. This experience, particularly that of the moratorium,
further increased the pressure for change. It is also suggested that
budgetary pressures were further exacerbated as a result of the post-
Falklands climbdown over the equipment cuts set out in the Defence
Review of 1981, the end of the '3 per cent commitment' and, latterly,
post-cold war cuts in defence expenditure.

It is certainly the case that in many areas of procurement the value
for money policy has led to significant changes in approach – sometimes
fundamental, sometimes qualitative. However, it is necessary to add

some qualifications to such an assertion, and it is with these qualifications that the chapter begins.

Continuities

Different commentators have identified either specific dates and/or the arrival of certain individuals at the helm of procurement as marking significant turning points in the tide of policy. In particular, the adoption of a range of reforms that have become associated with the government's 'value for money' initiative is often associated with Michael Heseltine, secretary of state for defence between 1983 and 1986,[1] not least because Mr Heseltine's arrival at the MOD coincided with the publication and subsequent implementation of *Value for Money in Defence Procurement*. This set out many of the aims of government policy on procurement. Alternatively, other commentators have emphasised the arrival of Peter Levene as chief of defence procurement (CDP) in 1985 as a critical point in the evolution of policy.[2]

It will be shown further on that both Michael Heseltine and Peter Levene have played a significant part in bringing about the new approach. However, many changes in policy were either under way or have their roots in initiatives that were taking place *before* the arrival of Levene or Heseltine. Indeed, a number of changes in the approach to procurement have their roots in developments that were taking place even before 1979 and the arrival of the Conservative government. Where relevant, these will be elaborated on when the new policies are described in more detail later. However, certain points need to be dealt with now.

Sir Frank Cooper has suggested that one can date the origin of the value for money approach 'well before the time it [is] conventionally dated. I'd go back to the middle of the 1970s ... there was a major impetus going, part of which came out of the Review of the Organisation of the Management of Defence which started in 1975/6.'[3] He suggests that the reason for the change in approach was the fact 'there was serious concern that too little money was being spent on equipment and too much on other things.' Added to this, of course, were the defence cuts undertaken by Labour in the mid-1970s. Indeed, by 1978 real terms expenditure on defence had reached a post-war nadir of £10,530 million (at 1980 prices) which represented 4.5 per cent of GDP, another post-war low.[4] In consequence, a conscious attempt was made to cut down on overheads and thus increase the resources given to the equipment budget.[5] Of course, to some extent the whole of post-war British defence policy could be characterised as an ongoing attempt to cut the fat from the defence budget, but from the early part of the mid-1970s onwards there was a pronounced change of approach which was marked by a concern to increase output instead of input.[6] There was a realisation on the part of the ministry that there would be little, and certainly not enough, extra money coming from government for defence. The concern to cut back on overheads therefore owed much of its *raison d'être* to the fact that the alternative would have meant either cuts in commitments or large cuts in the equipment budget.

It is certainly the case that the proportion of the defence budget devoted to equipment rose significantly from the mid-1970s onward, rising from 33.5 per cent in 1975–6 to almost 40 per cent by 1979–80 (and then up to a peak of 45.8 per cent in 1984–5). Moreover, this shift meant that despite the squeeze in the defence budget that occurred in the late 1970s, expenditure on equipment rose 16 per cent (in real terms) between 1975–6 and 1979–80.[7] Of course, this growth in expenditure was probably as much a reflection of the rising real cost of weapons as it was of a conscious and deliberate attempt to increase equipment expenditure. Nevertheless, the figures do show that faced with a choice of taking an axe to the equipment programme or making cut-backs elsewhere in the defence budget, the MOD opted for the latter approach.[8]

This is not to suggest that procurement did not suffer at all in the pincer squeeze of rising costs and finite budgets. Despite its favoured place in defence expenditure, economies were still necessary. Indeed, by 1977 *The Economist* could record:

> the now indefinite postponement of medium-lift helicopters for the army; delays in the procurement of Milan infantry anti-tank missiles, the cancellation of a squadron of Jaguar attack bombers ... the deferment of the navy's surface-to-surface Exocet missile and the lack of air defence equipment for the army.[9]

Thus, even given the protection afforded to the equipment budget the incentive to improve the output obtained from both the equipment and the non-equipment budgets persisted – the latter because it had to bear the brunt of the economies needed to finance the rising cost of weapons procurement, and the former because even these economies were not enough to protect it from cuts in forward programmes, necessitated largely by their own rising costs.

There were certainly some significant attempts to make the MOD more efficient. For example, after remaining broadly level between 1974 and 1976, civilian numbers fell by 20,000 between 1976 and 1979.[10] Thus, as Malcolm Chalmers has noted, the rise in equipment expenditure was at least partly paid for by a reduction of 3 per cent a year in non-equipment spending between 1974–5 and 1978–9.[11] Of course, this reduction in numbers needs to be placed in context. It formed part of what was an almost continuous drive by the MOD to reduce civilian numbers since a unified organisation was created in 1964. In this sense it represented a very traditional response to the problem of budgetary stringency. Nevertheless, the reduction in this period was very drastic and much steeper than anything that had gone before. Moreover, following as it did from many years of earlier reductions, it was no doubt all the more difficult to make.

The drive for efficiency also had effects in the government's research and development establishments. Dissatisfaction with the efficiency of the R&D establishments had been felt for some time.[12] By 1972 this dissatisfaction led to the government announcing the initiation of a series of studies into the scope for rationalisation of the R & D establishments.[13] By the following year the first of these studies was completed, and by 1980 the Strathcona Report could record that, despite an increase in workload, the R&D establishments had been reduced from 25 to 12, and that between 1974 and 1979 staff numbers had fallen by 14 per cent.[14]

The late 1970s also saw the beginnings of an attempt to shift the emphasis in research and development away from in-house agencies to industry, particularly with respect to development.[15] Thus by 1979 Lawrence Freedman could record, the 'trend is now to bring industry in earlier while requirements are still being formulated and to contract out to industry more of the design work. Some 70% of R&D funds are now spent extramurally.'[16] It will be shown later that this policy of devolving the development of weapons to industry and allowing it greater say in their design represents one of the elements in the present value for money approach. As such, it would seem that the roots of this particular aspect of 'value for money' can be traced back to the late 1970s.[17]

However, once again certain qualifications need to be added. First, the extent to which this policy had been realised by the end of the 1970s should not be exaggerated. By 1981 Plessey Company Ltd. could still complain to the Defence Committee that the efficient development of weapons was hampered by the fact that 'the ability of industry to input marketing and production information so that a trade-off between costs and performance can be made is ... limited.'[18]

A further initiative which has come to be associated with the value for money approach is the attempt to introduce more rigorous contracts for the development and production of weapons. Here too, Sir Frank Cooper has argued that a change in the approach to procurement was brought about by the review of the organisation of the management of defence which took place in the mid-1970s. He argues that, from this point on, 'progressively there was a tightening up of the management thrust towards more fixed price contracts, a thrust towards much better project management, changes in the way requirements were specified.'[19] This seems to be borne out by the Expenditure Committee's 1974 report which noted that, with regard to defence contracts, 'efforts are being made to introduce incentives to cover about half the development work.'[20] Additionally, in 1979 (before the Conservatives came to power) the Committee of Public Accounts recorded 'the Ministry informed us that they were determined to avoid cost-plus contracts wherever possible. Such arrangements required a good deal more monitoring and offered no assurance about ultimate costs.'[21] More important than mere statements of intent, the Committee of Public Accounts also noted there had already been some success in this area; from 1971–6 there had been a decline in the proportion of non-competitive risk contracts placed. However, in its 1979 report, the committee could record that this decline had been arrested and that the 'final results for 1975–6 and the provisional figures for the following 2 years showed the proportion of risk to non-risk contracts to be levelling out very close to the 1.5:1 ratio assumed in the Profit Formula calculations.'[22]

This is not to suggest that the attack on cost-plus contracts was pursued with the same intensity as it has been under 'value for money'. By 1979 cost-plus contracts still represented 22 per cent (by value) of all contracts placed compared to the 1 per cent they have come down to under 'value for money'.[23] Moreover, as noted in the previous section, cost-plus practices in the form of late pricing of risk contracts were still rife, with the Committee of Public Accounts able to report in the same year that one-quarter of risk contracts had not been priced by the time 75 per cent of the work had been done.[24] Despite this though, it seems clear that the attempt to move away from cost-plus contracts had begun by the late 1970s.

The latter half of the 1970s, therefore, saw significant changes aimed at improving efficiency in the management of defence and defence procurement. Perhaps more importantly than the actual policies implemented, a change in attitudes had been fostered by the financial problems of the late 1970s. Economic stringency had begun a softening up of the procurement establishment which would continue into the 1980s. It was already beginning to dawn on many in procurement that changes had to be made.[25]

In many ways though, these initiatives did not imply a fundamental reappraisal of the MOD's approach to procurement. Reductions in numbers and the rationalisation of bodies such as the R&D establishments did not represent a sea change, they were simply traditional responses to the problem of rising costs and shrinking resources. Despite efforts to move away from the use of cost-plus contracts they still represented nearly one-quarter of all contracts placed; out of ten contractors awarded contracts of over £50 million in 1978–9, seven were wholly or partly in public ownership[26] and most fundamental of all, competition was still at a premium with only 14 per cent (by value and number) of contracts placed competitively in 1979.[27] Reform was thus conducted largely within the confines of the established method of procurement.

There were very significant differences, therefore, between the attempts to obtain value for money in the late 1970s and those that would follow in the 1980s. Fundamentally, the concern to introduce competition into the procurement system which is at the heart of the present value for money approach had not been elaborated.[28] The same can also be said of other policies which make up the present approach. For example, the desire to encourage small firms into procurement and the privatisation of defence concerns were both policies that had not yet been voiced. Of policies that had been voiced, some would have to wait a number of years before being realised,[29] while others that were taken on board in the 1970s (the move away from cost-plus contracts for instance) were not pursued with the same fervour as would be the case in the 1980s.

Moreover, the attempts to introduce efficiency into procurement that characterised the late 1970s were not translated into an over-arching procurement strategy that was underpinned by government's oft-expressed ideological commitment to the principles that upheld it. Rather, they were much more the *ad hoc* responses of an organisation caught in the pincer squeeze of increasing costs and finite defence budgets.

Though there are continuities that run through the procurement policies of the late 1970s and the 1980s, there are both fundamental and qualitative differences which mark them out from each other. This will become more apparent later when the present approach is described in more detail. First, however, it is necessary to examine the reasons for the introduction of the value for money approach in the 1980s. These can be broken down into two broad categories – first, cost pressures, and second, the ideology of the government. The latter will be examined shortly. In the case of the former, there were a number of factors that combined to produce pressure on the defence budget and it is these which will be considered below.

Cost pressures on the defence budget

Cash limits Government expenditure, including that on defence, is planned on the basis of annual surveys which consider the amount of money that should be made available to departments several years into the future. Until the late 1970s expenditure was planned in volume terms, so that a department such as the MOD would decide how many tanks, planes, missiles, etc. it would require, and the total cost of these would be estimated on the basis of prices ruling at some date before the survey started (constant survey prices). However, this system presented certain problems of financial management for governments. Put simply, volume planning emphasised the primacy of providing a set level of goods and services over a concern to limit departments' annual expenditure. Moreover, the system of volume planning did not just allow departments to claim for any increased costs that fell to them as a result of general inflation, but it also allowed them to claim for any increases in the costs of the goods and services specifically required by them, over and above the general level of inflation. Thus, the MOD was able to claim money for rises in the cost of defence-specific goods and services above the standard inflation rate. This tended to operate to its advantage as inflation in defence goods and services, particularly defence equipment, was on average higher than inflation in the rest of the economy.[30]

However, while volume planning gave inflation protection to government decisions on the necessary numbers of schools, hospitals, and tanks, etc., such protection made financial planning very difficult. This was particularly so in times of high inflation, as volume plans had to be met by ever increasing expenditure. For instance, in 1974–5 the difference between outturn and total planned public expenditure was roughly £6.5 billion.[31] Moreover, as Peter Riddell has pointed out, the implied guarantee of financing irrespective of cost increases meant that individual departments had little incentive to contain prices and cost changes.[32] Indeed, I.P. Wilson has suggested that the practice of allowing the MOD to claim an allowance for defence-specific inflation

> gave continued encouragement to project officials to maximise their pay and price estimates. Pay and price increases were deemed unavoidable and therefore virtuous. On the other hand real increases were taken to indicate lack of project control and had to be offset by a reduction in the budget elsewhere.[33]

In a period of low inflation it may have been possible to live with the flaws in volume planning. However, the rising level of general inflation in the 1970s combined with relative increases in public sector costs placed the system under great strain, and in 1976 the Labour government introduced the cash limits system as an alternative to volume planning. Further reforms were also introduced by the Conservatives in 1981. The introduction of cash limits raised a number of problems for the MOD (as it did for other departments). The logic and intention of the cash limits system is that when annual inflation rises above that allowed for in a department's cash limits, the government will no longer automatically increase expenditure to accommodate it. Rather, it is the department which has to bear the burden of these extra costs through cuts to its programmes – in other words, a reduction in volume. Moreover, inflation has often been deliberately underestimated by governments as part of an attempt to keep public expenditure down.[34] Thus, the MOD entered the 1980s facing an annual problem of how to reconcile the requirement to spend within cash limits with the cost of planned commitments and equipment purchases. For example, prior to 1980–1 it had overspent against *volume* only twice since 1964–5, yet by the same year it found itself having overspent against *cash limits* for three consecutive years.[35] Moreover, even an overspend against cash limits did not necessarily mean that volume plans had been maintained. For instance, while the MOD's cash limit for 1979–80 was raised once in November and then again in February so that it eventually stood

£613 million above its original total, the ministry could still complain to the Committee of Public Accounts that because 'the gap between what we were allowed and the real increase in pay and prices was very large ... there was in fact a volume underspend of well over £180 million.'[36] Cash limits, therefore, while solving a crisis of financial management for government, created a crisis of financial management for the MOD.

In the early years of cash limits, the annual squeeze on volume implied by its operation was also compounded by the fact that though departments were not allowed to retain any underspend they might achieve, the Treasury was able to deduct an overspend in one year from the following year's budget. Thus, if the MOD managed to underspend its budget it effectively lost the amount of money it underspent. This meant that, particularly towards the end of each year, spending decisions were not necessarily determined by a concern to obtain value for money but simply by a concern to avoid losing money back to the Treasury. It was not a system geared to promote efficient procurement.

Of course, as already noted, the MOD's primary problem in the late 1970s and at the start of the 1980s was its constant overspending against budget. However, as the 1980s progressed the ministry did encounter the problem of underspending too. For instance, after obtaining an increase of £300 million in its cash limit for 1981-2 the ministry soon realised it was heading for a significant underspend at the end of the year and so advanced its monthly date of payment by a few days into the 1981-2 financial year. This allowed it to register an underspend of only £5 million in 1981-2.[37]

The MOD thus found itself in a situation in which it had to engage either in rapid and unplanned cut-backs to stay within cash limits, or in rapid additional expenditure to avoid an underspend. The system clearly had significant flaws if the primary aim was to make the defence budget work efficiently. Eventually, after much lobbying by the ministry, and after recommendations by the Defence Committee,[38] the Chancellor announced in July 1983 that the ministry would be able to carry forward up to 5 per cent of its gross cash provision into the next financial year where underspending occurred on the Votes covering equipment pro-curement and works.[39] In 1987 this flexibility was increased further when the Treasury agreed to allow an extra £400 million a year to be carried forward for the next three years.[40] Finally, the MOD negotiated a further agreement with the Treasury to allow unlimited end-year flexibility on the department's operating costs (Votes One and Two). While this latter arrangement excludes costs incurred on the procurement of major equipment such as a new fighter aircraft, it does include procurement costs arising from such things as the purchase of spares, fuel and ship-refits[41] and covers some £16–17 billion of defence expenditure. Thus, the ministry now has virtually unfettered freedom to carry over unspent money from one year to the next.[42]

Nevertheless, in the early and mid-1980s, the introduction of cash limits, by reversing the previous primacy of numbers over cash, exacerbated the strain on an already overstretched defence budget – particularly given that, in setting cash limits, governments frequently underestimated inflation in order to keep public expenditure down. Added to this, the absence of any carry-over facility meant the defence budget was managed very much on a stop-go basis, with expenditure being reined back or increased according to whether the MOD was underspending or overspending its permitted budget. It was a system in which prudent financial management sometimes had to take second place to the need to meet the cash limit.

Rising equipment costs If the system of cash limits attempted to place a lid on departmental expenditure, then the perennial problem of rising equipment costs ensured that severe pressure would be placed on this lid during the 1980s.

The problems inherent in the procurement system have already been examined in the previous section. The end result of these problems was ever-rising equipment costs (although, of course, this was not a problem confined to the UK).[43] For instance, the *Statement on the Defence Estimates 1982* calculated average annual cost growth over and above inflation of 6–10 per cent on the capital production costs of major equipment[44] and noted that 60 per cent of the defence equipment budget had proved liable to significant cost growth.[45] This meant that each successive generation of weapons cost significantly more in real terms than their predecessors. For example, a new artillery shell was double the price of its predecessor, the Type 22 frigate cost three times more than the Leander, and the Harrier aircraft four times more than the Hunter.[46] Such rises came home to roost on the defence budget. As the *Statement on the Defence Estimates 1982* made clear, since 1950 defence had seen a real terms rise in expenditure from £10.25 billion to over £14 billion and an increase in the proportion of the budget spent on equipment from 30 per cent to about 45 per cent.[47] Despite this, John Nott, then secretary of state for defence, could note:

> In 1950 the Navy had 12 aircraft carriers and commando ships, 26 cruisers, 111 destroyers, 165 frigates and 62 submarines. In 1980 the figures were 3 carriers, no cruisers, 12 destroyers, 54 frigates and 28 submarines ... in 1950 we had some 1,500 front line aircraft. The figure today is more like 500. In 1950 we had 1,100 tanks against some 800 today.[48]

Thus, in spite of the Conservative government's commitment to spend more money on defence, such cost increases placed increasing pressure on each year's budget and serious question marks over the UK's ability to procure both the range and numbers of equipment necessary to maintain its military commitments.

As the minister of state for defence procurement stated in the House of Commons in 1983, there was a very real need to 'counteract ... the road to absurdity – the apparently inexorable rise in cost between one generation of equipment and the next. If nothing were done to mitigate that trend, in about eighty years the entire defence budget would be sufficient to purchase just one tactical aircraft.'[49] This concern to bear down on the rising costs of equipment in order to keep the size of the defence budget in check was, therefore, an important factor behind the adoption of the value for money approach.[50] Thus, during the 1980s, ever-increasing equipment costs created a double bind for the government and the MOD in which defence spending was required to rise steeply in order to maintain commitments, yet such was the increase in costs that even this was not sufficient to do away with the need for cuts in the equipment programme (see below), or to dispel talk of a defence review. The government publication which heralded the new approach to procurement (*Value for Money in Defence Equipment Procurement*) had a point (though not one universally shared) when it suggested:

> It is of paramount importance – to the Services, the defence industries and all who work in them – that everything possible is done to halt (and where possible to reverse) the rise in defence equipment costs and ensure that the defence budget is spent in the most cost-effective way.[51]

Spending crisis The need to do something about the rising costs of defence equipment was dramatically demonstrated by the spending crisis

that occurred in the 1980–1 financial year. The defence estimates for
1980–1 originally set a cash limit of £10,125 million.[52] However, by
May the MOD's estimate of its likely expenditure during the year
suggested it would overrun this figure by some £500 million, an estimate
confirmed by a second forecast in June.[53] Thus, in July and August the
MOD found itself having to instigate three tranches of savings measures, totalling £160 million, £100 million and £90 million respectively.[54]
Despite such drastic cut-backs though, the government still found it
necessary to increase the cash limit for defence. First, it was increased
by £153.7 million as a result of the presentation by the Civil Service
Department of Revised Estimates for civilian pay on 4 July 1980.[55]
However, the primary area of overspend was on Vote Two, the equipment budget, and a further increase to the cash limit announced in
August effectively allotted an extra £277.5 million to the equipment
budget.[56] This was made up of an increase of £203 million in the cash
limit[57] and the transfer of £74.5 million of forecast savings in other
areas of the defence budget to equipment.

Despite this extra money and the cut-backs instigated by the MOD
earlier in the year, the government still found it necessary to take even
more drastic action. A moratorium was imposed on 8 August for an
initial period of three months.[58] The moratorium was, essentially, a ban
on new purchases[59] and lasted until 11 November when it was replaced
by a period of 'stringent discipline on new commitments'.[60] The
moratorium saved £100–150 million, with a further £15–20 million
saved by the subsequent period of stringent discipline.[61] The effect of
the measures to reduce spending throughout the year was eventually
estimated by the Reeves Report to have saved £400 million[62] although
figures given to the Committee of Public Accounts by the MOD
estimated the savings at £440–490 million.[63]

Thus, by the end of the year the defence budget had been increased
by £406.7 million, with £50 million abated in respect of the previous
year's overspending against cash limits a net increase of £356.7 million.
Of course, not all the pressure on the MOD's budget came from the
equipment Vote. As already noted, £153.7 million of the increase was
for civilian pay awards (and another £54 million for the armed forces
pay award). Nevertheless, this still left an increase of £149 million.
Moreover, the £54 million awarded for armed forces pay actually went
into the equipment Vote, giving a total increase in the cash limit
(excluding the civil service pay award) of some £203 million.

At the same time, the MOD had implemented cuts in expenditure worth some £400–500 million. Yet despite all this it still managed to overspend against the revised cash limit of August by £64 million. In theory, then, if no cuts had been made and the cash limit had only been increased by the amount necessary to fund armed forces and civilian pay awards, the MOD could have faced an overspend of some £617–717 million. Indeed, if no increase in the cash limit had been allowed at all, it could have found itself overspending by £820–920 million. The overspend did not result simply from the effect of rising equipment costs, there were a number of other factors at work which had combined to place pressure on the defence budget.

Economic downturn First, it should be noted that despite the increase in defence and procurement expenditure that had occurred under the Conservatives, the 1980–1 cash limit was £216 million less (at 1980 survey prices) than that planned by Labour before it had lost power two years earlier.

Another factor leading to pressure on the budget was the depression in the economy that had resulted from the government's economic policies.[64] The effect was to encourage firms with defence contracts to switch the spare capacity released by the lack of civil work into defence production, thus completing orders much faster than normal. Added to the speedier completion of contracts was the fact that firms were tending to bill the MOD faster than normal, spurred on by the high interest rates set by the government as part of its economic strategy.[65] The net effect of this was that the MOD found itself presented with bills it had not expected to pay until the following financial year. For example, of the £277.5 million awarded to the equipment vote in the Autumn revision of the cash limit, £75 million was for faster progress on orders and £24 million for faster billing.[66]

The problems caused by faster progress on defence contracts and speedier billing, resulting in part from the economic downturn, were compounded by a series of other factors.

The profit formula Since the late 1960s the profits allowed on non-competitive contracts have been determined by a Review Board for Government Contracts, which (until recently) set allowable profit margins every three years. Theoretically, the Review Board is required to set a rate of return equal, on average, to the overall return earned by

British industry.[67] In reality, however, practice has often failed to match theory.

This was the case during the 1980-1 period. The average profit rate allowed on non-competitive contracts for this year was 20 per cent, a rate of return set after the Review Board's 1977 Review and maintained in its 1980 Review.[68] Had the comparability principle been in operation in 1980-1 the allowed profit rate on non-competitive contracts should have been 15.3 per cent and not 20 per cent. According to the Public Accounts Committee, the cost to the MOD of each 1 per cent of target profit rate was £8.9 million. Therefore, in 1980-1 the defence industry received an extra £42 million, or nearly one-quarter more than the £178 millon it would have received if comparability had been operating.[69]

Moreover, as the then director general of contracts told the Defence Committee:

> Many firms through improved efficiency or pricing mechanisms achieve returns slightly in excess of [the target profit rate] ... indeed post-costing results over the period that post-costing has been taking place do tend to show that returns on average from that selected sample of contracts, secured two percentage points more than the relative *risk* target rate of profit.[70]

Thus, those firms working on non-competitive risk contracts (as opposed to non-competitive, non-risk, cost-plus contracts) may well have received even more profit than suggested by the above figures. The speedier completion of contracts was not, therefore, simply the result of a downturn in the economy but was also influenced by the fact that profits obtainable from non-competitive defence work were actually higher than in the rest of industry.

The block adjustment   The problems created by the faster completion of contracts were also exacerbated by the way in which the MOD assessed its budgetary requirements for the year. Because delay in the development and production of equipment is so universal, the expectation of slippage in development and production timescales is actually institutionalised within the budgetary process, where a reduction in the original estimate of expenditure is made to allow for delays in programmes. This reduction is termed the 'block adjustment' and in 1980-1 the block adjustment amounted to 19.4 per cent. Moreover, while the final figure published in the Estimates (the cash limit) is arrived at by deducting the block adjustment, in this case 19.4 per cent, and then adding an enhancement for inflation, the managers of individual weapons projects were authorised to spend up to the levels of expenditure estimated *before* the block adjustment was made (survey prices).

In 1980–1 this process meant that project managers were collectively authorised to spend up to the original estimate of £4,183 million, while the final estimate of expenditure, once the block adjustment and the cash limit enhancement had been taken into account, was only £3,731 million – a difference of £452 million.[71]

However, because of the speedier completion of contracts already noted, the expected slippage did not materialise. Added to this problem of course was the fact that individual project managers were working to a much higher budget and were, therefore, not necessarily aware of the need to put the brakes on their own expenditure at a time when the central management of the MOD was grappling with a major over-spend.[72]

Cost inflation A further factor leading to pressure on the 1980–1 budget was cost inflation in the development and production of weapons. As in previous years the MOD found itself under pressure on two fronts here. First, once again the allowance for inflation in the final cash limit was less than the full inflation rate. Added to this, equipment costs spiralled.[73] For instance, of the £277 million awarded to the equipment Vote in the August revision of cash limits, £210 million was for pay and price increases.[74]

Overspend as deliberate policy It should also be noted that in the case of at least one senior member of the PE, the overspend appears to have been encouraged as part of an attempt to discredit the cash limits system and thus persuade the Treasury to allow some flexibility in the MOD's annual budget (which subsequently occurred). To quote the official concerned:

> I used to say the best way of persuading the Treasury that we should not adopt in procurement this crazy business of closing the books every year, is to actually have an overspend one year ... So we deliberately set out to try and get an overspend ... .[in the year of the moratorium] I was still trying to spend, I was still trying to spend as much as I could.[75]

It is difficult to say whether this attitude was more widespread, but even

if he was an exception the official quoted above was in control of a
sizeable proportion of the procurement budget and his actions would
thus have had a commensurate impact upon the extent of the overspend.

The effect of the overspend A number of factors were, therefore,
responsible for the financial pressures the defence budget experienced
in 1980–1. Not all of these could be, or were, laid at the door of ministry
mismanagement. The earlier than expected completion of contracts and
the effect of higher interest rates on the speed with which contractors
billed the MOD were unfortunate consequences of the state of Britain's
economy and government economic policy. However, other factors highlighted already growing concerns about the way the ministry managed
its finances, and particularly the procurement of equipment. In some
cases immediate action could be, and was, taken to remedy the deficiencies revealed by the overspend. For instance, the Reeves Report
recommended that no systems controllerate should be block adjusted by
more than 2.5 per cent.[76] The ministry also introduced initiatives to
eliminate the problem of project managers working to the estimated
expenditure figures produced before the block adjustment and the inflation allowance in the final cash limit had been added.[77] Other measures
taken by the MOD included specifying 'not earlier' dates for the
completion of new contracts where appropriate[78] and requesting the
major defence firms to provide a profile of their expected rate of billing
in the forthcoming year.[79]

However, the problems represented by soaring equipment costs were
not so amenable to solution. Moreover, the overspend against the original
cash limit provoked much criticism of profligate defence spending, while
the cut-backs introduced to stave off an even higher overspend provoked
equally deep concern over the effect on the defence industry and the
services' operational capability. For instance, the moratorium had required contractors to introduce such measures as banning overtime,
reducing the number of days worked in the week and even imposing
alternate week working.[80] The smaller contractors, who did not have the
resources to wait out the trough in defence orders were particularly
hurt. It was even suggested the experience had encouraged some to leave
the defence market altogether.[81]

If the defence industry had been hurt by the MOD's cut-backs, the
services had fared even worse. For instance, expenditure on fuel was cut
by as much as £100 million.[82] This meant the Royal Navy had to

withdraw two frigates from a NATO exercise[83] and that restrictions on air flights had to be imposed.[84] Other cuts reported included the freezing of orders for Land Rovers, replacement aircraft for the RAF's Devons and Pembrokes, as well as those for more Hawk trainers.[85] The army even imposed cuts in the number of practice rounds to be fired by troops in training. Such cuts were, not surprisingly, the subject of some concern and comment.[86] The expression of these worries reached new heights during the Autumn public expenditure round of 1980 when, in the face of Treasury proposals to cut the defence budget from 1981–2 onwards, the service chiefs exercised their right to meet the prime minister and inform her of their opinion that further cuts could impair Britain's defences. This had not happened since 1976. Moreover, Francis Pym, then defence secretary, sided with the service chiefs and was even prepared to resign over the matter.[87]

Despite this, the MOD still found itself saddled with a budget reduction of £200 million a year up to 1983–4.[88] Furthermore, there seemed little prospect of an early end to the problem of rising costs and retrenchment in spending programmes. The MOD had already overspent in 1979–80 as well as 1980–1 and by the end of that year it was becoming increasingly clear that an overspend was very likely to occur in 1981–2 as well. Indeed, by April 1981 the MOD's forecasts pointed to an overspend of £700 million for the 1981–2 financial year, and by December of that year the government found itself once again having to announce an increase in the defence cash limit (this time of £300 million).[89]

Thus, the problems of 1980–1 did not add up to an isolated incident but were a symptom of more pervasive problems in the management of defence procurement. Moreover, the overspend and the inquiries it gave rise to highlighted not only the already known problem of rising costs but also severe deficiencies in the way procurement was managed – and the prospect was of even greater problems ahead if something was not rapidly done to ease the pressure on the defence budget. The MOD's answer to this was both to intensify efforts to make procurement more efficient and to engage in a defence review.

The defence review

Although the budget for 1981–2 was reduced by £200 million in the 1980 public expenditure survey, the government extended its commitment to increase defence spending by 3 per cent a year (although from this lower base) up until 1983–4. Indeed, by the time the defence review was published this had been extended even further to 1985–6.[90] Thus, the published summary of the review, *The Way Forward*, could note that the intended provision for 1985–6 would be 21 per cent higher than actual expenditure for 1978–9.[91] Yet despite this it was clear as *The Way Forward* stated, that 'even the increased resources we plan to allocate cannot adequately fund all the force structures and all the plans for their improvement we now have'.[92]

The review provoked strong opposition from the defence lobby, particularly among supporters of the Royal Navy, which it became clear was to suffer the brunt of any cuts. Indeed Keith Speed, the Navy minister, publicly spoke out against the cuts and was asked to resign as a result.[93] It is difficult to assess the success or otherwise of this opposition. However, it is worth noting that original reports had suggested the Royal Navy might be cut by almost a half, to about 30 frigates and destroyers,[94] with the loss of all of its remaining aricraft carriers.[95] Such drastic measures, however, were not taken; on the surface at least, it would appear that the naval lobby was successful in mounting a damage limitation operation against the defence review.

The conclusions of the defence review were eventually published in *The Way Forward* in June 1981. The axe, as predicted, fell on Britain's maritime commitments though not with as much severity as initial reports had suggested. The then current fleet of 59 destroyers and frigates was to be reduced to 50, and it was envisaged that by 1989 8 of these would have been withdrawn to a stand-by squadron, giving an effective fleet of 42.[96] Also, one of the navy's new generation of carriers, HMS *Invincible*, would be sold off, while an older carrier, HMS *Hermes*, was to be phased out, leaving only two carriers.[97] Additionally, two amphibious assault ships, HMS *Intrepid* and HMS *Fearless*, and nearly all the navy's auxiliary landing ships were to be phased out. Other cuts included the closure of the naval base and the Royal dockyard at Chatham, and a reduction in Royal Navy, Army and RAF numbers by 1986 of 8–10,000, 7,000 and 2,500 respectively. John Nott, then defence secretary, refused to disclose the financial information on which the review was based but *The Times* estimated the cuts would reduce MOD expenditure by £5,000 million over the following 15 years.[98]

However, the implementation of the Nott review was to be overtaken by the Falklands War, during which the Royal Navy utilised the very vessels Nott had proposed to cut. Consequently, the naval lobby was in a much more powerful position to argue its case, and the MOD subsequently drew back from a number of the review's more controversial recommendations. Indeed, by the time The White Paper on the lessons of the Falklands Campaign (Cmnd 8758) was published, in December 1982, the government had decided not to proceed with the sale of HMS *Invincible* and to retain the two assault ships, *Fearless* and *Intrepid*. Most significantly of all, it was declared that the number of destroyers and frigates in the active fleet would be held at 55 until 1984.[99] And in a press interview to coincide with the release of Cmnd 8758, John Nott stated the number would be held at this level until 1985.[100] This contrasted with the expectation in the review that the active fleet would be reduced to 50 by 1985–6.[101]

In May of 1984 the government went further and announced that up to eight ships – the full complement which the Nott review originally envisaged in the stand-by squadron – would, in fact, be run on and retained in the operational fleet.[102] As the *Statement on the Defence Estimates 1985* noted, 'there will be 53 front-line destroyers and frigates in the Fleet this year and none in the stand-by squadron.'[103] Once more this was a higher figure than that anticipated in the Nott review. Moreover, this remained the position throughout the 1980s. Thus, as the Defence Committee noted in its 1988 report on the surface fleet compared with the plans outlined in *The Way Forward*:

> There have been significant changes in the way the programme has in practice developed. The increased numbers of aircraft carriers, the retention of an amphibious capability and the maintenance of a larger number of ships in the active fleet as opposed to the stand-by squadron are indeed all enhancements of RN capability ... It appears to us that much of the philosophy underlying that paper [*The Way Forward*] has been quietly discarded.[104]

The costs of revision The changes to the Nott review, however, entailed an increased burden on the defence budget. The MOD attempted to offset this extra cost in a number of ways – for instance by extending the life of the Type 21 frigate from 18 to 20 years.[105] Nevertheless, it seems sensible to conclude that despite such attempts, the cost of running and manning these extra ships compared to the costs of maintaining them in a reserve fleet entailed a greater financial commitment than originally anticipated in the plans outlined by Nott. For example, just the two manpower intensive assault ships retained after the Falklands War required crews of some 550 men each,[106] and even the retention in-service of the ice patrol ship HMS *Endurance*, whose announced with-drawal had encouraged the Argentinians to invade the Falklands, added an extra £2 million a year to the defence budget.[107]

Thus, the naval lobby managed to limit the extent of naval cuts both before and after the review.[108] The aftermath of the Falklands War, though, did not just see many of the Nott review's planned cuts thrown overboard, it also resulted in the purchase of additional, or more modern weaponry. For example, during the conflict itself £200 million worth of improvements or new equipment were introduced which included the accelerated introduction into service of the Sea Skua anti-ship missile, Sub-Harpoon submarine-launched anti-ship missiles and the introduc-tion of laser guided bombs for Harrier GR3 aircraft. Moreover, as Cmnd 8758 stated, most of this equipment remained available for use by the services elsewhere.[109]

On top of this, the ships and equipment lost during the Falklands Campaign were all replaced. This represented more than a simple re-placement of equipment lost in the fighting for, as Cmnd 8758 noted, 'the replacement of ships and other equipment lost in the Campaign will enhance the capabilities of the Services, since replacements will be newer and in many cases more capable than their predecessors.'[110] For instance, destroyers and frigates lost in the war were replaced by the more modern Type 22 frigates, and three of these were of the new Batch III design.[111]

In addition to all this, it was also decided 'in the light of the conflict and in order to provide for the defence of the Falkland Islands'[112] that it was necessary to make a number of other, previously unplanned equipment purchases. These included 24 additional Rapier fire units, the purchase of 7 Sea Harrier aircraft and 6 Sea King ASW heli-copters.[113]

Clearly then, given the already intense pressure on the defence budget, the MOD would have been more than hard-pressed to finance such changes. However, it managed to fight and win a battle with the Treasury to ensure that the full cost of replacing equipment lost in the Falklands War would be met, in *addition* to existing plans for defence expenditure.[114] This meant the Treasury was not only required to finance the cost of the war and the islands' post-war defence, but also the cost of replacing lost equipment with newer, more up-to-date – and more expensive – versions. Moreover, the Treasury had attempted to limit its Falklands supplement to just one year, but it lost this battle too, and it financed the costs of the Falklands throughout the 1980s, although these costs were re-incorporated into the normal defence budget after 1989–90.[115]

Thus, for the services, particularly the Royal Navy, the Falklands War represented something of a lifebelt thrown to a last gasp drowning man. Indeed, it not only reversed planned equipment cuts, but also resulted in the purchase of more modern replacements for lost equipment and even additional equipment on top of that. Furthermore, the costs of the Falklands War, post-war defences and the replacements for equipment lost in the conflict were financed not out of the defence budget but out of the Treasury supplement. To a certain extent then, it was possible to accommodate the increased expenditure required by the post-Falklands revision of the Nott review.

However, despite this, the aftermath of the Falklands still left the government and the MOD facing serious financial problems. For instance, *The Financial Times* reported that while the Treasury had given in on the question of the Falklands supplement, it had done so in a compromise which preserved its insistence that the MOD should not be given an allowance for inflation higher than that permitted in the budgets of other departments.[116] Historically, defence inflation has been higher than inflation generally, so the MOD could have expected to lose by this. Additionally, although the ministry might not have been paying for its Falklands supplement, the government certainly was, and this entailed it producing for defence, via the Treasury, an extra £3,917 million over the period of its operation.[117]

In the wake of the Falklands War, defence was an even greater burden on government finances than it had been before John Nott had initiated his defence review, a review that had been launched on the grounds that 'when I [Nott] looked at the forward programme it was quite clear to me that the aspirations of the defence lobby had outrun the amount of money that was likely to be available.'[118] This meant that, from a government point of view at least, the incentive to reduce the costs of equipment was even greater than it had previously been. Moreover, the Treasury supplement only paid for the cost of the war, the construction and staffing of the Falklands Garrison, and the replacement of lost equipment; it did not include payment to help with the increased costs arising from the post-Falklands revision of the plans outlined in John

Nott's defence review. Such changes (excluding the increased cost of Trident and the costs of the Falklands) had added £2.4 billion to defence spending.[119] Thus, despite the Treasury supplement, the post-Falklands alterations added to the financial pressure on an already over-stretched budget.[120]

The ending of the 3 per cent commitment

If the government's retreat over large sections of the defence review had maintained and even added to the problems facing defence planners, there were even more problems in the pipeline. On coming to power, the Conservatives quickly reaffirmed Britain's commitment to the NATO goal of an annual real terms increase in defence expenditure of 3 per cent per annum which Labour had agreed to in 1977. This meant that by 1984–5 defence expenditure was, in real terms, 17 per cent above what it was in 1979–80. Additionally, the proportion of the defence budget spent on equipment had increased during this period from 39.7 per cent to 45.8 per cent which meant that spending on equipment had risen some 35 per cent (see Figure 2.1).

The significance of this was not so much in the dramatic increase in defence expenditure these figures represented but, first, in the fact that despite such increases the defence budget still found itself under constant strain. For instance, in the 1984–5 financial year, the services once again found themselves having to correct a potential overspend by implementing cuts.[121] Secondly, and of even more significance, the 1984 Public Expenditure White Paper announced that 1985–6 would be the last year in which the government would seek to implement the 3 per cent commitment.[122] For a defence budget which had been unsustainable during a period of very large and rapid growth, this was not the best of news.

This is not to suggest the end of the 3 per cent commitment had come out of the blue. As early as 1980 Francis Pym had indicated the MOD was basing its long-term planning on a working assessment of only 1 per cent real growth after 1985–6,[123] and in his 1981 defence review John Nott went further and 'insisted that we look at the whole ten year programme again and put it on nil growth from 1986.'[124] Thus, the prospect of an end to the 3 per cent was, in itself, a significant factor in encouraging the MOD to seek greater efficiency in its procurement process.[125]

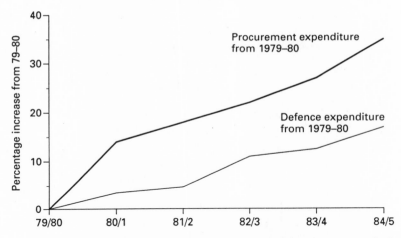

Source: Based on figures for annual defence expenditure (at constant 1993–4 prices) supplied by the MOD and figures showing the percentage of expenditure devoted to procurement given in Ministry of Defence, *Statement on the Defence Estimates 1983*, London: HMSO, Cmnd 895–II, p. 10; *SDE 1985*, Cmnd 9430–II, p. 8.

Figure 2.1 Percentage increase (in real terms) in defence expenditure and procurement expenditure from 1979–80

However, although the end of the 3 per cent commitment had long been included in the MOD's forward plans, and although it was attempting to increase efficiency, the Defence Committee rightly noted:

> Real increases in resources between 1978–9 and 85–6 provide a welcome increase in capability but despite the rationalisation of force structures proposed in Cmnd 8288 [*The Way Forward*] changes to the programmes since then will consume real resources in a way not foreseen in that June 81 White Paper. It is also the case that the increases over the period 79–86 have been presented as necessary corrective action following earlier underfunding ... [I]t seems unlikely that the real increases up to 1985–6 will be able to help out subsequent years to any marked degree at all.[126]

By 1986 it had become clear that the end of the 3 per cent commitment would not simply inaugurate a period of zero budget growth as assumed in the Nott review of 1981, but that the money allocated to defence for the coming years implied a real terms fall in the budget. Indeed, George Younger, then defence secretary, noted that bids for resources by the

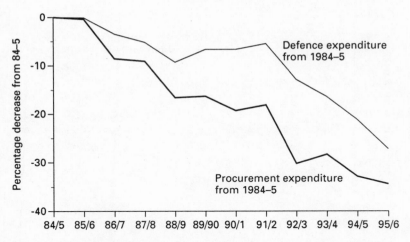

Source: Based on figures for annual defence expenditure (at constant 1993–4 prices) supplied by MOD and figures showing the percentage of expenditure devoted to procurement given in Ministry of Defence, *Statement on the Defence Estimates 1989*, London: HMSO, Cm 675–II, p. 9; *SDE 1990*, Cm 1022–II, p. 9; *SDE 1991*, Cm 1559–II, p. 9; *UK Defence Statistics: 1995 Edition*, p. 3.

Figure 2.2 Percentage decrease (in real terms) in defence expenditure and procurement expenditure from 1984–5

services exceeded funds available by about £1 billion a year. In response, he proposed yet more cut-backs.[127] These included reducing the provision for future mine systems and the complete abandonment of the army's Light Anti-tank Weapons (LAW) mine, along with plans to retrofit new towed-array sonars to Type 22 frigates.[128]

By 1989 planned defence expenditure for the year was almost 7 per cent less, in real terms, than it had been in 1984–5 (see Figure 2.2). Moreover, the equipment budget suffered an even larger reduction. This was in part due to the difficulties experienced by the MOD in recruiting and retraining personnel.[129] In addition, from 1985–6 any pay awards above the general level of inflation had to be financed from the defence budget rather than from a separate Treasury allowance as had been the case previously. On top of all this, service pensions rose faster than inflation.[130] Thus, either personnel numbers had to be drastically cut or the budget devoted to manpower had to rise. Unfortunately, the government had already initiated a very significant programme of cuts in both service and civilian manpower.[131] Consequently the procurement budget lost the favoured position it held in the early 1980s. This meant that whereas procurement accounted for 45.8 per cent of MOD expenditure in 1984–5, by 1989–90 it accounted for 41.1 per cent. Combined with the overall reduction in the defence budget this meant that between 1984–5 and 1989–90 defence equipment expenditure fell by 16 per cent, over £2 billion at 1993–4 prices (see Figure 2.2). After the heady days of the early 1980s when it had risen in leaps and bounds, the procurement budget found itself being brought back to earth with a bang. Thus, to quote Keith Hartley, 'the ending of the three per cent signalled a major budget squeeze during the rest of the decade.'[132] Indeed, even the prospect of its ending provided significant impetus to the search for efficiency in procurement.

Post-cold war cuts

The downturn in defence expenditure was not simply the consequence of a decision to end the 3 per cent commitment that had been anticipated in the early 1980s and automatically implemented. It was also a response, in part at least, to the growing rapprochement between the West and Mikhail Gorbachev's Soviet Union. Nevertheless, up until 1989 it is arguable that the reductions in defence expenditure that did occur were less a function of growing *détente* and more the function of a decision taken in the early 1980s (and then reaffirmed) to abandon the blank cheque approach to defence after 1986. Similarly, reductions in the procurement budget were more a consequence of the MOD's difficulties in recruiting manpower and the increased cost of pay and pensions than a considered response to a rapidly thawing cold war.

After 1989, of course, the traditional parameters of the security debate in Europe were transformed beyond all recognition: first by the revolutions in Eastern Europe, then by the dissolution of the Soviet Union and the emergence of a Russian state led by a pro-Western, pro-capitalist leader whose power was no longer drawn from the Communist Party. The MOD's response was to initiate the Options for Change defence review.

The ministry's deliberations were set out in two statements to the House of Commons on 24 July 1990 and 23 July 1991, as well as in a White Paper entitled *Britain's Army for the 90s*.[133] In his statement on 25 July the defence secretary announced cuts in service personnel of 18 per cent (later increased to 20 per cent), a reduction in the surface fleet from 'around 50' to 'around 40' destroyers and frigates, a halving of the submarine force and, most significantly, a halving of British forces in Germany. The defence secretary asserted that Options was different from previous British defence reviews in that it was undertaken in response to changes in the international environment rather than to a demand for savings from the Treasury. However, while Options for Change was clearly made inevitable by the events of 1989, it was equally a response to the mounting resources crisis implied by rising equipment and manpower costs on the one hand, and a declining defence budget on the other. Furthermore, it was clear to many commentators, including the Defence Committee and the chief of the General Staff, that despite the defence secretary's protestations to the contrary, the exercise was very much driven by a Treasury determined to extract a peace dividend from the end of the cold war.[134] Thus, changes in the international environment were less a reason for Options, more a face-saving rationale.

Inevitably, Options came in for criticism from both those concerned at the extent of the proposed cuts and those who argued they did not go far enough. However, the review did at least have the merit of appearing to propose a structure for the forces that was sustainable on the projected budget.[135] Subsequent to Options though, extra commitments were undertaken in Bosnia necessitating an increase in the number of planned regiments from 38 to 40, while a rising PSBR necessitated further cuts in the defence budget. Most notably, the Chancellor's autumn statement of 1993 proposed significant cuts in defence expenditure, particularly in 1996–7. In real terms, the budget for 1996–7, represented a cut of £750 million less than the previous plan for 1995–6. Moreover, the Defence Committee estimated that the real terms fall between the previously assumed figures for 1996–7 and the new ones amounted to a cut of nearly £1 billion, while reports in the press suggested the revised budget was actually some £1.5 billion less than the bids accumulated in the long-term costings.[136] The MOD's response was to adopt its traditional approach to a mismatch between resources and commitments. On the one hand it engaged in *ad hoc*, incremental cuts in personnel and equipment. On the other, it announced a Defence Costs Study entitled 'Front Line First' (FLF) designed to examine further ways in which efficiency savings could be achieved in everything from its chaplaincy services to its procurement practices. According to the MOD this produced the required £750 million worth of savings for 1996–7. It also expected an additional £100 million of savings over and above that figure for each of the years after that. On top of this, the 1994 Budget Statement produced expenditure plans for 1995–6 and 1996–7 which actually represented real terms *increases* of £220 million and £310 million respectively over previous figures.[137]

What did all this mean for procurement? First, the stated aim of the Defence Costs Study was to ring fence resources for the front-line fighting forces to protect them from any proposed cuts. Thus, the study was presented as freeing resources which could be channelled back into spending on the forces. On one hand, therefore, the study proposed reductions in support manpower of almost 19,000 by the year 2000, with the RAF and UK-based civil servants bearing the brunt of the manpower cuts (40 per cent and 38 per cent respectively). On the other hand, the savings were presented as allowing the MOD to make a number of 'highly significant enhancements' to front-line capability, including some £5 billion worth of orders and invitations to tender for new equipment. These included the announcement of an order for 7 Sandown minehunters, confirmation of an order for 250 Challenger 2 tanks and a production order for the mid-life upgrade of the Tornado GRI.[138]

Of all the equipment decisions announced, however, only the revelation that the MOD was considering the acquisition of Tomahawk cruise missiles was actually novel. Other projects had already been foreshadowed in earlier announcements or constituted confirmation of orders which had actually been frozen while FLF was in progress. Consequently, FLF's achievement was not so much in securing new equipment but in avoiding swingeing cuts in the equipment programme. Moreover, of the projected savings secured by the study it was notable that the majority (51 per cent) were to be achieved through further efficiencies in procurement and logistics support. Thus, while FLF may have afforded relative protection to the equipment programme, it actually formalised the incentive to search for savings in the conduct of weapons acquisition and maintenance. Equally, though the 1994 Budget Statement may have increased the money available to defence, this was done simply to cover the costs of the services redundancies proposed in FLF. There was no new money for defence procurement. Indeed, any benefits to defence procurement from FLF had to be viewed against the backdrop of a 22 per cent fall in procurement expenditure in the period from 1989–90 to 1995–6 and a 34 per cent fall from 1984–5 to 1989–90 (see Figure 2.2).

Although the reform of procurement had already begun before the end of the cold war, the cuts in defence expenditure that ensued from its demise certainly reinforced the incentive to continue the search for efficiency in weapons acquisition. Ironically, however, the scale of these cuts highlighted the already apparent flaws in the new approach to procurement and consequently increased the countervailing pressure on the government to disavow its commitment to competition in favour of a more interventionist approach to the defence industrial sector. As will be noted in subsequent chapters, this has meant that the MOD's value for money policies have continued to evolve in response to the financial constraints imposed on the procurement budget.

Government ideology – the influence of Thatcherism

Throughout the period of the value for money reforms there has been severe pressure on the defence budget as a consequence of rising equipment costs and, latterly, falling defence expenditure. Coupled with the manifest problems inherent in the procurement system, the need for reform of the weapons acquisition process was arguably undeniable and inevitable. In reality, however, the nature of the reforms undertaken can only be properly understood when account is taken of the influence of Thatcherism in determining the policy towards the defence industry.

To explain the reform of procurement policy as simply a response to pressure on the equipment budget is to exaggerate the influence of such pressures in bringing about fundamental reform in MOD practice. Indeed, the twin problems of rising costs and finite budgets are hardy perennials that the MOD has lived with ever since its inception, while the flaws in the procurement process had been well known and well documented for a good many years. These had even led to procurement reforms such as those recommended in the Gibb-Zuckerman Report of 1961, by Downey in the late 1960s and by the Rayner Report in the early 1970s. However, such reforms were largely of a technical or organisational nature rather than an attempt to change the very philosophy of weapons procurement. In contrast, the value for money approach introduced in the early 1980s represented a declared attempt to replace the cost-plus, preferred contractor approach with competition, privatisation, incentive contracts and a *laissez-faire* approach to the defence market. In short, while pressure on the defence budget and crises in the procurement system may have been necessary conditions for reform, they do not explain the actual direction that procurement reform took in the 1980s and later. Ultimately this was determined less by the constraints of the weapons acquisition process and more by the philosophy of Thatcherism, with its emphasis on 'sound' money, the belief in competition, free enterprise, and what Biddis has described as 'the provision of positive incentives rather than a negative cushioning, the privatisation of state-owned industries, [and] the encouragement of calculated risk taking'.[139]

As will be noted in later chapters, actual procurement practice has not always been as radically altered as the rhetoric of ministers might suggest, and inefficiency in procurement remains rife. Nevertheless, a significant change in the philosophy of weapons acquisition has occurred since the early 1980s. In particular, cost-plus contracts have been virtually eliminated, the use of competition in the allocation of new contracts has increased notably, and the defence industry has been swept up in the privatisation process. In the case of privatisation, for example, by the time Mrs Thatcher resigned British Aerospace (BAe) and Rolls-Royce had been floated as independent firms and BAe had acquired both BL (Rover) and the bulk of Royal Ordnance; those warship yards of British Shipbuilders which were profitable were sold off; Short Brothers was purchased by Bombardier of Canada; and private contractors were brought in to operate and manage government-owned facilities such as the Royal Dockyards and the Atomic Weapons Establishment.[140]

The reform of procurement was also characterised by the fact that many initiatives – in particular the competition policy – were introduced in the teeth of opposition from both the defence industry and the bureaucrats in the MOD. Indeed, it is notable that many of the key actors in the reform of procurement were either brought in from outside the MOD or, in the case of ministers, were appointed less for their knowledge of strategic issues than for their perceived ability to instil efficiency into the organisation. For instance, the appointment of John Nott as defence secretary was perceived to reflect the prime minister's wish to install someone who would bring Thatcherite rigour and efficiency to the defence budget.[141] Indeed, although Michael Heseltine has been given (and claimed) much of the credit for the introduction of the value for money reforms, it was during Nott's period in office that the proposals in *Value for Money in Defence Equipment Procurement* (the document which formed the basis of the government's new approach to procurement) were drawn up. Although not published until October 1983, when Nott had already left the MOD, the document was actually completed in 1982 and only held back due to discussions with the Treasury and because of the Falklands War.[142]

Nott's successor, Michael Heseltine, was also sent to the MOD because of his talent for managing and streamlining bureaucracies rather than his knowledge of strategic issues. Moreover, while much of the policy development may have been undertaken by his predecessor, Heseltine nevertheless found resistance to the new approach from within the ministry. For instance, he later complained to one interviewer that:

> The Ministry did not want me to introduce competition. ... I said look I'm not going to have this. We are being ripped off and I am going to subject these people to the sort of competition that I understand about ... In the end I had to do it ... but there were some pretty traumatic experiences on the route.[143]

Partly because the value for money initiative had encountered so much resistance from the defence establishment, Heseltine brought in Peter Levene from the defence industry to 'turn gamekeeper' and act as chief of defence procurement. As Levene himself has noted, one of his main assets in the eyes of Heseltine was that he came from outside the civil service network and was 'not totally bound up with the system'.[144] Levene's successor in the post in the early 1990s, Malcolm Macintosh, was also an outsider whose previous experience had been gained as an Australian defence official.

To a large degree, therefore, the value for money policies, particularly in their early years, were imposed on the MOD and the defence industry – often in the face of opposition. To some extent, this may explain the fact that, as will be noted in later chapters, implementation has often fallen short, and in some cases a long way short, of declared policy. It is also notable that in recent years, even declared policy has been moderated. In particular, the assertion that 'we don't conduct an industrial policy'[145] has been modified in the face of cuts to the defence budget and heavy lobbying from the defence industry, so that the MOD now expresses a greater willingness to take into account the long-term health of the defence industrial base (DIB). To the extent that there has been a dichotomy between declared and actual policy, and the more radical edges of the value for money approach have been softened in recent

years (see later chapters), it could be argued this reflects either the re-
orientation of Thatcherism under John Major and/or the success of the
defence establishment in first resisting, and then moderating, the value
for money approach.

Both these arguments may have a certain explanatory value, but
neither paints the whole picture. In many ways policy on defence
procurement, even in the mid-1980s, rested at the epicentre of the
contradictions inherent in Thatcherism – between its emphasis on the
free market on the one hand and a strong State on the other. The free
market approach required the introduction of competition and an attack
on the cosy corporatism that was the hallmark of procurement in the
1970s. This, of course, was what value for money was supposed to be
about, and to some extent it did achieve its aims. Indeed, even left wing
academics such as Dunne and Smith could conclude that: 'Thatcherism,
particularly after 1985, represented the most sustained attack on the
British military-industrial complex since World War II. This was as a
result not of Mrs Thatcher's personal involvement but of the application
of the economic ideology of Thatcherism.'[146] However, this represents
only half the story. At the same time that Thatcherism's free market
philosophy required an attack on corporatism in procurement, the
'strong State' element implied a commitment to strong defence. This
was reflected in the acquisition of Trident, the fighting of the Falklands
War, and the maintenance of relatively high levels of defence expenditure
compared with those of the UK's European allies – a feature of UK
defence expenditure which has persisted despite significant overall cuts
in the defence budget since the mid-1980s (see Chapter 8). It was also
reflected in a concern to maintain a wide-ranging defence force and an
industry capable of servicing it. Thus, in domestic procurement there
have been constant tensions between the concern to promote efficiency
in defence procurement on the one hand, and the concern to maintain
the defence industrial base on the other. This can be seen at work in a
succession of major procurement decisions – for example Alarm, Challenger, and the recent order for transport helicopters – where the MOD
has opted for British equipment of debatable 'value for money' when
compared to alternatives from abroad (see Chapter 3). Indeed on the
issue of defence exports, where the tension between the government's
concern to make the procurement pound go further and industry's
ambition to make procurement profits go higher is absent, Thatcherism's
emphasis on strong defence and the promotion of national economic

and security interests has led, if anything, to an intensification of the cosy relationship between the MOD and the defence industry. There has certainly been a substantial increase in the level of resources (both financial and political) mobilised by government to promote the sale of British defence equipment abroad (see Chapter 6).

Thus, while the free market elements of Thatcherism implied an attack on the procurement practices of the past, the commitment to strong defence actually implied a set of policies that were more in line with the preferences of the defence establishment and the traditional military-security bias of British foreign and defence policy (see Chapter 8). Indeed in the case of defence exports, far from attacking the corporatism of the 1970s, Thatcherism reinforced it. Consequently, as will be shown in subsequent chapters, the acquisition process in both the 1980s and 1990s has often been hindered by a dichotomy between policy and practice, and an inconsistency in approach. This has meant that the defining characteristic of the value for money reforms has not been the unleashing of market forces, as is often claimed, but rather, the Janus-like quality of policies that have had to straddle the contradictions inherent in the government's philosophy. The aim in the following chapters is to outline these contradictions and the consequent failure to eliminate both inefficiency in weapons procurement and the costly military-security bias of British foreign and defence policy.

Nevertheless it remains the case that, in terms of the genesis of the value for money reforms, while crisis in defence procurement created an imperative for change, it was the ideology (albeit a contradictory one) of Thatcherism which determined the direction that change would take.

3

Competition with limits

Competition statistics

According to the MOD, its previous preferred contractor approach has been abandoned and competition now lies at the heart of the procurement process.[1] Indeed, in the mid-1980s the MOD set itself the target of raising the proportion (by value) of competitively let contracts to over 60 per cent by 1990,[2] and currently aims to place at least 75 per cent of contracts competitively.[3] As part of this new approach the placing of any non-competitive contract over £10 million now has to receive ministerial approval.[4] The ministry has also adopted an American initiative termed 'breakout' which aims to identify the high value items in a spares package offered by a contractor and compete for them.[5] Primes are also encouraged to hold competitions when placing sub-contracts. This has been particularly stressed as a means of introducing competition into otherwise non-competitive prime contracts. The ministry has, in addition, adopted a number of measures designed to attract new and, particularly, small firms to defence work and thus increase the pool of potential competitors. For instance, it now produces a fortnightly *MOD Contracts Bulletin*, which advertises contracts where competition needs stimulating or where the contract value exceeds £500,000.[6] In the mid-1980s the Ministry also placed emphasis on competing for the production of equipment where it had funded development. However, difficulties were experienced in ensuring that adequate data was passed from the holder of the design rights to the producer. In consequence, policy has been modified and the MOD is now, in general, aiming to contract for design, development and production in a single package using option prices for production items established during the initial competition.[7]

Such initiatives would appear to represent a very significant and real

Table 3.1 Average level of competition in the five years to 1994–5

Type of competition	Per cent
Official competition (cat. 1 and 2) including amendments to contracts.	68.5
Competition (cat. 1 and 2) excluding amendments to competitive contracts and *amendments* to contracts let by reference to market forces.	52.0
Competition excluding amendments to competitively placed contracts and *all* contracts placed by reference to market forces.	40.5
Competition on new contracts excluding amendments to *both* competitive and non-competitive contracts.	68.7

Source: Calculated from statistics supplied by the MOD, April 1996.

attempt to introduce competition into the procurement system. Moreover, the statistical evidence would appear to support this view. For instance, by the early 1990s the number of firms on the Defence Contractors List stood at some 11,000, an increase of 4,000 since 1985.[8] More important, the proportion of competitively placed contracts (as defined by the MOD) has risen from 30 per cent of the total value of all contracts placed in 1979–80 to 73 per cent in 1994–5.[9]

However, while the level of competition has most certainly risen, the level of competition in the procurement system as a whole has not risen to the extent suggested by the MOD's statistics. For instance, in 1992 the Defence Contractors List (DCL) was cleansed of inactive contractors (those not receiving contracts for three years) bringing the total registered down to 8,000. Moreover, a recent National Audit Office (NAO) report has noted that of those companies registered on the DCL, only 53 per cent subsequently received an invitation to tender, and that that there was 'still a tendency to stick to tried and tested names'.[10] More recently the DCL has been abandoned and the MOD now refers to the DTI's Register of Quality Assessed Companies when searching for suitable contractors.

Furthermore, the headline figure of 73 per cent competition in 1994–5 exaggerates the real level of competition in the procurement system as a whole. This is due to a number of factors. First, the figures for

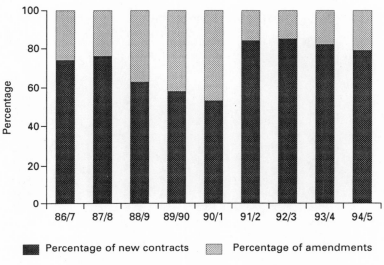

Source: Calculated from statistics supplied by MOD, April 1996.

Figure 3.1 Percentage (by value) of competitive contracts (category 1 and 2) made up of amendments to contracts and new contracts

some years are influenced by the placing of one or two large competitive contracts. For example, a particularly high level of competition was recorded in 1991–2, but this was because large competitive contracts were placed for both the Challenger 2 fighting vehicle and the Merlin helicopter. To obtain a more accurate measure of the level of competition it is necessary to calculate the average amount of competition over a number of years. Taking a five-year period to 1994–5, for instance, the average level of official competition comes down to 68.5 per cent (see Table 3.1).

Second, amendments to previously placed competitive contracts are actually included in the total of competitive contracts. Some amendments may simply be adjustments for inflation and therefore have no impact on the real cost of a project. However, adjustments for inflation are more commonly dealt with by what are termed contract price letters and therefore do not give rise to formal contract amendments. Thus, as the MOD itself has noted, 'the vast majority of amendments relate to real changes in the nature and cost of the contract.'[11] Such amendments, however, take place *after* the initial competition has taken place and

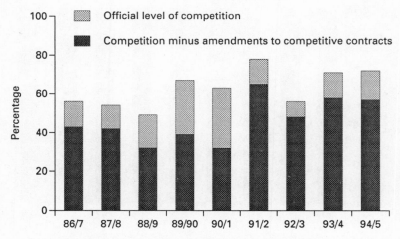

Source: Calculated from statistics supplied by MOD, April 1996.

Figure 3.2 Percentage of contracts (by value) allocated competitively

consequently are not subject to competition. Indeed, as will be suggested later, contractors may actually use amendments to contracts as a way of subsequently raising profits on competitively placed contracts. As can be seen in Figure 3.1, amendments to contracts account for a significant proportion of supposedly competitive contracts – almost 50 per cent (by value) in some years.

As a consequence of these factors, the real level of competition in the procurement system is actually much less than the MOD's official figures would suggest (see Figure 3.2). Indeed, if amendments to contracts are excluded, the average level of competition over the five years to 1994–5 (the most recent for which I have been able to obtain figures including amendments) comes down to just 52 per cent (see Table 3.1). Clearly, this is much lower than the over 60 per cent figure the MOD aimed to achieve by 1990 and the 75 per cent the ministry currently aims for.

This is not to to deny that the MOD has been relatively successful in placing a high level of *new* contracts on a competitive basis. For instance, if one considers only the proportion of new contracts placed competitively (excluding amendments to all types of contract, both competitive and non-competitive), the average level of competition over the five years to 1994–5 was nearly 69 per cent (see Table 3.1) – a higher level than suggested by the MOD's official competition statistics. However, this latter figure does not give a valid measure of the level of competition in the procurement system *as a whole*, excluding, as it does, the substantial amount of expenditure incurred on amendments to contracts.

A further question mark that can be placed against the MOD's competition statistics concerns the practice of defining competitive contracts as the sum total of competitively placed contracts (category 1) and contracts placed by reference to market forces (category 2). Unlike those priced by competition, the price of contracts let by reference to market forces is not arrived at following a formal competitive tendering process. Instead, such contracts, which tend to be for low-value off the shelf equipment, are priced through the use of informal competitive tendering processes and commercial price lists. It is questionable whether such practices should be regarded as truly competitive: informal competitive processes are more likely to encourage the use of established contractors and thus fail to guarantee the inclusion of all possible suppliers. This contrasts with the MOD's aim to increase the pool of suppliers in the belief that new firms may sometimes give better value for money. Additionally, while discounts are often obtained on commercial price lists, a doubt remains as to whether more extensive price reductions could be obtained by going out to formal competition.

A further problem related to this category of the competition statistics is that it includes contracts for equipment (for example, spares) listed on a company's commercial price list but for which the firm is a monopoly supplier. Clearly, if no other company is able to supply the kind of equipment required, the price agreed will be arrived at in a non-competitive context, so to include such contracts in the competition statistics is misleading.

None of this is to suggest that the MOD's use of contracts let by reference to market forces is necessarily inappropriate in those cases where it adopts this approach. Given that it is a strategy generally used in the purchase of smaller value items it is probably the case that the costs of undergoing a formal competitive tendering process would normally outweigh any potential savings. What is questionable, however, is whether such contracts should be included in the competition statistics, upon which they have a significant influence. Indeed if one excludes both contracts let by reference to market forces and amendments to competitively placed contracts, the level of competition in the five years to 1994–5 comes down to just 40 per cent (see Table 3.1), nearly 30 percentage points below the official level of competition claimed by the MOD.

Thus, while the level of competition has certainly increased since the early 1980s and the proportion of new contracts let competitively is even higher than suggested by the MOD's official statistics, the real level of competition in the procurement system as a whole is much lower than claimed. At best, it has averaged some 52 per cent, at worst just 40.5 per cent in the five years to 1994–5.

The headline figure for competition, however, only paints a limited picture of the way in which competition has been introduced into the procurement system. To gain a fuller understanding, it is necessary to examine both the way in which the structure of the UK DIB has served to limit the possibilities of competition in important sectors and the MOD's willingness to contemplate the use of overseas firms as competitors for procurement contracts.

Sectoral competition

In a number of major equipment areas, the implementation of competition has had to contend with the reality of monopoly suppliers inherited from the industrial restructuring of previous decades. Furthermore, this position has worsened, particularly during the late 1980s, as the UK DIB has been rationalised through takeovers and mergers. Consequently the UK now has, for instance, only one manufacturer in each of the following areas: helicopters, fighter aircraft, tanks, submarines and of heavy calibre ammunition. Clearly, this presents challenges for the MOD in implementing competition policies.

The rationalisation of the defence industry has largely been in response to a number of mutually reinforcing factors which have affected the European DIB in general – for example, shrinking defence budgets and rising weapons costs, combined with fears of increased competition from US companies suffering from a similarly dwindling home market. It is also a response to the Single European Act which, despite precluding defence, has affected many contractors who are part of industrial conglomerates with extensive civil interests. This is particularly the case for those defence sectors dependent on dual use technologies such as electronics and telecommunications, where competitiveness may depend on civil market strength. It is, furthermore, a response to Independent

European Programme Group (IEPG) initiatives to open up the European defence market to greater international competition and, therefore, integration.[12]

The implementation of competition policy has also had to take place against the backdrop of a 34 per cent fall in procurement expenditure since 1984–5 (see Figure 2.2). In a number of market sectors, therefore, there simply has not been enough work available to sustain more than one domestic supplier. As Peter Levene, then chief of defence procurement, acknowledged in 1991:

> Today things are different. The market runs down, we cannot pretend that we have to keep a large number of suppliers going when there is insufficient work for them ... if there is only sufficent work for one firm and two of them decide to merge ... then we would have a very weak position in objecting to that.[13]

Ironically, it is also the case that the MOD's own procurement policy has sometimes accelerated rationalisation of the defence industry, producing both new monopolies and increased market power for the major defence companies. For instance, competition took second place in the drive to have the £2 billion radar contract for the European Fighter Aircraft (EFA) (now renamed Eurofighter) awarded to a British company. In order to persuade the Germans to drop their opposition to a UK radar, GEC was allowed to purchase the troubled Ferranti's electronic and defence systems business. This was despite the fact that the MOD had previously been against such a move on the grounds that it would produce a monopoly in airborne military radar design and manufacture.[14]

The MOD's implementation of its own value for money policies has also served to promote the market power of the major contractors. For instance, privatisation resulted in the sale of Royal Ordnance's (RO) Leeds factory to Vickers, producing a monopoly in tank manufacture.[15] In addition, the ministry's policy of placing increasing reliance on prime contractors to manage large defence projects (albeit a sensible approach) and the reduction in the scale of the government's research establishments has inevitably increased the large prime contractors' command over the defence technology base. This trend has been exacerbated by the fact that the MOD's new approach requires companies to assume a larger share of the risk in the development of equipment, and sometimes to take on board any increases in development costs. Only the large contractors have the capital base to shoulder such costs.

Furthermore, the squeeze on profits implied by the operation of competition and the worsening relations between the ministry and industry that were a consequence of the new approach to procurement, were probably contributory factors in convincing firms such as Philips, Thorn and Ford Aerospace to withdraw from the defence market. These same factors have also encouraged other companies to leave specific defence sectors or products, promoting further concentration of the defence industry. Certainly, one industrialist interviewed has noted that competition led his company to withdraw from a particular product range,[16] while another noted:

> Seventy per cent of our business used to come from the MOD, it is now reversed, seventy per cent of our business comes from other customers ... it's a direct response to how the Ministry has behaved ... the current policy of the MOD in terms of how they do business.[17]

It is notable in this context, therefore, that a recent survey found only half of the companies invited to submit competitive bids for projects actually did so.[18]

The implementation of competition has also evolved in a context in which ever greater emphasis has been placed upon ensuring that large national champions have the size and strength to compete both in an emerging European defence industrial base and in the global market. Increasingly, therefore, the maintenance of competition within the UK DIB has had to take second place to the need to ensure that Britain's principal defence companies have the necessary capabilities to operate in these larger markets. This was certainly the justification offered by the MOD for allowing Vickers to take over Leeds RO. It is also noteworthy in this respect that the ministry has recently modified its defence export policy so that it will now support only one UK bid for each potential export order from overseas;[19] previously the ministry had supported every company pursuing an export order, even if they were competing against each other. Clearly, backing individual companies abroad is difficult to reconcile with the promotion of competition at home, and is likely to advantage the major defence contractors who already have extensive contacts and experience in overseas markets. As one industralist has noted: 'by a process of elimination eventually we are going to have national champions anyway.'[20] Similarly, the MOD has recently made it clear that while it remains concerned to promote competition in collaborative equipment programmes with other nations, it

would nevertheless be prepared to sacrifice competition in some programmes in order to promote greater collaboration and the restructuring
of Europe's defence industry.[21]

The concern to promote the UK's major defence contractors as
leading players in the European and global defence market is perhaps
most notably reflected in government policy towards British Aerospace
(BAe), whose growing pre-eminence has been facilitated by the generous
terms on which the government sold both Royal Ordnance and Rover
to the company. Similarly, the language of the MOD's support for a
BAe proposal to merge its missile business with Thomson CSF of
France suggested the ministry was less concerned about the implications
of domestic competition than it was anxious to see the company being
built up as a leading player in the European defence market.[22] More
recently, the MOD's decision to split an order for the next generation
of air transport planes between Lockheed's Hercules and the European
Future Large Aircraft (FLA) was influenced more by its concern to
maintain BAe's position in the European aerospace industry rather than
the intrinsic merits of an FLA procurement.[23] Thus, despite the
ministry's commitment to competition, it is difficult to avoid the conclusion that it has facilitated the creation of a corporate defence giant
which concludes 2,000 contracts a year with the MOD[24] and whose size
has led one French industrialist to comment, 'The problem for the
British government is that it now has two ministries of defence – one
called the Ministry of Defence and the other called British Aerospace.'[25]
Indeed, it is notable that recurrent speculation about the possibility of
a merger between BAe and GEC has also been accompanied by reports
of MOD equanimity at such a prospect. For instance, the government's
decision to allow GEC to go ahead with its bid for VSEL was widely
considered to mean that it would not stand in the way of a bid for BAe.
If such a merger were to go ahead, it would create one of the largest
defence companies in the world, with annual defence sales of some £10
billion a year.[26] This is not a development that would sit easily with the
stated aim of maintenance of competition in the domestic market.

This is not to suggest that actual policy has been completely at odds
with the competition initiative. As already noted, the MOD has made
active efforts to try and bring new firms into the defence market, particularly in the software and telecommunications fields.[27] The MOD also
opposed GEC's first attempt to take over Plessey on the grounds that
it would reduce competition in defence procurement.[28] Subsequently, of

course, GEC's second attempt was permitted by the Monopolies and Mergers Commission (MMC) after the company made a number of changes to its bid aimed at satisfying the ministry's concerns.

Nevertheless, it is clear that in a number of sectors the ministry has effectively retreated from the commitment to maintain competition, a retreat that has been determined by a number of factors. First, rising weapons costs and (from the mid-1980s on) declining defence budgets meant that equipment orders were no longer available to sustain more than one company. Second, the advantages of having one large national champion competing for contracts in the European and global market-place became clearer. Third, the politics of the day made other considerations such as privatisation or the winning of an order for the UK DIB more important. Ironically, the pursuit of the MOD's competition policy has also accelerated rationalisation in some sectors and encouraged the increasing predominance of the major prime contractors.

Thus, the MOD's headline figure for the level of competition does not give a full picture of the nature of competition in the procurement system. In reality, competition is either more or less extensive depending on the market sector under consideration, and many of the sectors where monopolies exist are responsible for the high value products which make up a significant proportion of the equipment budget. Even where competition does exist it is sometimes nominal, with one major contractor possessing exceptional market predominance. For instance, in the five years from 1985–6 to 1989–90 BAe (British Aerospace) was awarded 84 per cent of contracts for guided weapons systems, with its only other rival as prime contractor (and then only in certain types of systems) being Shorts, which received 14 per cent (the remainder going, in contracts for repairs, to other companies).[29] Similarly, the MMC have noted that, prior to their merger, GEC and Plessey received over 70 per cent of MOD expenditure with all major electronics companies.[30]

This is not to deny that the MOD has attempted to bring new and small contractors into the defence market. However, it is the major contractors who receive the vast majority of MOD payments. For instance, in 1993–4 the top three prime contractors accounted for 24 per cent of MOD equipment expenditure, and the top five 31 per cent.[31] Furthermore, it is only the major contractors who have the size, expertise and experience necessary to take on the MOD's major high-technology, high-value weapons projects. At this level the ministry has, in spite of its commitment to competition (and indeed sometimes because of its own procurement policies), presided over a decade during which the UK DIB evolved into a market with fewer major contractors, many of which exercise monopoly control and/or exceptional predominance in important defence sectors. Consequently, for some of these firms at least, the MOD's competition policy may not have affected them to the extent suggested by the headline competition figures. For instance, it is notable that the percentage of competitive contracts awarded to GEC and Plessey prior to their merger was consistently lower than those attained by the MOD throughout the procurement system as a whole.[32] Furthermore, the predominance of major companies often holding monopoly control over certain product areas has implications for the way in which such firms can offset the effects of competition in some product areas by clawing back their losses in areas where they suffer little or no competition. This is a point that will be returned to later.

Of course, the rationalisation of the UK DIB can be seen as a sensible response to cut-backs in defence expenditure and the evolving nature of the European and global defence markets. It has, however, placed constraints on the operation of competition policy within the domestic DIB. Clearly, such constraints do not necessarily imply that competition has been undermined. For example, the MOD has emphasised its willingness to appoint prime contractors who are not the main platform builder but integration specialists – an approach adopted, for instance, in the appointment of Loral ASIC as prime contractor for the EH101 helicopter. The ministry has also underlined the fact that it is prepared to buy equipment from abroad when better value for money can be obtained. However, as will be shown below, despite this shift in formal policy, the extent of the ministry's commitment to international competition (even in the late 1980s), has been less than wholehearted, thus placing a question mark over the thoroughness with which it has been prepared to operate its competition policy to date.

Buy abroad

By the end of the 1980s and the beginning of the 1990s the MOD was emphasising its greater willingness to consider tenders from overseas companies. For instance, Peter Levene stated '[W]e have no predisposition to favour home producers nor to discriminate against them. We are there to obtain the best value for money for the defence budget.'[33] However, this greater official emphasis on international competition needs to be put in perspective. For instance, the policy was not put into place immediately following the election of the Conservative government in 1979; indeed, despite its commitment to the free market in other areas, the new government appeared to be almost as protectionist as its Labour predecessor. For example, in 1981, despite noting there was nothing really to be gained for British industry by the MOD buying expensive and uncompetitive products, John Nott, then defence secretary, could note:

> Ninety per cent of everything we procure is from British industry or our collaborative partners and that is on the basis of a conscious decision. Indeed, the industrial implications flowing from our decisions are very much in our mind always. Indeed, it is quite often the case that it would be cheaper to buy off-the-shelf of a long production run from overseas than to buy from British industry on what is by necessity a shorter production run.[34]

In fact, the percentage of equipment purchased overseas fell consistently from 8.8 per cent in 1978–9 to 4.4 per cent in 1982–3. In comparison, 31 per cent of domestic demand for manufactured goods in general was met from imports in 1983.[35]

Subsequent to the formal enunciation of the ministry's value for money policy, the official position on the question of international competition was typified by one minister, who informed Parliament in 1984:

> The government considers that the acceptance of UK tenders which are internationally uncompetitive does not lead to a sustained increase in employment in the economy as a whole. It is accepted that there may be short-term employment benefits in particular sectors of the defence industry, but the adverse effects of uncompetitive purchases on the economy through higher public sector borrowing, interest rates, rate of inflation or the exchange rate lead to increases in unemployment in other areas.[36]

Moreover, this period also saw the cancellation of the GEC Nimrod AEW and the purchase of US AWACS, which was interpreted as signalling a greater willingness to buy abroad. However, this was only half the story. As one minister noted in 1986:

> Although we will not always buy British regardless there would have to be good justification for turning to overseas suppliers in the face

of UK competition – justification that might not be provided by small differences in price alone.[37]

Even Peter Levene, whose brief it was to extend competition, could note in the mid-1980s:

> to have the impetus of competition occasionally from abroad – and we will obviously only use it where we deem it to be appropriate for one reason or another – is no bad reason to keep people on their toes. But we have to use it carefully we have to use it appropriately and we have to use it sparingly.[38]

However, in the 1988 Public Expenditure White Paper the MOD announced a greater readiness to consider non-UK equipment where it offered greater value for money, and the Defence Committee concluded this might signal a new policy towards the defence industrial base.[39]

One example of this greater willingness to countenance overseas competition can be seen in the Anglo-French reciprocal purchasing initiative, launched at the end of 1987. As a result of this initiative each country now publishes its contract opportunities in bulletins available in the other, and companies tendering for requirements in either country are assured of equal consideration for development contracts valued between £1 million and £10 million, and for production contracts valued between £1 million and £50 million. Between 1988 and 1991 this led to £68.5 million/Fr 651 million worth of business being exchanged – an approximate balance.[40] A greater willingness to buy abroad can also be seen in the fact that when the MOD re-launched its New Suppliers Service (now called the Defence Suppliers Service) at the end of 1988 it made clear it was not confining its search for new suppliers to the UK.

Rhetoric versus reality

Despite the apparent shift in policy noted above, in reality the extent to which the ministry's formal commitment to overseas competition has been matched by practice is questionable. For instance, the extent to which the value of contracts awarded under the Anglo-French reciprocal purchasing initiative represents business that would not normally have been placed in each country anyway is debatable. This is particularly so given that some 26 per cent of expenditure by the UK and 66 per cent of expenditure by the French represents sub-contracts placed by prime contractors rather than direct contracts placed by the respective govern-

ment's purchasing organisations.[41] It is also notable that the department's *Contracts Bulletin* is published only in English. Furthermore, it
is official policy that certain sectors and particular defence programmes
should remain off-limits to overseas buyers (such as naval shipbuilding
and certain 'nuclear elements'); indeed there is a list of areas, formally
endorsed at ministerial level, where international competition does not
apply.[42]

Even where overseas competition has been pursued, it is nevertheless
the case that procurement decisions have ultimately been influenced less
by price and more by protectionism. For example, John Lovering has
noted that a tender from the British Marconi company was accepted
despite being some £100 million above that of the competing American
company Gould Incorporated; in the satellite industry the MOD refused
bids from two consortia of British and American companies and asked
the two British contenders for a combined bid, which was accepted
despite its higher price; and the MOD purchased the more expensive
Alarm missile rather than Texas Instruments' Harm.[43] Indeed, Alarm
was chosen despite the fact that Harm was, in the words of the Defence
Committee, 'already substantially developed, offered less risk, and the
opportunity of an earlier in-service date', and despite the fact that
'professional opinion in the RAF ... preferred Harm.' By 1988 Alarm
was 'some £260 million over budget and several years behind schedule'.[44]

Since the late 1980s international competition has been particularly
emphasised, but despite this, equipment decisions still have not always
been taken on the level playing-field of price and performance. For
instance, according to a number of press reports, the decision in
December 1988 to place a development contract for Vickers' Challenger
2 tank was taken against the wishes of the chief of defence procurement,
who backed the American Abrams tank. The UK company had argued
that 10,000 jobs and £2–3 billion worth of export orders would be at
stake if the contract did not go its way. It also reported that Vickers
received support from Lord Young, then at the DTI. As the RUSI
noted: 'Many believed the Abrams would win the day over the "paper
tank" ... what happened in the first three weeks of December is an
indication of the strength of the economic lobby.'[45]

Subsequently Vickers also received the production order for the new
tank. The MOD has argued that despite the award of the development
contract to Vickers, a very real competition took place between the same
companies for the production order. It should also be noted here that

the Challenger apparently performed rather better than expected in the Gulf,[46] while the Abrams confirmed its reputation as a 'gas guzzler'.[47] However, as the Committee of Public Accounts noted on another question, once a development contract has been let to a company, the financial commitment already made and the significance of industrial considerations are likely to make it even more difficult for the government to choose a non-UK option.[48] It is hard to escape the conclusion, therefore, that whatever the merits of the respective contenders, the crucial decision on the new battle tank was actually taken in December 1988 and, whether intentionally or not, the overseas contenders actually represented just so many stalking horses.

More recently, the Cabinet approved a mixed order of 22 British-built EH101 helicopters and US Chinooks to supplement the UK's existing fleet of transport helicopters. This was despite the fact that the RAF had recommended an all-Chinook order, despite the fact that a mixed order cost £300 million more and despite the fact that Boeing, the makers of the Chinook, had offered a 200 per cent offset deal for an all-Chinook order. The extra cost was justified on wider industrial and employment grounds.[49]

Thus despite the stated commitment to competition, the percentage of equipment actually procured abroad has persistently remained at or below the 10 per cent mark. Although this is higher than in France (3 per cent) which has an explicitly protectionist approach to procurement, it is substantially less than in states such as Sweden and Holland, who procure 35 per cent of their equipment from overseas,[50] though it is fair to say they have smaller domestic defence industries of their own.

In response to such statistics, the MOD has argued that the low percentage of expenditure going abroad reflects the fact that competition has made UK firms more efficient and able to offer better prices than overseas competitors who operate in protected markets.[51] Moreover, one senior procurement official has argued that American companies are often unable to gain competitive advantage from the significant economies of scale that their huge domestic market offers because:

> Quite often what we want may be different, maybe something they have to produce specially, so they don't have that advantage and they are not efficient ... if you buy a standard product off the line from them then clearly you would buy at an advantageous price. If you want something made to your requirement which may be different from their standard, then they do not benefit from economies of scale

because it's a special and then they are in fact on a par with everybody
else because they are no more efficient and frequently less efficient
than companies in this country.[52]

This is a view supported by a series of questionnaires/interviews
undertaken by Keith Hartley among American and European aerospace
producers between 1977 and 1980, in which these some firms claimed
that British producers could be cheaper than American on smaller orders
(up to an output of 200 units).[53]

Thus, the figures given above may well underestimate the extent to
which the MOD is prepared to go out to international competition.
However, even excluding those equipment areas (reportedly few in number) exempt from international competition on security grounds, it is
difficult to believe that the operation of real international competition
would not produce a larger figure for equipment procured abroad,
simply as a result of the price advantage that economies of scale give
American companies if for no other reason. As the then ex-defence
secretary, Michael Heseltine, told the Westland Inquiry: 'there is prac-
tically nothing that you cannot buy cheaper from the US.'[54] Moreover,
ministers' claim that the British defence industry is more efficient is
often supported by reference to its success in the global marketplace.
However, as will be noted in Chapter 6, this success itself is, in reality,
chimerical. In addition, the comments of the MOD official quoted above
beg the question, why can't the UK buy more standard products off the
shelf? As will be suggested later, the advantages of this approach could
be significant, and the fact that the MOD may not be pursuing it as
vigorously as it might suggests it has not been prepared to exploit the
potential economies available from international competition to the full.

Finally, as the example of the Challenger development contract shows,
formal policy has to contend with the fact that major procurement
decisions tend to be made by ministers of state, often at Cabinet level.
Thus, such decisions have often reached an interface, where political
considerations have taken priority over stated policy. This is perhaps not
surprising given the preponderance of domestic monopoly suppliers in
key equipment areas. Indeed, the MOD essentially conceded as much
in its evidence to the MMC when it initially opposed the attempt by
GEC to acquire Plessey. As the MMC Report noted:

> if there was a monopolistic United Kingdom producer of equipment
> it could more effectively lobby to try to ensure that MOD did not

buy abroad and this would clearly be in the interests of such a producer. The MOD said it was a feature not only of the United Kingdom but of the United States and of all the countries in Western Europe that, in defence markets, if procurement authorities tried to move into a competitive international market they found that the domestic companies used their political influence and political pressure to restrict that possibility.[55]

Current policy

It is clear that a combination of post-cold war cuts in defence expenditure and intensive lobbying by the defence industry have now led the MOD to moderate even its rhetoric on international competition. The aerospace industry for example, has been particularly active in pressing its claims for government support, most evidently in the National Strategic Technology Acquisition Plan (NSTAP) developed for the civil aerospace sector in 1992; in evidence given to the House of Commons Trade and Industry Committee in 1992–3; to the House of Lords Select Committee on Science and Technology in 1993–4; to the House of Commons Defence Committee in 1995; and through the Technology Foresight exercise.[56]

The MOD for its part has responded to these dual pressures with a flurry of initiatives. In conjunction with the DTI, the Defence Manufacturers Association (DMA) and the Society of British Aerospace Companies (SBAC) it has commissioned a study of the defence industry's value to the UK economy. It has also initiated the development of a National Defence Strategic Technology Acquisition Plan (NDSTAP) for defence aerospace and is formulating a Technology Plan for the defence industry as a whole. The intention behind these measures is to give the government a clearer understanding of the technologies and industrial capabilities it is deemed necessary to retain, either for strategic or industrial reasons, and to ensure that such factors are taken into account 'as an integral part of our defence procurement process.'[57] The MOD has also indicated that its definition of vital strategic capabilities will go beyond what is currently a very narrow list. Given that key capabilities are often vested in companies that are domestic monopoly suppliers, it seems likely that in particular sectors at least the commitment to competition will, in future, be sacrificed as a function of explicit policy (as opposed to the *ad hoc* industrial interventionism of the past). To quote one minister:

Those key technologies and industrial capabilities must be retained. If you have choice in delivering that technology, in terms of research and development, or capability, in terms of a procurement decision, if you have choice, because there are two or three companies, then, of course, the principle of competition will apply. If you end up with one single source of that capability and technology, our procurement policy may have to change in order to retain that capability or technology.[58]

It is equally clear that a buy-British policy will now be more explicitly applied, at least in some sectors of the defence industry. For instance, the chief of defence procurement has recently noted:

if the price of retaining the sonar capability were, say five times the cost of buying it offshore, the Government would clearly think very carefully. But if the cost of retaining it in the UK were, say 20 or 30 per cent then you might judge it to be strategically worthwhile.[59]

The MOD has also pointed to the decision on the procurement of EH101/Chinook transport helicopters cited above as evidence of its greater willingness to protect the domestic defence industry, even at extra cost (£300 million in this case) to the defence budget.

This more explicit buy-British approach may well be offset in some of those defence industrial sectors defined as non-essential, by a greater willingness to pursue international competition even if this necessitates the sacrifice of domestic capability. Certainly ministers appear to have accepted that a shrinking defence budget has made the maintenance of an all-round defence industrial base an increasingly difficult goal. As one minister has noted: 'it is not possible for us to maintain an expertise in every single area of defence technology. I think in the past we have sought to maintain expertise in too many areas.'[60] Thus Roger Freeman, when minister of state for defence procurement, could note, 'I have no problem with some calibres of ammunition being manufactured in France because France will rely on us for certain calibres. That is mutual interdependence.'[61]

Nevertheless, in the mid-1990s even the MOD's rhetorical commitment to international competition has clearly been watered down and, while it may be willing to sacrifice certain defence capabilities in the face of a shrinking budget, the general thrust of *formal* policy appears to be towards the extension of protectionism for Britain's major defence companies. As already noted, the reality throughout the 1980s and 1990s has been that, despite a declared policy to the contrary, a buy-British bias has operated in many sectors. It may, therefore, be that the new approach will simply formalise what has been happening anyway, rather than extend further protection to the defence industry. Either way, while international competition certainly offers the MOD a way of reconciling the existence of monopoly suppliers at home with its commitment to competition, and while the MOD has claimed to pursue this approach, the reality of both past and current policy has been more varied. In practice, the policy commitment to international competition has been applied highly selectively, with overseas contractors excluded from some sectors (and possibly excluded from more in the future), at best used as stalking horses to drive prices down in others, and being given the opportunity to compete on a relatively level playing-field in still others.

The MOD's commitment to retain key capabilities also has implications for the effectiveness of using integration specialists other than the platform manufacturer to compete for the role of prime contractor on a project. While a concern to maintain a particular capability does not preclude this option, where such a capability is vested in a monopoly supplier it would require all competing proposals to source from just that one supplier, thus undermining the effectiveness of competition.

Summary

This chapter has examined the extent to which competition has actually been implemented in the UK procurement system. It has argued that while the MOD has been relatively successful in placing new contracts on a competitive basis, the competition figures exaggerate the level of competition in the procurement system as a whole, particularly when amendments to contracts are taken into account. It has also suggested that the MOD's approach to the maintenance of competing units within the UK DIB has varied according to time, circumstance and industrial sector. While the ministry has encouraged and promoted competition in some areas, in a number of major equipment sectors it has not only had to contend with the reality of inherited monopolies but also the creation of new ones – sometimes as a result of its own procurement practice. Moreover, despite claims to have abandoned a buy-British policy, particularly in the late 1980s, the MOD has persistently acted rather like a failed weight-watcher, unable to resist taking one more bite of its protectionists cake. Furthermore, post-cold war cuts in equipment expenditure and pressure from the defence lobby appear to have persuaded the Ministry to moderate even its formal commitment to international competition.

Thus, while the MOD has certainly taken significant strides in the direction of competition, it has not quite become the byword in procurement claimed by the ministry, and more recent initiatives would suggest a move away from this supposed goal rather than towards it. The question remains, should the MOD pursue the route of competition or does the development of a defence industrial policy and an explicitly buy-British approach, at least for some sectors, actually make more sense? In addressing this question it is clearly necessary to examine the advantages and disadvantages of the MOD's competition policy. In particular, the question of whether competition has really produced savings is central, and it is this issue that Chapter 4 will examine.

4

The costs and effectiveness of competition

Savings from competition

The MOD has justified the move to competition on a number of grounds (which will be examined below). Primarily though, it has argued that through competition it is able to obtain equipment at lower prices and therefore make the procurement budget go further.[1] For example, Peter Levene, on becoming chief of defence procurement (CDP), noted that savings 'should be in excess of 10%',[2] a target confirmed to the Defence Committee by MOD officials.[3] Additionally, in 1989 the deputy under-secretary (defence procurement) estimated that competition 'ought to give average savings of 10–15%'.[4] Moreover, since the onset of competition the ministry has cited a number of studies which appear to confirm the success of the policy in driving down prices. For instance, the *Statement on the Defence Estimates 1984* (1984 SDE) reported that analysis of a number of competitive programmes had revealed an average saving of over 30 per cent; in 1988 savings of over £400 million (16.6 per cent) on 10 contracts with total costs of £2.4 billion were reported, and in 1994 the NAO noted that 'extrapolating from a range of projects' the department estimated continued savings of roughly £1 billion a year resulting from competition.[5]

However, selective estimates of the savings that have accrued from a few programmes may not necessarily reflect the effect of competition on the procurement budget as a whole. This is certainly the view of one senior MOD representative, who has argued that 'the total savings would be less than would be arrived at as a number by extrapolations of the examples that have been quoted. The true savings would be substantially less than the claimed apparent savings.'[6] Furthermore, savings have to be estimated by calculating what the ministry *would* have spent had it not gone to competition. Thus, the results of such hypothetical statistical analyses are open to question. As one MOD official told the Defence Committee: 'we have to make a certain judgement or even a guess about what we would have paid.'[7]

To compound this problem, the ministry uses an amalgam of methods in calculating savings. Thus, published savings are often expressed against different criteria. For example, in the 1988 SDE, savings on some equipment were expressed against the cost of equipment being replaced, other savings were expressed against the MOD's estimates of what equipment would cost, others were expressed in comparison with the best previously quoted price, and still others were expressed against other tendered prices.[8] Clearly, the criteria used can have a significant influence on the level of saving calculated.

Added to these problems is the fact that savings are sometimes given in terms of unit production costs and sometimes in life-cycle costs, while in other cases it is not stated whether savings were estimated in terms of life-cycle costs, unit costs, or initial purchase price, leaving one to presume (perhaps wrongly) that these are savings on initial purchase price. Given the suggestion on the part of some critics that the ministry's competition policy has produced low initial purchasing costs at the expense of higher total life costs, this is clearly an important omission, and makes it difficult realistically to assess claimed savings. In a number of examples given it is also noted that other factors, such as economies of scale, the introduction of new technology, and batch ordering had also played a role in bringing down prices but no indication is given of the extent to which these, rather than competition, have produced savings.[9] Indeed, in the case of the £20 million saved on the purchase of three Upholder class submarines, the impression given by George Younger in a statement to Parliament was that this was all the product of competition[10] when, in fact, half of this saving had come from placing the order for all three submarines with a single group (Vickers).[11]

Clearly, it may well be that some of the vagueness of presentation and variation in the criteria used to assess savings results from the difficulties of estimation and from the different nature of equipment purchased. Nevertheless, such practices place further question marks over the statistical usefulness of the MOD's figures. Thus, while apparently significant, the evidence that competition has produced savings for the defence budget is open to question on a number of fronts. First, the selective nature of the examples begs the question, what about the other competitive procurements? Second, the fact that the savings recorded are estimates of what MOD *might* have had to pay in the absence of competition undermines their statistical value, as does the fact that savings on different pieces of equipment are given according to different criteria.

Despite the questions that can be raised about the ministry's statistics, its various reports of savings are certainly impressive. Moreover, many MOD representatives have concluded, on the basis of their own experience, that competition has produced significant price reductions in specific procurement programmes. It may well be, therefore, that competition has produced savings in the expected contract price for a number of individual projects.

However, procurement by competition, and the MOD's particular application of this approach, has a number of problems associated with it which involve other costs of one kind or another and these need to be borne in mind when evaluating the benefits that competition has brought to the procurement budget. There are also problems of implementation which are likely to reduce the benefits of competitive procurement.

The costs of competition

As already noted, while competition may well produce reductions in the price of *individual* equipment purchases, a proper assessment of the savings produced also has to take into account a number of other factors which may increase the costs of competition both to the MOD and to the nation. This was certainly the position for the latter in the case of the ministry's purchase of the Tucano aircraft from Shorts. In financial terms this represented a good buy for the ministry. Competition reduced the expected cost by £60 million and the fixed price nature of the contract meant cost overruns were borne by Shorts. However, the arrangements to privatise Shorts meant that other government departments probably ended up paying for the company's losses on a contract which encountered such problems that the first aircraft was delivered 18 months late.[12] Whether the British taxpayer, as opposed to the MOD achieved value for money on the Tucano contract is, therefore, debatable.

A similar situation also arose in the procurement of the Auxiliary Oiler Replenishment ship (AOR). A fixed-price contract (subject to inflation adjustment) was placed with Harland & Wolff in 1986 and the MOD claimed it had made substantial savings when, in competition, the company reduced its price to £127 million. Subsequently, however, the project suffered a delay of two years and eight months and significant cost escalation. Moreover, as Schofield has noted, 'the Auditor General's detailed analysis leads to the inescapable conclusion that competition had a negative impact. Insufficient consideration was given by the MOD to the contractor's capability of tackling demanding technical specifications within a tight budget.'[13] The fixed-price contract negotiated with the contractor largely indemnified the MOD from any price increases (in 1992 the ministry estimated its final bill would be £140 million). Nevertheless, because of delays in the production of designs from Harland & Wolff, the ministry also agreed to pay Swan Hunters (the contractor for a second AOR) between £8 and £13 million in compensation. Moreover, as part of the privatisation of Harland & Wolff, the Northern Ireland Economic Development Board provided some £53 million of support to the company to complete the contract. Thus, although the Ministry of Defence was largely protected from the flaws in its procurement process, it was, nevertheless, the taxpayer who ultimately paid the bill.[14]

A more significant and ongoing cost pertains to the fact that competition, by definition, requires a number of firms to devote R & D resources to the *same* set of problems. This implies costs for both the defence industry, the MOD and the country. For instance, a recent NAO survey found an average of 6.4 tenders were invited for each contract, with half the companies invited actually submitting bids. Indeed, the ministry has been criticised for running competitions involving as many as 40 firms[15] and for running second or even third rounds of a competition. The MOD has responded to such criticism by asserting that it will, in future, restrict both the number of companies invited to tender for individual contracts (to no more than six)[16] and the number of rounds in a competition.

Nevertheless, the costs to industry of placing competitive bids are substantial. Even bidding for a relatively simply item such as a military vehicle can cost the contractor as much as £1 million.[17] Indeed, the NAO have estimated that competition (excluding expenditure borne by companies who ultimately decide not to tender) costs the defence industry some £400 million a year.[18] Moreover, encouraging the replication (sometimes several times over) of such significant levels of R&D activity arguably implies costs to the UK in that it promotes the inefficient utilisation of the UK's scarce R&D resources and personnel.

As one MOD representative has noted, in reference to just one equipment contract:

> We went out to competitive tender for a piece of electronic equipment. Nineteen firms put in proposals ... in at least one of the case it cost the firm £200,000 to make the proposal. ... But it's not the money I'm concerned with, I'm concerned with the number of specialist engineers and scientists and the amount of man-months involved in £200,000 worth of work, and the fact that you did that nineteen times over of which only one team is going to have a productive output because you've only got one winner. It seems to be a gross misuse of a resource.[19]

This is particularly the case if Peck and Scherer's observation, that companies tend to use their most able personnel in the formulation of competitive bids, holds true for the UK.[20]

The costs to the MOD

Competition and the way in which it has been applied also involves a number of costs for the MOD. First, most if not all of the annual £400 million costs of bidding incurred by industry will be passed back to the MOD via charges against overheads on future contracts. Clearly, this one factor alone makes a significant dent in the estimated £1 billion a year of savings from competition.

Second, the ministry's estimates of competitive savings do not apparently factor in the administrative costs of competition.[21] When competition was initially introduced there appears to have been an assumption that it would reduce such costs on the basis that competitive fixed-price contracts require less monitoring than cost-plus ones. However, the experience has been rather different. For instance, one official has noted that the earlier conception that project offices could be run down under fixed-price contracts led to occasions where the ministry 'had the wool pulled over its eyes.'[22] Indeed, in 1988 the ministry's own report, *Learning from Experience*, rejected the notion that fixed-price contracts required less monitoring, although the kind of monitoring required is very different. For example, under cost-plus, monitoring is of costs incurred and allows MOD participation in development decisions. Under fixed price, monitoring consists of observing progress and verifying that key milestones have been reached.[23] Furthermore, competition actually involves higher administrative costs at the tender stage. For instance, there is the cost of advertising tender opportunities, sending out invitations to bid and details of the equipment specification, as well as providing a de-briefing for losing companies on why their bid failed. The evaluation of every bidder's tender also adds to costs, involving people in project management, finance, contracts, and the R&D establishments in assessing proposals from each one of the competitors. Indeed, for the contracts branch alone, the ministry has estimated the cost of competition at 0.5 per cent of the value of each contract.[24] Given that the value of competitively placed new contracts, where formal competitions can be assumed to have been run (i.e. new category I contracts) amounted to some £3,238 million in 1994–5, the administrative costs of competition in this one branch alone amounted to roughly £16 million in the same year.

Another cost for the ministry lies in the fact that the process of tender evaluation appears to build in delays to the procurement process. For instance, one survey of defence contractors found the ministry was taking longer to assess bids.[25] This is perhaps not surprising given the heavy demands made on personnel at the tender stage and the under-staffing that characterises many important sections of the MOD. In one sense such delay may be perceived in a positive light by the ministry as it puts off expenditure to a later date and may thereby help to balance its shrinking budget in any one year. However, delay also has a number of costs attached to it. For example, the introduction of more modern equipment is pushed back and the purchase of spares can go into a sort of 'competitive black hole' while the bidding process takes place. Thus, a price has to be paid in terms of operational effectiveness. Furthermore, it is often the case that older equipment requires extra maintenance, both because it may not incorporate more modern R&M (reliability and maintainability) features and because it is likely to break down more frequently as it comes to the end of its life. This, of course, results in extra expense. Indeed, the Defence Committee has recorded its concern that 'delays and changes in the placing of firm orders, arising from the decision to seek more competitive contracts may in fact lead to higher costs.'[26]

Competition has also produced costs in that its over-enthusiastic application has sometimes led the ministry to place contracts with firms that have subsequently not been able to do the job required. For instance, one MOD official has noted that the claimed savings from competition do not [bring] into the reckoning the cases where following the competitive route orders have actually been placed with companies who have fallen flat on their faces in actually delivering the equipment ... a slavish pursuance of the competition policy has produced a situation in which work has been awarded to contractors who appeared at the time of the competition to be the most promising source of supply but in the event have not been able to perform. ... When, under the gospel of competition [companies] ... have been encouraged to move into other fields, although their general competence has not been in question their particular and peculiar competence has, and there are more than a handful of major cases of that kind.[27]

Competition and whole-life costs

It has also been argued that, particularly in the earlier years of the competition policy, an undue emphasis on the initial purchase price of equipment has meant that equipment has been procured which will cost more in the long term. The MOD has of course emphasised that its concern to bring down prices through competition does not imply it is prepared to sacrifice quality or long-term equipment costs for short-term price considerations. However, it is certainly the case that if price has not been made the sole consideration, it has become the prime consideration. As one defence minister has noted, value for money 'principally means getting the best price'[28] or as another has stated, the ministry's current procurement philosophy is 'a philosophy which is going to look for price advantage – not being the only determining factor but being a key determining factor.'[29]

Of course, there is nothing intrinsically wrong with this aim. Indeed, if one accepts the criticism that past procurement policy has resulted in overpricing and the incorporation of unnecessary and expensive high technology, then such an aim makes sense; the ministry's insistence that it can square the circle of low prices and high quality not only appears reasonable, but sensible. However, the central thrust of the criticism levelled at the MOD's emphasis on initial price is that it has been overemphasised to the extent that sub-standard equipment has sometimes been purchased, and that because of inadequate performance and/ or poor R&M, such equipment may actually cost more in the long run (either in reduced military proficiency or pounds and pence). For instance, one company has noted: 'Although the "value for money" approach has led to savings in the public purse, its basis is not so much an assessment of value, but more the acceptance of the lowest priced bid.'[30] One defence trade association has also told MPs that 'industry suspects that MOD tend to go for the lowest price regardless.'[31] It is certainly the case that most defence industry representatives can recall at least one occasion in which the ministry's emphasis on initial purchase price at the expense of other factors has led to problems later on. For instance, it is alleged that in one case a contract which was partially NATO funded was let to the cheapest bidder even though the contractor proposed to use a different computer language from that preferred, and that having let the contract the ministry found itself confronted by Nato's insistence that it be done in the original computer language. This has entailed the ministry placing an additional separate contract with the company.[32] Another supplier has also recalled losing an order for equipment normally supplied to the MOD by his company to a firm which

> went in undercutting us by ... getting on 20% and I know for a fact having kept in touch with the Projects Office that the Ministry were having one hell of a time ... it was late, it was wrong, the quality was not right ... [With us, MOD] were not on a competitive tender and they ended up with two superb articles of kit ... at the same time we made a fair old profit, and the taxpayer didn't perhaps get terribly good value for money. At the other extreme they get something which is perhaps 20% cheaper, goes in service late and gives a lot of problems, now it's a subjective value ... who's getting the best deal?[33]

Competition would appear to have influenced the consideration given to whole-life cost in another way too. It seems the more formal relationship between the MOD and industry engendered by competition, and the fact that under competitive contracts it is the firm that shoulders the cost of any price overruns, has meant that companies are only prepared to do what is in the contract – no more and no less. This begins at the tender stage where, as one member of the defence industry has noted:

> In putting a bid together you would look to see if MOD ask for something and if they did not you would delete it from the tender because that would make it cheaper – this would often affect its life-cycle costs ... let's say ... each hinge has got a grease nipple, and each grease nipple costs you a pound fifty, so you say ... 'what do we want those for?'

Well if we don't put those on, within a couple of years the doors will be all seized up.
Do they ask for it?
No
Delete them. And you just go through it deleting, deleting, deleting until now people don't put them in the first place. The customer gets no more no less than they ask for. You put in something they don't ask for, it doesn't do any good because somebody else will see it and undercut you. So you end up with a door which after a couple of years has seized up solid and that's actually something that's happened.[34]

Furthermore, the move away from the 'cosy' cost-plus relationship to the more formal contractual relationship produced by competition has led to examples of antagonism and even litigation between the MOD and contractors. In such circumstances sensible and practicable steps to reduce costs may be inhibited.[35]

In addition, if any changes aimed at reducing life-cycle costs are implemented at the suggestion of the MOD *after* a fixed- or firm price contract has been let, it makes it easier for companies to avoid shouldering the cost of any overruns, (as they should under fixed- and firm price arrangements) by arguing the overruns are due to ministry-induced changes.[36] Moreover, any further contract let to cover changes to an equipment's specification designed to improve its whole-life costs will be done so in an essentially non-competitive situation, with all the disadvantages this entails for negotiation of the price of such changes. Clearly this places the ministry in something of a quandary. On the one hand it is likely to be discouraged from making changes beneficial to whole-life costs because of the above factors, but if it does make such changes, the above factors may result in the changes costing more than will be saved from any reduction in whole-life costs that may be achieved. This was the problem the ministry encountered in the development of the Phoenix (a remotely piloted air reconnaissance vehicle). Despite the fact that the NAO have described the project's contracted reliability requirement as 'inadequate', the ministry decided against changing the reliability requirements because the original contract had been awarded under firm price competitive conditions and any alteration would have required technical, programme and price changes.[37] This is in contrast to the old preferred contractor approach which, despite its many faults, is seen by some as having provided a system in that allowed far more give and take on both sides over such issues. Under cost-plus contracts, a company would have a positive incentive to point out any additional work to be done on a contract as this would be financed by the ministry

It would certainly appear to be the case that, particularly in the early years of the competition policy, the MOD's primary consideration in evaluating tenders was short-term acquisition price. Moreover, it would seem that in at least some cases these considerations, together with the pressures competition places on firms to sacrifice R&M efficiencies, may have resulted in the procurement of inferior equipment likely to prove more expensive in the long run. Indeed, towards the end of the 1980s the ministry itself appears to have recognised this as a problem when it introduced a range of initiatives designed to bring about the reduction of whole-life costs and ensure that R&M be given sufficient priority in the procurement process. This is not, however, to discount other factors influencing the shift in emphasis given to R&M. For instance, awareness of R&M as an issue had been growing in the MOD and in overseas defence ministries for a number of years. Moreover, the rising costs of military hardware and the decline in defence budgets precipitated by the end of the cold war made increased R&M an attractive proposition for defence ministries concerned to effect savings without cutting commitments or weapons programmes. In addition, investigations into the question of R&M by the Committee of Public Accounts, the Defence Committee and the National Audit Office in 1989 and 1990[38] also concentrated the minds of officials on the issue.

Reliability and maintainability

From the late 1980s onwards the MOD have gradually given more attention to the problem of reducing the whole-life costs of equipment. For example, it has implemented a number of measures aimed at reducing the cost of spares procurement by 10 per cent.[39] These include improvements in the size and frequency of batches to maximise economies in ordering, competition for the supply of spares by firms other than the original manufacturer and, since July 1987, a requirement that spares packages be labelled with the price of their contents. These measures have certainly brought about significant individual savings. For example, the price of a £161 track guard was challenged and consequently reduced to £32 – resulting in an initial saving of some £19,000. In another case the price of a £100 lever was brought down to £24, resulting in an initial saving of £3,000.[40]

Other measures have been introduced aimed at achieving significant savings in the cost of unreliable and hard to maintain equipment. Indeed, the ministry aims to achieve savings of £250 million per annum over the next twenty years.[41] Such measures include a 1987 Procurement Executive Management Board (PEMB) strategy for improving the reliability of equipment. Recommendations have been made to strengthen the role of the Directorate General of Defence Quality Assurance on R&M, and in particular for it to provide reliability inputs to the Equipment Policy Committee,[42] which now requires all proposals for the procurement of major items of equipment to be supported with information on whole-life costs. In 1989 a Directorate of Reliability was created to give greater attention to the issue of R&M, and the following year an action plan was produced which included provisions for R&M in contracts, improvements in data collection, and an increase in the number of R&M specialist staff.[43] Indeed, by 1993–4 all new contracts contained provisions for availability, reliability and maintainability (ARM),[44] and, as the Defence Committee have noted, increasingly the MOD are punishing contractors who fail to achieve reliability targets by withholding payments.[45]

However, despite these initiatives there is still a great deal of pressure to take the short-term view. To quote one MOD official: 'getting a spend-to-save measure through is very difficult ... there is a very definite pressure to save money in the short term and let the future look after itself.'[46] This problem is exacerbated by the fact that while the ministry have initiated measures designed to improve life-cycle costing techniques, these are likely to be least accurate in precisely those new, high-risk, innovative programmes which often constitute the more expensive of the MOD's projects. Historical data will be of only limited value in such circumstances, and estimates of R&M, particularly in the early stages, will have to rely more on engineering research and risk analysis. Additionally, the testing of R&M during development is always open to the criticism that, however rigorous the conduct of such tests, the actual level of R&M in any equipment will, as one former procurement official has noted, not become clear 'until quite a number have actually been made and are in use.'[47]

Thus, the influence of R&M in procurement decisions is subject to the problem noted by one MOD representative responsible for R&M:

acquisition cost is something you can quantify in hard terms ... life-cycle cost is only an estimate and one inevitably has a lower degree of confidence in the figures ... and if the estimate of life-cycle costs is a lower life-cycle cost, but today's price is more, then there is always difficulty in actually finding the money in today's budget.[48]

Even where R&M is built into a development programme as is now supposed to be the case for all major equipment procurements, many firms told the Defence Committee in a 1990 Report that, to quote GEC-Marconi, 'R&M requirements are the first areas to be modified in the face of other programme pressures.'[49] Similarly, a survey of defence companies conducted for the NAO in 1994 concluded that a 'significant number' reported the importance of R&M being downgraded by the ministry as a result of conflicts arising with other performance aspects. The survey also concluded that the means of R&M demonstration specified by the ministry were often inadequate. For example, failure definitions were considered deficient or inappropriate, as was the timing of tests, which in some instances were not completed until the equipment had been in service for two years. The NAO's survey of 14 projects undertaken since 1989 also found that while the ministry's commitment to R&M had improved, six projects had nevertheless encountered problems of one sort or another, and the ministry had sometimes encountered difficulties in translating the R&M required into contractually binding provisions.[50] With respect to this latter point it is also notable that the NAO found only one contractor that gave a firm yes, when asked whether the ministry had succeeded in enforcing R&M requirements.[51]

The new Directorate of Reliability has also proved somewhat ineffective and has now been subsumed within a revised central structure. Furthermore, while the number of R&M specialists has risen from 30 in 1989 to 85 today, all but 10 of these additional posts have arisen as a result of changes in the way the ministry counts R&M specialists in the organisation, rather than representing real increases in staff. A report commissioned by the MOD in 1989 actually recommended that the number of R&M specialists should be increased to between 120 and 180.[52] In reality, therefore, a substantial shortfall still exists. In addition, the ministry's definition of an R&M specialist is simply any person employed in an R&M post. This fails to take account of the fact that the NAO found staff in 8 out of 10 R&M cells (where over half of the MOD's R&M specialists are deployed) had limited or no prior experience of R&M, and its survey of industry concluded that R&M

project officers did not have adequate knowledge and background in the appropriate disciplines. Furthermore, while it takes up to two years in post to develop the necessary R&M experience, staff in the MOD's R&M cells only remained in post for four years on average.[53] It may be that such staffing limitations are partly due to the difficulty of recruiting and retaining people with the relevant expertise and experience as a consequence of the scarcity of UK specialists and also more attractive salaries in industry. However, if the Defence Committee is correct in its assertion that 'the size and quality of the specialist R & M organisation is a significant tangible measure of the relative importance that MOD attaches to R&M'[54] there would still appear to be some way to go before it is given the priority it requires – budget and recruitment difficulties notwithstanding.

It is also notable in this context that responsibility for drafting specifications for development work, including R&M, has increasingly been passed to contractors. The risk inherent in this trend is that contractors will deliberately refrain from specifying their obligations clearly and in a manner that renders achievement easily measurable. Such a risk is, of course, exacerbated by the fact that the ministry still has only limited and often inexperienced staff available to review contractors' R&M specifications. It is further compounded by the fact that the ministry's quality assurance procedures have not been as rigorous as they could be. This was most notably demonstrated in the case of a contract let to the company Airwork in 1992 for the modification of up to 134 Tornado F3 aircraft. Four competing tenders were originally submitted and Airwork was eventually selected. It should be noted here that, under the ministry's initiative to place a proportion of repair and maintenance work with industry, the RAF's own in-house organisation was not allowed to bid. The ministry's quality assurance procedures provide for the assessment of contractors' quality management systems and for surveillance audits by the ministry, but the latter are limited to those areas identified as representing particular risks. In the case of Airwork, a number of quality deficiencies were identified. However, the ministry received written confirmation from the company that the deficiencies in its working processes had been rectified and, in accordance with *normal practice*, the contractor simply certified that the work on the Tornados had been carried out correctly. *No formal inspection of the completed work was undertaken by ministry staff.* In April 1993, however, work was suspended by the ministry following what the Defence Committee described as a 'fortunate accident' – the discovery by an RAF technician of damage to aircraft that had undergone modification. A more detailed examination found significant damage to the 18 aircraft that had by then entered the Airwork programme. Indeed, the centre fuselage sections of 16 aircraft required major repair or replacement before they could be returned to operational service and all 18 were originally described by the ministry as not airworthy.

Shortly before discovery of the problems on the Tornado F3s, Airwork also won a competitively placed contract to carry out modifications to 23 Hercules aircraft, undercutting the price paid to the main contractor for this kind of work by a third. Again, however, problems were discovered (on 10 aircraft) part of the way through the modification programme. These included incorrect positioning of transmitters, holes in the wrong place, parts fitted in the wrong place and unapproved changes to the design. Subsequently, limitations were applied to the 10 aircraft to restrict the use of air deflector doors which are used during the deployment of paratroops.[55]

In both cases the ministry has taken action to recover the costs of rectification from the company but in the former case the company has had to pay only £5 million of a potential £20 million bill. In addition to the £15 million so far shouldered by the MOD there was also of course a cost in terms of operational capability which, were it not for the good fortune of early detection, could have been significant. More worrying still is the evidence of flaws in the ministry's quality assurance procedures. The Defence Committee has called for reforms of these procedures but even if these are properly instigated this still begs the question of whether similar problems have yet to come to light.

A further problem in the MOD's approach to the issue of R&M is that responsibility for this question is distributed among different agencies within the ministry at different stages of an equipment's development. Thus, for instance, each of the service's R&M advisors is responsible for the R&M input at the staff requirement stage, but it is the PE's advisors to each of the controllerates who deal with development and production. This fragmentation of responsibility for R&M was one of the main complaints of a number of companies that gave evidence to the Defence Committee when it was compiling its report on R&M. For instance, Vickers noted: 'Hitherto a number of MOD agencies have been involved at different stages of projects in relation to R&M requirements. This has resulted in a somewhat disjointed approach where apparent conflicts have arisen.'[56] A better organisational system may be one in which responsibility for R&M is centralised in one agency responsible for the co-ordination of general R&M policy and initiatives, as well as R&M input throughout the life of equipment. The Defence Committee has rejected this notion on the grounds that it would distance R&M specialists from project work and defence contractors, and reduce the control that project managers have over the use of R&M expertise. However, a centralised agency would not only give cohesion to policy and implementation but also coherence to the career structure and training of R&M specialists, which would help overcome problems of staff recruitment and retention in this area.

One problem already noted is that, in placing a premium on firms producing to the lowest possible cost in order to obtain the highest possible profit, firm and fixed-price contracts probably discourage contractors from doing anything beyond meeting the minimum level of R&M stated in a contract, even though it may be possible to achieve a higher and more cost-effective level. For instance, one company has noted privately that while one piece of equipment it produced had met its R&M requirements, there were still elements of it that were not up to standard.[57] One solution to this problem may be found in the greater use of incentives and warranties. Incentives can take the form of bonuses paid to the contractor for demonstrating that a specified level of reliability has been achieved, while warranties require the contractor to assume responsibility for repairing or replacing items that fail during the warranty period. The MOD does occasionally use warranties; for instance, of the 14 projects examined in the NAO study noted above, four included specific warranties. The ministry has emphasised, however, that under the Sale of Goods Act and English law it is able to claim remedy for defects during the first six years of an equipment's life anyway and that the injudicious use of warranties might actually undermine its legal rights. In consequence, it considers the case for warranties on a project by project basis.[58] The MOD appears even less enthusiastic about the use of incentives and there are certainly problems associated with them. For example, statements of reliability are not easily formulated and are often open to different interpretations (this was the case with Shorts' development of the Tucano for instance[59]), a situation which can obviously lead to disagreements over the level of R&M achieved and, therefore, the level of extra payment a contractor might expect. As with warranties it can be argued that if used unwisely the ministry may end up paying extra money for a level of R&M it could expect anyway.

However, where they have been used R&M incentives have sometimes resulted in quite dramatic savings in life-cycle costs. One example is the contract for the Hawk where the inclusion of a sliding bonus for the contractor led to an estimated saving of £5.5 million over the equipment's life.[60] It should also be noted that the US DOD has successfully used R&M incentives for many years. For instance, on the contract for the F18 aircraft R&M incentives encouraged the contractor to improve the Mean Time Between Failure from the minimum 3.7 hours to 8.3 hours.[61] Thus, the possible benefits from the use of R&M incentives could well be significant. Moreover, some of the cited problems regarding their use apply equally to the ministry's more common practice of simply setting R&M requirements and targets, for instance problems of definition, interpretation and contractual enforcement. Indeed, these are problems also associated with the use of fixed-price contracts – a mainstay of the value for money approach.

This still leaves the possibility that the use of incentives and warranties may involve the ministry paying for a level of reliability it would expect to obtain anyway. However, as the ministry improves its life-cycle data and modelling techniques, and if it fulfils its commitment to increase the number of R&M specialists (as it ought to), it should become better able to predict the level of R&M obtainable. It could then build in appropriate warranties and incentives which would encourage firms (in the interest of greater profit) to not only meet *minimum* levels of R&M as under the present system, but to ensure that R&M is as high as possible.

Perhaps the most important initiative necessary to bring about improved R&M, however, is the development of defence equipment which contains a much lower proportion of untried technology and consequently less risk of failure.

On one level the MOD's competition policy and its R&M initiatives can be said to represent contradictory elements in its value for money approach, with the former producing pressures that tend to emphasise initial purchase price and lead to the downgrading of long-term, life-cycle costs, and the latter attempting to give R&M considerations the emphasis they deserve. In the early years of competition in particular, the emphasis may well have been on initial purchase price at the undue expense of other factors. Ironically, however, the problems competition raised in respect of whole-life costs, together with the criticism these produced, were at least contributory factors in persuading the ministry to pay more attention to life-cycle costs as the 1980s came to a close. However, while the various initiatives recently introduced by the ministry certainly represent a marked improvement on its past attitude to whole-life costs, a number of question marks remain over some of the reforms. In particular, the continuing shortage of experienced R&M officers is likely to be costly. Furthermore, there is no one agency which is responsible for R&M input throughout an equipment's life, and, while the ministry's caution about using warranties is understandable, there does appear to be a case for greater use of incentives. It should also be noted that the MOD's record on R&M has been one of fine words and occasional initiatives that have foundered on the rock of institutional pressures to emphasise short-term acquisition costs (see Chapter 1, Cost increases, slippage and their causes). These pressures still exist and indeed have been added to by the operation of competition, casting doubt on the effectiveness of the ministry's R&M measures. Last but by no means least, probably the most significant aid to improved R&M that exists within the purview of the MOD is to refrain from the use of untried, state-of-the-art high-tech equipment which pushes performance to the very edge of what is technically possible.

The effectiveness of competition

Not only does competition produce additional costs which need to be taken into account when assessing the ministry's claims for the success of its new approach, there are also a number of ways in which the competitive process can be fixed. Another problem is that the apparent savings achieved when a competitive contract is first placed can be clawed back by contractors, or offset on non-competitive contracts.

First, however, it should be noted that industrialists privately complain that firms with little or no chance of success are sometimes encouraged to bid by the ministry simply to create the illusion of competition,[62] a feature of the new approach also noted by the NAO.[63] Thus, as Schofield has noted, there may well be informal 'rules of the game' at work which means that companies know who is most likely to win a particular contract.[64] Obviously, to the extent that this does occur it may ameliorate (though not necessarily eliminate) the downward pressure on prices that competition supposedly induces.

Even where a proper competition has been undertaken, the achievement of a competitive fixed price does not guarantee this will represent the final cost of a product. Once a contract has been placed it is likely there will be numerous changes to a weapons project. Indeed, it is extremely difficult for a buying agency to ensure such changes will not be made, particularly given the complex nature of most weapons programmes and the fact that development takes many years, during which the nature of the threat may change and the technology on which the weapon is based may advance. As a contract will already have been let, the company will be able to negotiate the price of any amendments to it in an essentially non-competitive situation. An illustration of the effect this can have on the eventual price of equipment is provided by the competitively placed firm price contract to develop a Satellite Earth Terminal. This contract experienced 193 specification changes worth some £9.3 million – an increase of more than 20 per cent on the original contract value.[65] To quote Pace on the American experience of post-competition changes:

> It is an old and true saying that defence contractors make exceptional profits on changes. No matter how competitive was the initial procurement, a contractor is always in a sole source position when negotiating contract changes.[66]

The British experience would appear to be similar; as one UK contractor noted:

> I am aware of companies who say we will put in this price but we know we will get so many contract changes as the time goes on that we will be able to make our money up in that sort of way.[67]

It is notable, therefore, that the NAO's *Defence Procurement in the 1990s* found 11 of the 37 projects it examined had been subject to significant specification changes which had impacts for costs (in excess of 10 per cent) and/or in-service dates. And the 1993 Major Projects Report (MPR 93) found specification changes on the department's major equipment projects resulted in a net cost increase of £110 million.[68] Moreover, this latter figure probably underestimates the extent to which firms can increase profits on such changes as many are introduced with the aim of reducing overall costs (that is, by reducing performance requirements) when projects are already going over-budget. Clearly, while overall costs may be reduced, companies may still be able to negotiate relatively higher profits on such post-competitive changes, thus undermining the value for money obtained in any initial agreement. It is more pertinent therefore to note that MPR 93 found specification changes resulted in cost variation (both up and down) in 40 per cent of projects showing a change in price.[69]

Furthermore, the ministry has now abandoned its earlier policy of running separate competitions for both development and production and is now, in general, committed to contracting for design, development and production of equipment in a single package. So, although contracts will include a series of option prices designed to take into account possible changes in the ministry's requirements, the sheer length of such contracts will make it extremely difficult for the MOD to take account of every possible change to the specification. This is particularly the case given that changes often arise in response to unforeseen technological developments or threats. As the NAO rather politely put it:

> care is needed to ensure that a sufficiently broad range of option quantities is established since, if this is not done, any changes to the quantity required will involve negotiations to adjust the contract price in which the Department may not be in a strong position.[70]

The fact that something as basic as VAT was omitted from the estimates of cost on the contract for the Satellite Earth Terminal hardly inspires confidence in the ministry's ability to detail long-term requirements with sufficient rigour. Although the contract was firm price, the ministry had to finance the extra cost as it was not originally detailed – this basic error added £10.5 million to the final bill.[71]

A further way in which contractors can claw back profits on competitive (and also non-competitive) contracts is through negotiations on variation of price (VoP) clauses. These are clauses which uprate the agreed price in line with inflation. Because of the sheer longevity of many defence projects, contractors are often only prepared to offer a price on condition that such a clause is included. Indeed, the NAO have estimated that up to 20 per cent by value of the ministry's procurement contracts have VoP clauses, and actual VoP payments averaged £188 million for each of the three years up to 1991–2. However, a recent NAO report found that, in negotiations with contractors, the ministry often departed from its own guidelines on VoP payments and when this occurred it usually committed itself to payments over and above those mandated by the guidelines. Moreover, the ministry has admitted that, up until 1993, it did not, as a matter of practice, calculate the costs of deviating from its VoP guidance. The most notable example cited by the NAO was that of a competitively placed production contract let to IBM Asic for 44 EH101 Merlin helicopters. The MOD not only deviated from its own guidance but also failed to calculate the costs of doing so. This amounted to an extra £72 million on top of the original tendered price.[72]

Fraud and corruption

Companies can also fix competitions themselves by bribing officials to ensure they are allocated contracts in preference to their competitors. The incidence of such corrupt practice on the part of UK procurement officials appears relatively low when compared with other countries (for example, the USA) and UK industry in general. However, as is noted below, this may simply reflect the inadequacy of the department's arrangements to detect fraud in procurement, and those examples that have come to light may well represent the tip of an iceberg. It is certainly the case that the introduction of competition against the backdrop of a declining defence budget and rationalisation in the industry has increased the incentives for firms to ensure, by fair means or foul, that they receive contracts which could mean the difference between business survival or extinction. Certainly, a number of high profile corruption cases have recently come to light:

- In November 1993 Gordon Foxley was found guilty of taking bribes of £1.3 million from three overseas companies (Gebruder Junghans of Germany, Fratelli Borletti of Italy and Raufoss of Norway) to place both competitive and non-competitive contracts with them. These offences took place over a five-year period up to 1985 and covered some £33 million worth of contracts. The origin of a further £2 million held in bank accounts has yet to be identified and it must be concluded that the money relates to further bribes offered to secure contracts in addition to those so far identified. With regard to the overseas companies involved, the MOD has temporarily banned them from bidding for new contracts and has begun civil actions against both the companies and Gordon Foxley to recover the amounts paid as bribes. However, the ministry has also made it clear that as long as some sort of financial restitution is forthcoming and the companies publicly apologise for their behaviour, they could receive defence contracts in the future.[73] In the long term it seems the companies will receive little more than a slap on the wrist and a request to say sorry. It is difficult not to contrast this with the government's more usual response to law and order issues, where, for instance, single mothers can find themselves incarcerated in prison for not paying their television licence fees.

- In December 1993 James Taylor was found guilty of receiving five payments, totalling at least £24,000, in 1986 from Gordon Foxley for information on a tender which helped the company Simmel bid for and win a £12 million contract for a new mortar flare for the Army.

- In April 1994 Bernard Trevelyan was found guilty on four charges of corruption involving receipt of bribes amounting to £8,652 and one charge of attempted corruption when he solicited a payment of £28,580. He received payments from the Managing Director of IMVEC Limited in exchange for secret technical and financial details on arms contracts. In the late 1980s the company won arms contracts worth over £3 million. The most significant was for the supply of a system that allowed the continued use of armoured vehicles after tyre deflation. This contract was placed in 1989 after competitive tender and was for £1.9 million.[74]

Fiscal inducements are not the only means by which contractors may influence the procurement process. The 'revolving door' syndrome, whereby former MOD officials move on to jobs in the defence industry, raises serious questions about the extent to which firms may be improperly securing contracts. As the ministry itself has noted, 'impropriety could arise if there was a case of a job being the reward for a contract being given.'[75] It could also arise if former officials improperly used knowledge or contacts gained in office to ensure their current employers' success in future competitions. Moreover, while both civil servants and military personnel are required to seek permission before taking up a post with a contractor with whom they have had dealings, the vast majority of such requests are approved without any waiting period. For example, of 4,422 business appointment applications approved in the 10 years to 1995, only 328 (7.4 per cent) were subject to a waiting period and only 242 (5.5 per cent) were subject to a ban on the involvement of the applicant in a specific project or area of work.[76] In just the two years to December 1994 some 35 applications to join BAe and its various subsidiaries were approved.[77] This contrasts with practice in the USA where there is a five-year blanket ban for officers joining contractors. It is notable in this context that, in February 1995, a leaked printout from an MOD computer revealed that companies who had been the heaviest recruiters of former ministry staff had had the most success in winning consultancy contracts placed by the Department in the previous two years. One of the most successful companies was EDS-Scicon Defence Ltd., a new American company owned by General Motors. The company managed to acquire 27 consultancy contracts in just two years.; it also happens to have recruited some 13 ex-MOD staff – a figure only exceeded by British Aerospace. Similarly, GEC-Marconi, which is third in the list of top recruiters, gained eight consultancy contracts. In contrast, most firms were lucky to win one or two contracts per year and even big consultancies which had not recruited ministry staff over the two-year period had been given no more than three contracts.[78]

The possibility of corruption in the allocation of contracts has three implications for the success of competition. First, where the outcome of a competition is fixed by a firm it may well be that 'value for money' is eroded either as a result of the ministry paying a higher price than it would in a normal competition or as a result of procuring equipment which is sub-standard – whether sub-standard in absolute terms or relative to that being offered by competitors. Second, the corrupt allocation of contracts may cause the demise of potential competitors or their exit from the market sector in question, thus eroding competition. Third, where corruption results in the award of contracts to overseas companies this results in costs both to the UK economy and to the Treasury in the form of lost tax revenues. For instance, in the case of Gordon Foxley, the award of contracts to overseas companies resulted in the loss of jobs at Royal Ordnance. Taking this into account, one anti-corruption pressure group has estimated Foxley's activities cost the public purse over £100 million.[79] This has to be set against the supposed efficiencies instilled in the procurement process as a result of competition. Moreover, this estimate does not take into account any losses that arose from the additional payments of £2 million made to Foxley and against which he was not charged.

Another way for contractors to offset the effects of competition is for them artificially to inflate the cost of equipment supplied non-competitively. Indeed, this would appear to be the more common method of fraud in defence procurement rather than bribery of officials. Public Concern at Work, a pressure group that campaigns on issues related to malpractice in the workplace, has noted all the calls made to their confidential telephone hotline concerning fraud in the defence industry have involved concerns about the artificial inflation of contract costs.[80] In one example, which occurred before the advent of competition, a former employee of the company Aish & Co accused it of overcharging the MOD. After an investigation of nine contracts valued at some £2.6 million the firm was required to repay excess profits of £421,000. Subsequently the ministry reclaimed a further £600,000.[81]

Theoretically, such overcharging should not be possible as the price of non-competitive contracts is supposedly set by the government's profit formula which allows companies to charge for the costs of manufacturing an equipment, plus a fixed percentage of profit on top. In non-competitive contracts the ministry has access to the details of a company's expenses and should, therefore, be able to determine whether claimed costs are correct. Moreover, post-costing exercises are undertaken on a proportion of non-competitive contracts in order to verify that contractors' bills are not excessive. In reality, however, there is always an element of negotiation in arriving at a price because cost estimates on a major project which might last 10 years or more are difficult to pin down with any real precision. Thus, where a contractor is a monopoly supplier it will often be in an advantageous position when it comes to negotiating the price of the various elements that go to make up the cost of a project, particularly where there is an urgent need for the equipment concerned. Additionally, the contractor can, simply through the adoption of a better negotiating strategy, convince the ministry that the costs involved will actually be higher than the contractor has privately estimated. To quote one member of the defence industry on his experience of negotiating the price of the man-hours expended on a project:

> You have got to negotiate a number of hours, you have got to convince the other side that this job really needs 1500 hours or whatever, hoping in your heart of hearts that you can really do it in 1200 ... we take every opportunity of flexing the margins up because of the ones where it's too tight.[82]

This would certainly appear to have been the practice followed by the main warship builders. As a 1985 NAO report noted:

> the main warship builders have consistently underrun estimated main build-hours on MOD non-competitive contracts and in some cases earned the maximum profits allowed; this throws doubt on the accuracy of the estimates of labour input on which pricing was largely based.[83]

Indeed, the report found that in 19 out of a sample of 22 major warships ordered since 1973 (mostly under non-competitive risk contracts), agreed estimates were greater than the actual or forecast outturn by an average 15 per cent. Moreover, the ministry's own estimates were initially more accurate but price negotiations with the firms had led to settlements nearer those of the shipbuilders. It is also notable that between 1985 and 1993, the return on capital achieved on all non-competitive risk contracts has been consistently higher (by an average of 10 per cent) than the target rate of return set by the government.[84]

The ability of contractors to get away with inflating costs during contract negotiations has been made easier by the fact that the ministry suffers from a severe shortage of qualified accountants. For example, the Defence Committee noted in 1989 that the number of accountants was over 15 per cent below target across the Procurement Executive[85] and in another report it pointed out that a significant number of accountancy posts that are filled are held by under-qualified staff. Indeed, in 1989 the ministry had 106 out of 363 posts for qualified accountants either vacant or filled by under-qualified staff.[86] Moreover, in 1991 some 70 per cent of the MOD's professionally qualified accountants were aged over 50. As the Committee of Public Accounts has noted, given the age distribution of staff, the shortage of qualified pricing accountants 'may soon reach crisis proportions'.[87]

Firms can also attempt to offset any losses on their competitive contracts with the MOD by switching some of the costs on to non-competitive contracts they may hold, particularly where the work involved on the two contracts is similar. As Pace has commented on the American experience:

> If a contractor performs related work on many different types of contracts ... it may be advantageous to 'manage' the allocation of certain marginal costs, particularly those related to research, tooling, production set-up, inventory and so forth. It is also possible to shift

the allocation of work itself e.g. from a space vehicle production contract to its launch support contract.[88]

Or, as one UK defence industry interviewee put it:

> In executing it [the contract] you have got a facility funded by that which you can use for some other project which doesn't have to bear that cost and if you're clever you can do that quite a lot, you get something set up and you say we'll run two or three things through ... you try and get other things through the same overhead.[89]

This would appear to have happened in one case cited recently by Public Concern at Work: an employee of a European defence manufacturer discovered the costs of bidding for a procurement contract were charged to the MOD under the guise of work completed on an existing contract. Another time, unfunded civil work was booked to the ministry. The company also bought computer hardware for civil and non-MOD work and charged it, once again, to the ministry. When the employee raised the issue with his superiors he was sacked. He then brought a claim for unfair dismissal which the company settled with a payment of £25,000 – over twice the maximum sum the relevant tribunal could have awarded. Although the company certified that all matters concerning the financial malpractice had been notified to the ministry, the settlement also forbade the employee to contact the MOD. Thus, he does not know for certain whether the ministry has indeed been notified of all his concerns and he has not been able to detail his allegations directly to the ministry. In total, the fraudulent practices employed by the company involved some £500,000 of MOD funds.[90]

The ministry does operate a system of post-costing which aims to both deter and detect overcharging and cost migration. However, only a proportion of contracts are post-costed, although these often represent contracts which the ministry is concerned may involve some element of over-pricing and generally include most contracts over and above a certain price threshold. Nevertheless, while roughly 1,200 contracts eligible for post-costing are placed each year, only about 80 a year are post-costed, covering only 50 per cent by value of eligible contracts.[91] Indeed, most small value contracts are not post-costed, yet such contracts account for expenditure of around £280 million a year. As the Committee of Public Accounts has noted, 'significant improperly gained profits may occur on smaller value contracts. Since these may not be selected for post-costing MOD may not be identifying the true extent of excess profits.'[92] Indeed, the standard contract conditions for post-costing are not normally written into contracts below a value of £150,000[93] although large excess profits can nevertheless be made on such relatively small contracts. For instance, in the case of Aish & Co cited above, the contracts on which overcharging occurred included a batch of 10 which were all under the £150,000 limit and on which the company made a total excess profit of £100,000.[94] Given these factors, it is perhaps unsurprising that an Audit Office investigation of a number of contracts not post-costed by the ministry found five in which excessive profits had been made.[95]

Even where the ministry is able to identify instances of excess profit it is only able to claw back the amount of profit it can demonstrate was obtained as a result of inequality of information; that is, as a result of the contractor possessing information of which the ministry was unaware. As Peter Levene told the Committee of Public Accounts,

> if those figures proved at the end of the day to be inaccurate, that may just be because the contractor made his best genuine estimate which we accepted and in fact it was found to be different. If we found that the contractor actually knew and had not given all the information to us, we would regard that as inequality of information and seek to get that money back. As to whether that was something which we regarded as a fraud in the criminal sense rather than as overstatement of costs, clearly we would have to look at it again on a case by case basis.[96]

Obviously, establishing there was inequality of information may not always be easy, particularly given the shortage of qualified accountants within the MOD noted above. Moreover, unless the ministry decides to take legal action for fraud, the only punishment the contractor receives for such a practice is that it is required to pay back the part of any excess profit the MOD is able to establish was obtained as a result of inequality of information. However, legal action is rarely taken. This is partly because of the difficulty of proving allegations of fraud, but it may also be due to the presence among ministry officials of what the NAO has described as 'a great deal of confusion about the distinction between fraud, sharp but acceptable practice and a genuine mistake.'[97] Thus, the deterrent effect of the post-costing system is limited. Indeed, given that contractors do not even have to pay back the interest earned on any excess profit, the present system may be said to offer not only limited deterrence but a positive incentive,[98] especially given that the sums involved can be quite large and can be made more significant by the simple expedient of holding back the cost certificates necessary to undertake post-costing – a practice which is quite common. Indeed, actual refunds are sometimes not made until 'several years' after completion of a contract.[99]

One alternative form of deterrent might be for the ministry to use a contractor's pricing record in determining future contract decisions. This does occur occasionally, with some firms being debarred from being awarded certain contracts or certain kinds of contracts (for example, non-competitive ones). However, competitive contracts are priced through the competitive process and whether a firm inflated its costs on a previous non-competitive contract might, therefore, be less important to the ministry than the fact that it put in the lowest priced competitive bid. Moreover, many non-competitive contracts are defined as such precisely because the tendering firm holds a monopoly (at least in the domestic market). Thus, the MOD may be faced with the dilemma that if it does not buy from the firm in question, it will not be able to buy from anybody. Additionally, if the ministry refused to allocate contracts to firms which it deemed had earned excess profits then it would have few contractors left to employ. For example, a 1987 review undertaken by the ministry found that of the 66 UK-based contractors listed in the 1985 SDE as receiving over £5 million, 31 had been subject to post-costing since it was introduced; out of this total, 23 had made refunds. Included in this latter figure were 15 who had been found to have manifestly failed to provide the ministry with equality of information at the time of pricing (although in all but one of these cases the ministry deemed this had not been wilfully done).[100]

It is also notable that, unlike the US Department of Defense, the MOD does not reward 'whistle blowers' who inform on their companies. Instead, such people have generally been left to suffer the consequences of their actions without any support from the government. For example, Jim Smith, the employee who revealed the cases of overcharging at Aish & Co cited above, was sacked and has suffered years of unemployment for refusing to overlook his company's fraudulent activities. However, while the MOD have now clawed back almost £1 million from the company, Smith has not received a penny in compensation from the government. This is despite the fact that the Committee of Public Accounts recommended such action and despite 300 MPs having signed an early day motion calling for compensation.[101]

Thus, given that discovery is difficult and punishment often neg-ligible, the introduction of competition against a backdrop of falling procurement expenditure may provide firms with a greater incentive either to fix the outcome of competition through the bribery of officials or to recoup losses by artificially inflating the costs of non-competitive work. Establishing an undeniable correlation between the introduction of competition and a rise in the reported cases of procurement fraud is difficult, however, as the period since the introduction of competition has also seen the inception of measures to raise staff awareness of fraud, partly in recognition of the fact that competition may increase firms' propensity to defraud the MOD. For instance, the NAO has commented:

> The MOD accepts that current procurement policy, involving in-creased emphasis on competitive and incentive contracts may put more pressure on some companies to protect profit margins by cutting corners or allocating costs incorrectly and may even tempt some to defraud the ministry. The anti-fraud initiative is therefore part of the MOD's wider procurement initiatives.[102]

It should also be noted that the incidence of fraud in UK industry generally has been on the rise in recent years. However, the increase in the level of reported procurement fraud since the introduction of com-petition has been dramatic. For example, between 1977 and 1988 36 potential fraud cases were referred to the MOD Police for investigation, most in the last three years of this period.[103] In contrast, the period from 1985–94 has seen 191 cases of alleged procurement fraud – an average of over 19 cases a year. In only 25 per cent of these cases were there sufficient grounds for prosecution.[104] The ministry has argued that at £22 million for 1993–4, the value of possible fraud under in-vestigation (not all of it procurement fraud) still remains relatively low when compared with other countries or to its £9 billion procurement budget. However, in absolute terms it is still a substantial sum. More-over, given the shortcomings in the ministry's detection procedures, the apparent inability of staff actually to recognise fraud when confronted by it, and the frequent absence of meaningful punishment, it seems likely that the current level of fraud simply represents not so much the tip of an iceberg but the first carriage of a very long gravy train.

Summary

While the MOD claim that the introduction of competition has wrought significant savings, the methodology underlying its estimates of savings is somewhat dubious. Moreover, the ministry's calculations do not factor in the costs of competition. These include the £400 million costs of bidding for contracts shouldered by industry. Not only does this promote the inefficient utilisation of the UK's scarce economic resources, but most if not all of this cost is actually passed back to the department via charges against overheads. Similarly, the ministry does not take into account the costs of administering competition; for the Contracts Branch alone, this amounted to some £16 million in 1994–5. Nor does the MOD take into account those instances where competition has protected the ministry from price rises on projects but where other government agencies, and thus taxpayers, have ultimately had to pick up the bill.

The benefits of competition also need to be weighed against the possibility that the introduction of competition, particularly in its early years, may have led to an overemphasis on initial purchase price at the expense of performance or whole-life costs, both by the MOD and the contractors bidding for projects. Moreover, while the ministry has now introduced a series of measures designed to address the issue of R&M, there are still weaknesses in the MOD's procedures which raise doubts as to their efficacy.

There are also a number of factors which may serve to ameliorate or offset the effects of competition. The ministry's practice of artificially creating competition where no real competitor exists may mean that, in some cases at least, the full impact of the competitive process is diluted. A contractor may also attempt to recoup losses on competitively placed contracts by negotiating favourable prices on any contract changes introduced after a competitive contract has been let. Contractors may also ameliorate the effects of competition by bribing officials to fix the allocation of contracts. In addition, companies can attempt to recoup losses by inflating prices on non-competitive contracts and by transferring the costs of competitive contracts to non-competitive contracts. These two latter practices should, theoretically, be detectable by the ministry's post-costing process. However, this process is by no means watertight in practice as not all contracts are post-costed and, even where they are, establishing that a contractor has deliberately misled the MOD is not easy – particularly given the ministry's failure to implement

US-style initiatives to encourage 'whistle blowers' to come forward. Even the deterrent value of the post-costing process may not be particularly high, given that the department only claws back the amount of excess profit it can establish as being due to inequality of information and does not even require contractors to pay back the interest earned on such excess profits.

Consequently, the introduction of competition may have changed the way in which defence companies maximise profits on their work, but the purported savings it has brought would appear to be something of a mirage.

5

The cost of non-Europe

The rising cost of weapons procurement and declining defence budgets has made co-operation with other countries, particularly in the development of equipment, an increasingly attractive option for European defence ministries concerned to reduce costs, maintain prestigious military programmes and retain key defence industrial capabilities. This has been particularly the case in the post-cold war era as weapons expenditure has fallen in response to the decline of the Soviet threat. For instance, from 1985–94 the procurement of major weapons by EU member states fell by almost 30 per cent in real terms and since 1984 defence exports have halved.[1] At the same time, weapons costs have continued to rise. Consequently, the nature of the arms dynamic in the 1990s has been such that keeping up with the military Joneses has also required increasing collaboration with them on the procurement of common weapons systems. The UK is no exception, with the MOD currently involved in some 46 collaborative projects, primarily with France, Germany, Italy and the USA. Indeed, at least ten of the 25 largest defence equipment projects involve some degree of collaboration.[2]

The intention in this chapter is to examine the ministry's policy towards collaborative procurement and the restructuring of the European defence industrial base. It will be suggested that UK policy is riddled with contradictions. On the one hand the MOD recognises that, as presently constituted, collaborative procurement is a recipe for cost growth and delay in weapons programmes and has consequently declared its preference for a greater emphasis on the competitive allocation of contracts. It also recognises that the pursuit of autarky and protectionism has resulted in supply and demand structures in Europe which promote inefficiency. On the other hand, the ministry is now placing a more formal emphasis on the protection of its domestic defence industry and is expanding its list of those sectors deemed strategically important. It has also been concerned, for various reasons, to limit the institutional reforms that might presage the development of an open European defence market relatively free from protectionism.

In order to place MOD policy in its proper context, however, it is first necessary to outline in more detail the inefficiencies that are generated by both the process of collaborative procurement and the structures of supply and demand throughout Europe.

The structure of demand

Weapons procurement in both NATO and Europe has long been criticised for promoting inefficiency on a number of grounds. First, states have traditionally been concerned to preserve domestic defence industries. Consequently, both domestic and collaborative procurement have been characterised by policies of national preference. At the domestic level this means that national companies have been preserved through the operation of protectionist procurement policies which deliver a continuing flow of orders to home contractors, irrespective of the performance and value for money offered by potential overseas suppliers. Indeed, within the EU, intra-European trade is minimal, accounting for just 3–4 per cent of total procurement of major conventional weapons by EU states in the 1988–92 period.[3] At best, as in the UK, overseas competitors are largely used as stalking horses in an attempt to exact concessions on price and performance from domestic firms. Consequently, both in Europe and NATO, each state produces much of its own equipment thus eliminating potential efficiencies (both financial and military) that could be derived from the rationalisation of costly R & D programmes, economies of scale, and the standardisation of equipment, training and support. This fragmentation of demand is best illustrated by comparing the US and European markets. In the US, which has a much higher level of defence expenditure, there is one market, with one defence budget and one buying agency. In NATO Europe there are 13 and in the EU 15, separate markets in which each buying agency practices policies of national preferment, resulting in a proliferation of both equipment models and contractors.

Where collaborative procurement is undertaken, it is characterised by national concerns and bargaining about the level of workshare allocated to each partner's domestic firms. Consequently, as Sandler and Hartley have noted, 'work is often allocated on the basis of political equity and bargaining criteria and not on the basis of efficiency, comparative advantage and competition.'[4] At worst, this results in each country being allocated specific tasks with the result that states seek work in areas in which they would like to acquire new technology. As the UK's chief of defence procurement has noted, this leads to a situation in which 'instead of playing to the strengths of Europe, in terms of those companies best fitted to do the work, you often put together a collaborative programme which is an amalgamation of the worst.'[5] In its more benign form there is only an overall level of workshare agreed, with individual decisions reached as far as possible on the basis of competition. This nevertheless still implies lower efficiency than if the most competitive and able firm was chosen for each task. Moreover, at the production stage, potential efficiencies accruing from economies of scale are mitigated by the fact that each participating country often sources production with a domestic manufacturer. In addition, collaborative projects are generally criticised for being marked by problems in harmonising the technical requirements and delivery schedules of partner nations as well as excessive bureaucracy and delay, generally resulting in higher costs and longer timescales than experienced in single nation projects. Indeed, it is generally assumed that overall development costs on a collaborative project can be multiplied by the square root of the number of partner nations. Thus, on a four-nation project, one would expect a doubling of overall development costs when compared to a purely national programme. Of course, because these increased costs are distributed between the partner nations collaboration is still considered to work out cheaper than a purely national option.

Many of the problems of collaboration can be seen at work in the four-nation Eurofighter project. The project is already three years late and the estimated cost to the UK has increased by over £2 billion. According to the National Audit Office (NAO), one of the prime causes of delay has been the 'rigid worksharing requirements specified by nations'. These led to delays in the selection of equipment as well as marked industrial inefficiencies. For example, drawings for the electronics of the head-up display were produced in the UK and the items fabricated in three different locations before being returned to the UK for final assembly and testing.[6] In another instance, the UK manufacturer

Smiths Industries had to constrain the design of an avionics sub-system to permit participation by suppliers from the other three partner nations.[7] To add to the problems generated by the workshare arrangement, the management of the project is labyrinthine and cumbersome. For instance, the management structure put in place by the collaborating governments involved over 500 meetings in 1994, with up to sixty people attending some. The cumbersome nature of this bureaucracy is perhaps best illustrated by the attempt to streamline it – a task which took a whole year and resulted in hardly any change.[8]

Clearly, the traditional pursuit of autarkic military-industrial policies has only served to generate Europe-wide inefficiencies in both national and collaborative procurement, as has long been recognised by academics and practitioners alike. For example, in 1960 Hitch and McKean noted the potential for savings consequent upon specialisation and international trade in defence equipment arguing, for instance, that if ten allies each requiring 100 planes concentrated production in one manufacturer instead of splitting it evenly among themselves, a cost saving of 40 per cent would be achieved. In 1975 Thomas Callaghan argued that NATO procurement was characterised by duplication of R & D, short production runs which failed to exploit potential scale economies and duplication in logistics support all of which contributed to a waste of resources which exceeded $10 billion per year. In 1988, the European Parliament produced a report, *The Institutional Consequences of the Costs of Non-Europe*, which estimated the potential economies that could be realised by opening national defence markets in the EC at 10–20 per cent, or 5 billion ECU.[9] More recently, a 1992 report from the European Commission, *The Cost of non-Europe in Defence Procurement*, estimated an open European defence market could bring savings of between 8 and 17 per cent, or 5–11 billion ECU per year, on existing expenditure in Europe.[10]

Despite the acknowledged benefits of an open European or NATO market, and despite a plethora of initiatives, progress to date has been limited by industrial protectionism and the concern to retain the largest degree of military self-sufficiency possible. For example, a Military Production and Supply Board concerned with promoting standardisation and improving procurement methods was set up in NATO as early as 1949. In 1950 this became the Defence Production Board, but the change of title did little to alter the lack of progress towards an efficient procurement strategy. Two years later a European Defence Community was proposed which, had it come to fruition, would have included a centralised procurement system. Unfortunately, the EDC never saw the light of day. A further attempt to rationalise NATO procurement came in 1959 with the creation of the NATO Basic Military Requirements (NBMR) procedure. The objective was to establish NATO-wide military requirements which could then be developed in common by the countries procuring the equipment. However, national industrial concerns ruled the day and despite agreement on 49 NMBRs, 7 were procured from existing national stocks and no weapons were developed specifically to meet an NMBR. In 1966 the system was abandoned. It was succeeded in the late 1960s by the Conference of National Armaments Directors. Along with NATO's Military Committee it is the organisation within the Alliance currently concerned with issues of interoperability and collaboration. However, it has more modest aims than the NBMR, principally providing a mechanism under which two or more countries who agree a common requirement and establish a collaborative equipment project can bring it under the NATO umbrella.[11]

Nevertheless a plethora of European institutions have continued to make recommendations for the creation of a common defence market. In 1978 the European Parliament produced a report which highlighted the waste of defence resources resulting from the duplication of R & D, unco-ordinated purchasing, and the duplication of training as well as repair and maintenance of equipment. It recommended the creation of a European armaments procurement agency with the aim of creating a single EC market in defence equipment. The same year also saw the publication of a report from the Western European Union (WEU), the Dankert *Report on Arms Procurement*, which argued that the efficiencies generated from an integrated European defence industrial base (DIB) would be such that it would have no need to export arms to the Third World in order to be self-sustaining. One year later, the Greenwood Report was submitted to the EC. This again considered the potential benefits available from a common European defence procurement agency and a European defence industrial management authority but concluded, not surprisingly given the autarkic instincts of national governments, that such proposals were unrealistic.[12] In 1983 the subject of a common European defence market and manufacturing base was yet again revisited, this time in the Fergusson Report produced under the auspices of the European Parliament.[13]

One of the more significant drives towards the creation of a common

European market came about as a consequence of the 1986 Single European Act and the commitment to develop a single market in civil goods. Because many defence companies have extensive civil interests and because many defence sectors are increasingly reliant on dual-use technologies where competitiveness may depend on strength in the civil market, the SEA has spurred some rationalisation in the European DIB. On the demand side, the SEA also committed member states to closer co-operation on the political and economic aspects of security. Although this formulation circumvented the military/defence aspects of security, the EC's responsibility for the technological and industrial conditions for security, the wider integrative trends presaged by the SEA and their impact on the defence industrial sector meant the SEA was to catalyse thinking about the Community's role in European security.[14]

Of supposedly equal if not greater significance for the defence market was the 1988 IEPG Action Plan. The Independent European Programme Group (IEPG) had been formed in 1976 and consisted of the European nations integrated into the NATO military structure and also France. The aim was to create a non-NATO European forum to promote, facilitate and monitor armaments co-operation. However, it had been largely moribund until 1984 when the decision was made to give it a more enhanced role. One consequence was the production of the Vredeling Report in 1987 which led to the development of an action plan to create a more open European defence equipment market. Included in the 1988 Action Plan were initiatives aimed at harmonising military requirements, the development of a common military research programme and the creation of a permanent secretariat for the IEPG in Lisbon. In particular, the Action Plan required a greater willingness on the part of governments to dismantle obstacles to competition from the defence industries of their European counterparts. However, the Action Plan also allowed that, while competition should operate in individual projects, the principle of *juste retour* could be retained over a number of projects. It also permitted positive discrimination in favour of the less developed defence industries of Greece, Turkey and Portugal. As Sandler and Hartley have commented, 'on this basis the Action Plan seems designed to benefit producers rather than consumers and taxpayers!'[15] In both intent and outcome the market opening steps produced by the Action Plan have been modest, to say the least.

A year after the development of the IEPG Action Plan it was the European Parliament's turn once more to consider the question of a

European defence market, this time with the publication of the Ford Report on European arms exports. This argued that a common European defence market would allow manufacturers to amortise R & D costs, achieve economies of scale in production and thus reduce the need to maintain capacity through arms exports. The Report called for a common arms sales policy to be developed through the mechanism of European Political Co-operation (EPC) and called on the European Commission to clarify the interpretation of Article 223 of the Treaty of Rome. Article 223 notes that: 'any member state may take such measures as it considers necessary for the protection of the essential interests of its security which are connected with the production of or trade in arms, munitions and war materials.'[16] Ever since the inception of the European Community in 1958, Article 223 has been invoked by member states to protect national defence industries from Community competition and monopoly regulations. Indeed, exemptions have actually been applied to a broader range of products than those outlined in a Products List established in 1958 and not updated since. Even before the Ford Report the Commission had signalled its interest in expanding its remit to cover defence industrial issues, but following to the SEA and the Ford Report of 1989 its campaign became increasingly active. For example, in March 1989 the new internal market Commissioner, Martin Bangemann, called for a Commission role in directing arms production and exports. The Commission also proposed the abrogation of Article 223 under the Maastricht Treaty,[17] a proposal which was unacceptable to key governments such as the British and the French. The call to delete Article 223 was also taken up by the European Parliament in the Poettering Report published in April 1991. In addition, the Report called upon the Commission to consider creating an independent agency to monitor and control the production and sale of arms.[18] Despite such recommendations from both the Commission and the EP, the outcome of the negotiations on the Maastricht Treaty was a much more gradualist approach to the integration of West European defence procurement. The treaty did nevertheless declare, albeit in rather ambiguous language, that one of its objectives was 'the implementation of a common foreign and security policy [CFSP] including the eventual framing of a common defence policy, which might in time lead to a common defence.'[19] Moreover, the four topics agreed upon for joint action under CFSP included disarmament and arms control in Europe, as well as the control of arms exports. However, decision making remained essentially intergovernmental with only a minor role for the Commission and the EP, and, as already noted, Article 223 was retained. In addition, a proposal to include industrial and technological co-operation in the armaments field among the list of topics agreed for joint action was ultimately dropped.

However, the Maastricht negotiations highlighted the bifurcation between European and Atlanticist conceptions of the most appropriate security institutions for a post-cold war Europe. The former was most strongly associated with the French campaign for a more concrete European defence and foreign policy identity, and the latter with the British insistence that nothing should undermine the sanctity of NATO as Europe's paramount defence organisation.[20] The outcome was a compromise which gave a more significant role to the Western European Union (WEU). The WEU has its roots in the Brussels Treaty Organisation (BTO) established in 1948. With the failure of the proposed European Defence Community in 1954 the membership of the Treaty was expanded and it was renamed the Western European Union, although until the 1980s, when it was revitalised by the French, it remained very much an institutional backwater of symbolic rather than practical value. The revitalisation of the WEU was confirmed in 1987 with the adoption of the *Platform on European Security*. This established the WEU's dual role as a forum for EC members to discuss defence and security issues on the one hand and as the European pillar of NATO on the other. It was this very duality which made it attractive to the diplomats at Maastricht, from which it emerged as an institutional bridge between NATO and the EU over a variety of defence issues.

As part of its enhanced role, the WEU secretariat was moved to Brussels, and in 1993 the IEPG was merged into the WEU and renamed the Western European Armaments Group (WEAG). This continued the IEPG's rather limited work in such areas as harmonising defence equipment requirements, procurement standards and running the EUCLID (European Co-operation for the Long Term in Defence) technological research programmes.

The Declaration on Western European Union annexed to the Maastricht Treaty also called for enhanced co-operation between the member states in the field of armaments, with the aim of creating a European Armaments Agency. Further to this end the WEAG established an *Ad Hoc Study Group* to consider the possible creation of such a body. The organisation has also been involved in a study by a joint EU/WEU *informal group of experts* on the options for a European armaments policy including the harmonisation of equipment requirements and procurement policies.[21]

Concurrent with these developments, in May 1994 France and Germany announced their intention to set up a bilateral armaments agency designed to reduce the cost of bilateral project management. This was presented as a possible stepping stone towards a fully fledged European armaments agency. They also proposed to establish it within the WEU and make it open to other WEAG members. However, a few months later the two countries tabled proposals for an agency with wider objectives than just programme management and which appeared to preclude participation by other states at the outset. Other countries would only be able to participate at a later date after key decisions, such as the location and operating methods of the agency, had been taken. This led to objections from other European states, including the UK. In consequence, while a meeting of WEAG defence ministers in November 1994 agreed to 'consider favourably' the Franco-German initiative, it was only on the understanding that the organisation would be open to all members from its inception.[22] The meeting also agreed that 'conditions do not currently exist for the creation of an agency conducting the full range of procurement activities on behalf of member nations'[23] – thus laying to rest the more ambitious plans for the agency. Subsequently, at the beginning of 1996, the French and Germans decided to start the agency, and shortly after Britain committed itself to joining. Thus, a European armaments agency of sorts has now come to fruition; however, it has been agreed that the agency will begin life with a staff of just six and with the limited aim of pooling finance and personnel activities on projects which have already been agreed. The operational offices managing individual projects will remain separate entities and it remains unclear when the agency will be empowered to draw up contracts itself.[24] Moreover, unlike the proposed WEAG agency, the narrowly drawn membership of the Franco-German-British body means that the agency – as it currently stands at least – looks rather like a state-level cartel of the major European arms producers. From the perspective of the smaller European defence countries, this is not necessarily a welcome development and may even encourage them to buy from cheaper US producers, inhibiting the development of a truly European defence market.

Nevertheless, the new organisation arguably has the potential to develop into a fully fledged European procurement agency. Moreover, in the run up to the Intergovernmental Conference, the Commission has continued its campaign to promote both a more efficient European defence market and its own institutional competence over military industrial issues. For example, in 1992 it produced the report on the cost of non-Europe referred to above, and two years later an expert advisory group presented an interim report to the external relations commissioner calling for the development of common European equipment requirements. The commission also produced a further communication in January 1996 which recited the arguments for a more integrated procurement policy and called for the extension of Community competition policy to defence and a more restrictive interpretation of Article 223.[25]

At present, however, the reality is that fifty years of institutional huffing and puffing on the subject has resulted in only the most limited of moves away from the knee-jerk protectionism that has characterised European defence industrial policy. To the extent that progress has been made in recent years it has been driven by the general dynamic of political integration in the EU and the dramatic decline in national defence budgets which has created an imperative to spread the costs of weapons procurement. Ranged against these pressures, however, has been the particularism of national governments concerned to preserve military autonomy and the sacred cows of their domestic defence industries. Ironically, however, the pressure for European integration in the military-industrial sector has also been driven by the supply-side restructuring of these self-same defence industries, both at the European and the global level.

Structures of supply

The annual output of defence equipment in the EU is currently worth an estimated 50 billion ECU and accounts for 3 per cent of total industrial output.[26] However, as noted above, the European defence sector has experienced a dramatic fall in demand from both domestic governments and overseas export markets. In consequence, the major European defence companies have experienced a series of crises. For example, partly (though not solely) as a result of falling defence orders British Aerospace came close to collapse in the early 1990s before engaging in a restructuring and rationalisation exercise which involved the shedding of 25,000 jobs in its defence operations between 1989 and 1995.[27] Since 1990, the German military aircraft group Daimler-Benz Aerospace (DASA) has suffered successive losses every year (apart from 1991) and in 1995 it incurred losses of DM2 billion, prompting a programme of restructuring involving job cuts, the transfer of some production to Asia, and the abandonment of its stake in the ailing Dutch aircraft maker Fokker.[28] In France, several major defence companies incurred heavy losses in the 1990s. Indeed, by 1996 French public defence sector debts amounted to over £5 billion. In response, the French government has committed itself to a fundamental reorganisation of the defence industry involving privatisation, the proposed merger of the aerospace group Aérospatiale with Dassault, and the loss of a predicted 50,000 jobs by 2002.[29] Across Europe as a whole over half a million jobs have already been lost in the defence sector since 1984.[30]

Despite the scale of job losses in the European defence industry, to date rationalisation has largely taken place within national borders. In the UK, a large part of the industry is now grouped around British Aerospace and GEC, with the latter's takeover of VSEL, the submarine/shipbuilding company, only the latest round in the concentration of the UK defence industry. In Germany, since the early 1980s much of the defence industry has been progressively concentrated around the DASA empire. In Italy, the defence scene is already dominated by Finmeccanica, while in France, the proposals for reform of the industry announced in early 1996 mean that it will probably be concentrated around a privatised Thomson CSF and a merged Dassault-Aérospatiale. Cross-border takeovers have been much less common and have tended to be by large firms in one country of smaller ones in another.[31] For instance, BAe bought the German firm Heckler & Koch and incorporated it into its light arms business.

This is not to suggest that co-operation between firms has not taken place, nor that the companies themselves are not interested in the creation of an open European defence market. Indeed, in recent years there has been a proliferation of cross-border alliances of one sort or another. To date, however, such inter-firm alliances have tended to take the form of either specific partnerships formed for the purpose of bidding for, or working on, collaborative projects such as Eurofighter, or joint ventures at the divisional level of major corporations. Examples of the latter include the merger of the helicopter interests of Aérospatiale (French) and DASA (German) to form Eurocopter; the merger of the airborne and underwater sonar business of GEC (British) and Thomson CSF (French) to create Thomson Marconi Sonar, and the pooling of the missile divisions of BAe (British) and Matra-Défense (French). The significance of such inter-firm co-operation should not be under-estimated. While such projects are industry-led they require the consent of each partner's domestic government, and to the extent that this has been forthcoming it represents a relinquishing of autarky and an accept-ance by governments that things cannot stay the same in the European defence market. Equally, it is recognised by the companies undertaking joint ventures that such businesses will either need to develop independ-ently of their parent companies or that one of the partners will become dominant.[32]

Potentially, therefore, this polygamous profusion of alliances at the project and divisional level in the European DIB represents the first step on the road to an integrated European defence industry. However, the obstacles are great. First, there is a mix of public and private companies across Europe which makes merger even more problematic than it is in a purely private system. Second, while governments are certainly more willing to concede the necessity for cross-border mergers in principle, they are often reluctant in practice. Thus, for example, BAe and Matra's negotiations over the pooling of their missile divisions have been hampered to some extent by the French government's reluctance to agree to the merger. Furthermore, while the major industrial actors acknowledge the advantages of concentration, in practice they are also reluctant to relinquish control over particular projects or their own commercial activities; while they acknowledge that an open defence market implies both winners and losers, much of the industrial courting undertaken has been done with a view to shoring up corporate positions rather than with the aim of consummation in a cross-border corporate marriage – and certainly not one that involves giving up one's own name! Moreover, while joint ventures may be a useful mechanism for combining the technological capabilities of the companies involved, they have not resulted in the rationalisation of plant that occurs in the civil sector. Indeed, production generally continues to be maintained in both countries, in deference to the protectionist instincts of governments which tend to make production within their territory a virtual pre-condition of a sale. Consequently, the European DIB has not yet ex-perienced the kind of mergers at corporate level, between European

Table 5.1 Relative fragmentation of European and US markets

Sector	Companies in USA	Companies in Europe
Warplanes and helicopters	5	10
Tanks and APCs	2	10
Missiles	5	11
Warships	4	14

Source: Dick Evans, 'European defence consolidation – challenge and opportunity', *RUSI Journal* (February 1996): 13.

defence giants such as BAe, DASA or Aérospatiale, which would produce the rationalisation necessary to bring down development and production costs and improve efficiency.

In contrast, in the US, with its single market and single buying agency, rationalisation has proceeded apace leading to the phenomenon of the 'super prime' – companies such as Lockheed Martin (formed by the merger of Lockheed and Martin Marrietta in 1994) which is the world largest defence firm, with an annual turnover equivalent to 15 months of French government defence equipment spending.[33] In consequence, despite the fact that the US market is substantially larger than the European market (and seven times bigger than the largest national European market), there are far fewer companies in each sector of the US market (see Table 5.1).

As a result, the average size (as measured by arms sales) of the 10 largest US defence companies is now twice that of the 10 largest EU defence companies,[34] offering economies of scale, technological resources and financial muscle that their European counterparts can only envy. Indeed, the sheer size of these new US defence companies is a further factor spurring calls for rationalisation of the European market – calls coming from both industry and national governments concerned at the growing dominance of US companies in the international marketplace and the threat even to EU markets that is presented by these defence behemoths. For example, the Dutch government recently chose attack helicopters from McDonnell of the US instead of the Tiger models offered by Eurocopter, partly because they believed they would save $115 million; and the French were angered by the British decision to purchase US Apache helicopters (albeit as part of a co-production deal with Westland of the UK) rather than the Franco-German Tiger. This threat from the US 'super-primes' is perhaps best illustrated by the fact that, inclusive of intra-EU trade, some 75 per cent of major conventional weapons imported by individual EU members came from the US in the period 1988–92. Moreover, this occurred in a context in which the level of defence imports has been rising, such that in 1991 the EU's trade in major conventional weapons actually recorded a balance of payments deficit.[35]

Consequently, both European governments and defence companies recognise the need to end protectionism and inefficiency in the European DIB and move to a more open market. It is a recognition of long standing, but in the post-cold war era it has gained increased support due to falling defence budgets, continued rises in equipment costs, the general dynamic of integration in the EU and the threat from the American super-primes. However, while both governments and industry agree in general on the need to overcome the fragmentation of the European market, when it comes down to particular procurement or policy decisions the position adopted is more often one of not now, not here and not in my defence industry. Indeed, in some respects, the very same cuts in defence spending and loss of markets to US primes that have prompted the realisation of the need to develop an open market have reinforced the preference of many governments to protect their domestic industries at all costs. Consequently, both industry and government throughout Europe has adopted a rather Janus-like approach to integration in the defence sector – willing the ends but not the means and thus condemning the development of an open European market to evolution at a positively glacial pace.

Much of the motivation to rationalise the European defence market comes less from an intrinsic concern to improve efficiency and increase competition and more from a concern to protect defence industrial interests in the new post-cold war environment. Thus, one view of a future European arms market, associated in particular with the French, is of it operating a 'préférence européenne' in procurement, in order to protect the European defence industry from US competition. This is not, it has to be said, a universal view; for example, the British are more strongly associated with a commitment to open international competition. However, as is noted below, this has as more to do with the particular security concerns of the UK and the importance of the US market for its defence industry than with an intrinsic commitment to international competition. Moreover, if domestic procurement policy is anything to go by, the UK's commitment to open competition will be adhered to more in the rhetoric than the observance.

A note of warning may be sounded here. Just as defence firms lobby their domestic governments to adopt preferential procurement policies, the European defence industry lobbies Brussels to do the same at the European level. For example, individual firms such BAe and Aérospatiale have their own offices in Brussels from which they lobby the Commission and other bodies. In addition, European firms have come together in the European Defence Industries Group (EDIG) to put forward an essentially protectionist perspective on the formation of the European arms market. Moreover, given that the companies to emerge from a rationalised defence industry would be giant corporations wielding enormous economic muscle, the lobbying power of such actors would probably be enhanced – even at the European level. The risk is, therefore, that any European market that does evolve will simply replicate the protectionism, subsidisation, inefficiency and absence of competition that characterises national markets – a phenomenon Keith Hartley has described as being akin to 'all the worst features of the common agricultural policy simply being translated into defence markets.'[36]

The UK and collaborative procurement

Up to and including the 1950s, collaborative programmes were looked upon with some suspicion by the UK. However, the 1960s and 1970s saw their growing acceptance as a means of procuring defence equipment; and the Conservative government which entered office in 1979 was equally prepared to countenance this approach. Nevertheless, although John Nott initiated a British–German investigation into the scope for rationalising Europe's defence industries (which was inhibited by the complexities involved and the resistance of the Procurement Executive),[37] it was not until the appointment of Michael Heseltine that the MOD appeared to take any significant steps to promote collaboration. Mr Heseltine's tenure saw the creation of a new post of chief of defence equipment collaboration (CDEC) and a Defence Equipment Collaboration Board 'to give focus to the existing informal arrangements within the Department for dealing with collaborative matters.'[38] The creation of the post of CDEC probably had much to do with the need to find somewhere to shunt the then chief of defence procurement (CDP), David Perry, in order to make way for Peter Levene – a view given credence by the fact that the post was discontinued when Perry retired in 1987. However, the fact that this post, rather than any other, was created for Perry still said something about the ministry's commitment to collaboration.

In addition, Heseltine played a significant role in breathing new life into the IEPG by suggesting the simultaneous adoption of 10 new projects and IEPG meetings at ministerial level. Indeed, as chair, he called for more collaboration 'even if it causes pain to some entrenched national interests'.[39] At the first ministerial meeting it was agreed that: all significant projects would be referred to ministers at the staff target stage so that collaboration could be considered from the outset, military staffs would be directed to work towards closer harmonisation of operational requirements and timescales, work would be set in hand to identify a number of co-operative technology projects, and a study would be commissioned to look into ways of improving the effectiveness of the European armaments industry (this eventually resulted in the Vredeling Report). The sudden departure of Michael Heseltine over the Westland affair appeared to represent a set-back for collaborative procurement in that it lost an important supporter and because the Westland affair itself appeared to place a damper on the prospects for further Anglo-European collaboration.[40] However, the budgetary difficulties faced by all defence ministries meant incentives to collaborate remained strong, and the MOD has not been an exception. Indeed, as already noted, it currently participates in some 50 collaborative projects, and ministers have noted that any new major defence procurement has to be viewed as an internationally collaborative project.

The ministry's motivations for engaging in collaboration are similar to those of its partners. First and foremost, it considers that, despite the diseconomies involved in collaborative procurement, it achieves savings by sharing the costs of equipment with partner nations. Indeed, on development costs the department subscribes to the square root formula outlined above, whereby costs are assumed to double in a four-nation project but nevertheless produce savings for each nation. However, it should be noted that a 1991 study by the NAO found that on collaborative development projects, the rise in costs from those originally anticipated when the collaborative route was chosen was much higher (24 per cent) than for purely national projects (14 per cent). Consequently, the NAO questioned whether the cost savings predicted on collaborative projects were actually achieved in practice.[41] At the production stage, the ministry's view is that there are few, if any, cost savings to be achieved from collaboration. Indeed, the unit cost of a collaborative programme can actually be higher than a national one. For example, for NFR90 the MOD estimated production costs would be £36 million more than on a national project (an increase offset by estimated savings of £160 million in development).[42]

The MOD also sees collaboration as a means of achieving standardisation and inter-operability within the NATO Alliance. Not only does this offer the prospect of scale economies in the production and holding of spares but it also helps to reduce the variety of equipment operated by different NATO forces, producing a commensurate increase in military effectiveness.

European collaboration is further perceived as producing a more efficient utilisation of European R & D resources and thus strengthening the European DIB in the face of competition from the US. Nevertheless the government has been careful to emphasise its commitment to its traditional links with the USA and has been happy to engage in collaborative projects with US companies, as examples such as the Harrier GR5/7 and the Joint Tactical Information Distribution System (JTIDS) demonstrate. However, the ministry considers that collaboration with US firms has been of limited success given that the US has traditionally been reluctant to transfer technology abroad, and given that the disparity in size between UK and US firms has usually resulted in domestic firms acting as junior partners in any collaborative project.[43] In contrast, the MOD views European collaboration as 'the more important field of opportunity'[44] and has supported attempts, such as the IEPG Action Plan, to build up the European DIB in the face of US competition. In addition, it is equally clear that the ministry has undertaken a number of projects in Europe because these have been seen as both a means of maintaining UK defence capacity in specific sectors and a means of strengthening the European DIB. For example, the MOD's decision to procure MLRS 1 (Multiple Launch Rocket System) through European collaboration rather than direct from the US was influenced by pressure from France and Germany for it to opt for this route so as to 'maintain the principle of European unity'[45] (as well as the opportunity to obtain work for UK companies). It may well be that the second source of supply represented by the European facility will reap dividends by creating the possibility of competition between the two producers for future supplies. However, it should also be noted that the decision to opt for European production was at the expense of a small increase in cost and a four-year delay to the programme. The Defence Committee has also expressed doubts about the decision to develop a new light attack helicopter in collaboration with the Italian government rather than to purchase the American Apache.[46] Furthermore, the decision to purchase the Eurofighter, formerly known as the European Fighter Aircraft (EFA), (although justified by the MOD on the grounds that it was the only aircraft capable of meeting its requirements) has been questioned by some commentators who consider that the American F-18 would have been a cheaper option.[47] Indeed, one senior MOD representative has stated:

> I am sure we would have got better value for money from buying from the US, we would certainly have got a cheaper aircraft ... [one argument was] if we did not participate in EFA and bought American aircraft that would be the end of Britain's manufacturing capability in aircraft and that would have been politically an extraordinarily difficult decision to take.[48]

It would appear, therefore, that in some cases at least, while the MOD has formally committed itself to the abandonment of a buy-British policy, it still seems prepared to operate a buy-European collaborative policy both to benefit UK industry and to maintain the strength of the European DIB.

The ministry has been keen to extend its value for money approach into collaborative projects, illustrated by its support for the various initiatives outlined in the IEPG Action Plan for example. Indeed, as in other procurement areas, defence companies have argued that the ministry has taken its enthusiasm for its value for money approach too far. In particular, it has come in for criticism for insisting on running domestic competitions to decide which company will act as the country's lead contractor for each particular collaborative programme, thus delaying UK entry to the project, and to the discussions as to which company and country will do what. However, the NAO have noted that in seven out of the ten projects it examined, companies were selected without competition – generally because they were the only domestic choices available.[49] The MOD have also argued for work on collaborative programmes to be shared more rationally, with each participating company developing complete sub-systems rather than passing work on particular components from one to the other.

The ministry's support for defence collaboration has not yet been translated into an increase in the proportion of its equipment budget going to collaborative projects, a figure which has consistently hovered around the 15 per cent mark. Nevertheless, the MOD's support for collaboration has deepened, particularly since the late 1980s, and it now expects that most significant new equipments will be produced collaboratively. Indeed, it seems likely that there will be a marked rise in the proportion of UK equipment expenditure devoted to collaboration. Trevor Taylor, for example, has suggested that collaborative projects could soon account for as much as 40 per cent of UK equipment spending.[50]

The UK and the structure of supply and demand in Europe

The MOD certainly has attempted to extend the principle of competition to collaborative projects, sometimes in the face of opposition from partner nations. It is also formally in favour of a free and open European defence market which it considers would be to the net advantage of the UK defence industry. However, like many other aspects of its procurement policy, the concern to extend competition to collaborative programmes and the commitment to an open European defence market is fraught with contradictions. First, as noted in earlier chapters, the ministry's application of its general competition policy has been less diligent than it claims. Second, it is now moderating its formal commitment to competition and placing a greater emphasis on maintaining the UK defence industrial base, even if this means paying more for particular types of equipment. Similarly, at the European level, the ministry has indicated it is prepared to promote collaboration, even if this sometimes means sacrificing its policy of seeking competing bids in all major procurement programmes.[51]

Third, while the ministry has declared its preference for an open European market in which procurement decisions are made on the basis of value for money, its current notion of such a market is, in reality, circumscribed by domestic industrial concerns. Thus ministers have been prepared to concede the need for 'cross-dependency' in the supply of equipment, but such mutual interdependence appears only to be envisaged *within* equipment sectors rather than *across* them. For example, Roger Freeman when procurement minister could envisage

British dependence on the French for ammunition but only for some calibres, and only in a context in which the French were dependent on the UK for other calibres. This acceptance of cross-dependence also appears to be hedged by exceptions for a number of sectors considered too important to give up (for example, naval shipbuilding, design of military aircraft and military aero-engines) as well as the condition that where cross-dependence does occur, the impact on the defence industrial base of the countries concerned 'should be broadly the same.'[52] The ministry may have declared its commitment to the goal of an open European defence market but it has obviously decided to take the scenic route towards it.

Fourth, industrial concentration within countries has already produced, and is likely to continue to produce, increasingly dominant suppliers able to wield both formidable market power and considerable influence when it comes to lobbying for their interests at the national and European level. This would appear to dilute the potential for open competition across Europe. The MOD has argued that rationalisation does not have to dilute competition and that mergers or associations between a home company in one sector and a foreign company in another may actually enhance the opportunity for Europe-wide competition between different industrial groupings while still allowing each country to take up some work from projects undertaken. Thus, for instance, a link-up between BAe and a European aeroengine company or Rolls-Royce and a European aircraft manufacturer would be viewed with equanimity by the ministry.[53] However, transnational mergers are unlikely to be as neat as this. Indeed, for obvious reasons, firms will have strong incentives to engage in anti-competitive mergers and alliances.

Fifth, as noted above, the application of competition to collaborative projects undertaken by European states is ultimately hindered by the realities of oversupply, market fragmentation and the autarkic military-industrial policies pursued by each state. Ironically, however, the wider politics of British domestic policy on Europe have meant the government has been consistently reluctant to contemplate the kind of institutional reforms that would presage the development of an open European defence market. Thus, the UK's emphasis on inter-governmentalism, the NATO Alliance and the 'special relationship' with the US, as well as the government's need to appease the Eurosceptics in its own party, have generally left Britain fighting a rearguard action to limit the impact of proposals designed to develop the kind of European defence identity which is arguably a prerequisite for the dissolution of state-centric procurement policies. Consequently, it has placed emphasis on a project-led restructuring of the European market rather than on institutional reforms designed to create a new structure of demand that would lead to an open European market. Thus, it has been concerned to limit the remit of any European arms agency and has actively campaigned against the idea of a common European defence or developments that might be interpreted as the first step towards the creation of a common European army.

Both at Maastricht and in the run up to the 1996 Intergovernmental Conference (IGC) to review the treaty's provisions, the British government remained committed to a European security architecture which stresses the priority of NATO and conceives of the WEU (Western European Union) as a bridge between NATO and the EU. Consequently it has resisted the notion of simply folding the WEU into the EU. In addition, the UK has been reluctant to see national control of defence issues diluted by moves to extend majority voting or the role of the European Commission and European Parliament. For example, while the MOD has declared its support for an open European market it has also made clear that it is against the abolition of Article 223.[54] Similarly, while the British have been prepared to envisage the Union moving towards a common defence policy (so long as it is compatible with NATO), they have been far less enthusiastic about moves to a common defence, a position made clear in the Anglo-Italian proposals drawn up during the negotiations on Maastricht and reflected in British insistence that the term 'might' should be included in Article J.4 of Title V of Maastricht, so that it refers to 'the eventual framing of a common defence policy which *might* in time lead to a common defence' (my emphasis).[55]

Not surprisingly, therefore, the UK's attitude to the Franco-German proposal for a European armaments agency has been at best equivocal. On the one hand, the government was concerned (along with its domestic defence companies) not to be left out of any such organisation for fear that its absence from a forum making key decisions about the future of the European defence market would disadvantage British industry; on the other hand, however, it has been equally concerned to limit the scope of the agency. Indeed, it was only once the more ambitious plans for the agency were laid to rest at the November 1994 Noordwijk meeting that Britain began actively to consider participation.[56] Thus, Roger

Freeman, then defence procurement minister, responded to the Franco-German proposal by suggesting a much more limited 'joint projects office' which would handle collaborative programmes which were well defined and had agreed specifications, and would place orders on the basis of open competition rather than in proportion to the amount of equipment ordered by each country.[57] Indeed, though Britain has now signed up for membership of the agency it is clear that its vision of the body is of an organisation with a limited mandate. The British view is of a body that will have a single head but a complex matrix of projects with different countries participating in them, and of a body which will take 'decades' to evolve into a proper functioning armaments agency. The UK also believes it will be 'some time' before ministers could delegate 'some procurement decisions' to such an agency, although a first step could be delegation of decisions on some sub-contracts, or some items that could be open to competitive procurement throughout Europe which were not of an essential strategic nature.[58]

The British, in line with their declaratory commitment to competition, have also rejected the notion that members of the agency or indeed any other European procurement entity should commit themselves to operating a European preference in weapons procurement, as advocated by the French for instance. However, as with much of British procurement policy, the reality of the MOD's formal position on this issue is not quite so clear-cut. As already noted, there have already been occasions when the UK appears to have operated a buy-European preference. Moreover, prior to Britain eventually joining the Franco-German agency both states made it clear that membership was conditional upon the British joining a collaborative project to develop a multi-role armoured vehicle (MRAV), despite the MOD's reservations about the specifications already agreed between France and Germany. Subsequently, the British have indeed joined the programme, and the extent to which their concerns have been addressed remains unclear. Whatever the merits of the decision to participate in MRAV, it is clear that future governments will continue to be under consistent pressure from other EU states to operate a European preference in procurement decisions. Similarly, the influential defence industrial lobby in the UK has also argued for European industry to be favoured at the expense of competition from the US.[59] It would be surprising if pressure from other EU states and the British defence industry was not factored into future decisions.

At the same time, however, there are also countervailing pressures which favour the procurement of at least some equipment from the US. First, the principal concern of British policy makers since the end of the Second World War has been the maintenance of the 'special relationship' with the USA, and in particular the American commitment to NATO and European defence. To the extent that a buy-European policy would sour relations with the US, it would not be welcomed by the UK. Second, as the MOD itself has noted, the US is often the sole source for equipment which it is uneconomic to develop elsewhere.[60] In addition, UK companies such as Rolls-Royce and Dowty have established an important presence in the American market, and the UK is involved in a significant number of collaborative projects with the USA (20 in 1996).[61] The US is also Britain's second largest export market after Saudi Arabia, with the UK providing 40 per cent of US defence imports[62] though this still leaves the US operating a healthy defence trade surplus with the UK. For example, the MOD consider that the balance of trade is about 2:1 in favour of the US, and the European Commission has calculated the US:UK balance of trade on major conventional weapons at roughly 4:1.[63] However, in comparison to other EU states Britain has been far more successful at penetrating the US market; according to the Commission, in the period 1988–92 Britain was the leading European exporter of major conventional weapons to the US, and Britain's trade balance with the US compares very favourably with an average of 10:1 for the EU as a whole. Indeed, French exports of major conventional weapons to the US amounted to just $3 million between 1988 and 1992 (compared with $543 million for the UK) – a trade balance of roughly 125:1 in favour of the US.[64] Thus, compared with other EU states the UK has done relatively well in its defence trade relationship with the US. Moreover, British access to the lucrative American market is aided by reciprocal access to the UK market. As the MOD have noted, the trade surplus in favour of the US is 'a factor which is useful in our attempts to counter protectionist moves on Capitol Hill. We argue that if the fertile UK market is to remain open then so must that of the US to afford UK companies the opportunity to bid for a greater share of defence work.'[65] Operating a 'fortress Europe' policy may not, therefore, be in the interests of the British DIB as a whole. In comparison the French, who are one of the strongest advocates of European protectionism, have little to fear from any tit for tat US action against such protectionism.

While the MOD certainly regard Europe as the more important field for the promotion of collaboration and co-operation in defence procurement and though the MOD does appear to have operated a buy-European policy on a number of occasions, both the wider security relationship with the US and the defence industrial interests of the UK dictate that the British market does not become totally closed to American firms. On the one hand, therefore, Britain's declared resistance to a European preference in procurement would appear to have about as much substance as its supposed commitment to international competition in domestic procurement; and just as protectionism at home has been cloaked in the language of international competition, the same would appear to be the case at the European level. On the other hand, just as protectionism at home has occasionally been modified with a view to obtaining the price advantages that US companies can offer, as well as access to the US market, this is likely to be the MOD's ideal for a future European defence market. Consequently, the perceived gap between the ministry and some other EU countries on this issue is probably greater in rhetoric than in practice. This is not to deny that a gap does exist; however, it is a gap determined not by the MOD's philosophical commitment to competition but rather the perceived security benefits of the 'special relationship' and the interests of the British defence industry.

Summary

The European defence market is characterised by structures of both demand and supply which actively promote inefficiency. It is also dominated by contradictions. At one and the same time it is cosseted by the protectionism of national governments, yet suffering from chronic oversupply and falling defence expenditure. It is a market in which both governments and industry recognise the need to relinquish autarky and policies of national preference, yet like a junkie trying to kick the habit, they keep coming back for one last fix.

In many ways, the record of the MOD in recent years has been better than most. It has argued for greater competition in collaborative weapons programmes and it has argued against the more extreme 'fortress Europe' conceptions of a future European defence market. However, British policy has not been immune to contradictions of its own. The emphasis on competition in Europe is now being played out against the backdrop of a greater formal commitment to protectionism at home and a declared willingness sometimes to sacrifice competition to achieve collaboration in Europe. Moreover, while the MOD has embraced the notion of an open European market at some point in the future, currently ministers are only prepared to envisage very limited steps towards this goal – and even such steps have been hedged by conditions. Furthermore, for various reasons, the government has generally been concerned either to limit or to prevent institutional reforms within Europe which might presage the development of an open European market, whether it be on the question of folding the WEU into the EU, the notion of a common European defence, or on giving the Commission greater authority over defence industrial issues. Even on the issue of a European armaments agency, while it has been concerned not to be left out of such a potentially influential body, its vision is of an organisation with a very limited mandate which *might* develop into something more substantial – but not yet. Similarly, while the ministry has rejected the idea of fortress Europe, there have been occasions when it has operated a buy-European preference. Moreover, its rejection of fortress Europe is predicated not on its supposed commitment to international competition but rather on a rose-tinted perception of the benefits deriving from the 'special relationship' with the USA and a concern to preserve the Atlantic interests of its client industry.

Of course, the ministry has deepened its commitment to collaborative weapons procurement both inside and outside the EU. To the extent that this facilitates intra-European co-operation on procurement it is no doubt a positive development. However, the prevalence of the *juste retour* principle combined with excessive bureaucracy and delay means that collaborative procurement is more part of the problem than any form of solution. As presently constituted, collaborative procurement acts as a mechanism for preserving domestic defence industries that can no longer be supported solely by national defence budgets, and whose breadth is no longer justified given the internationalisation of defence production and the overcapacity that characterises the European DIB. Moreover, the project-led approach to industrial restructuring which emphasises the extension and reform of collaborative practices as a means to engineer a more open European market, is ultimately undermined by the 'one last fix' syndrome that permeates Europe's defence ministries – including the MOD. In addition, while collaborative procurement may result in

reduced costs for each partner, a system of procurement which can lead
to a doubling or more in the overall cost of a programme is very far from
the ministry's goal of an efficient use of defence monies.

6

The cost of British arms exports

Since the arrival of the Thatcher administration in 1979 the British government has adopted a more aggressive approach to the sale of arms. On the face of it at least, this approach would appear to have paid dividends – according to the MOD, new orders for 1995 amounted to £5 billion.[1] Moreover, defence exports currently sustain some 90,000 jobs (see Table 6.1) and help maintain capacity in the British defence industrial base (DIB). Not surprisingly, therefore, in the context of relatively poor economic growth, a weak balance of payments and swingeing cuts in domestic weapons procurement the government has been keen to trumpet defence exports as a bright star in a rather dull economic firmament. Furthermore, they are considered to produce a virtuous circle of benefits from which everyone gains; for example, as the head of the MOD's Defence Export Services Organisation has noted: 'UK defence exports are a major success story. This has been good news for the British economy, for employment, and for the maintenance of our technological base.'[2] Moreover, ministers have explained this success story as a product not only of better marketing but of the introduction of competition into domestic weapons procurement contracts, arguing that exposure to the rigours of the free market at home has produced a leaner and fitter industry better able to compete for orders on the international scene. As Jonathan Aitken noted when minister of state for defence procurement:

> I think the companies themselves would admit that their competitiveness in today's international markets owes a great deal to the competitive procurement policies of the Ministry of Defence since the mid 1980s. Yesterday's painful disciplines have given birth to

many joyful successes in today's export market and that is the biggest single factor behind ... record-breaking export figures.[3]

The aim in this chapter is twofold. First, to analyse Britain's defence export performance in an attempt to show that the picture of success – in particular success built upon the foundation of domestic competition policy – requires substantial qualification. Second, to consider whether UK defence exports make a positive or negative contribution to British military, economic, and political security. Here it will be suggested that far from providing a virtuous circle of benefits, defence exports erode both military and political security, and that even their economic advantages are dubious.

There are a number of statistical sources which can be drawn upon to analyse UK defence export trends. First, the MOD publish an annual estimate of defence exports derived from a combination of Customs and Excise Tariff headings that can be reasonably allocated wholly to defence, and estimates of additional exports of military aerospace equipment produced by the Society of British Aerospace Companies (SBAC). However, exports of some types of equipment that have both a civil and a military use are not identified, as is the case for some non-equipment projects such as military construction. The MOD also gives figures for the level of defence export *orders* obtained annually by the UK. Again, however, reliance on these figures is problematic as export orders can take a number of years to be executed and their value can thus be eroded by inflation. In addition, orders do not necessarily translate into actual sales. The two principal independent sources of data on defence exports are the Stockholm International Peace Research Institute (SIPRI) and the US Arms Control and Disarmament Agency (ACDA). SIPRI, however, limits its analysis to the trade in major conventional weapons, including the licensed production of such weapons; ACDA's coverage of the arms trade is much broader. For example, ACDA also includes such categories as small arms and ordnance, dual-use equipment when its primary mission is identified as military, and the building of defence production facilities. Military services such as construction, training and technical support are also included for all nations except the USA.[4] The statistics published by ACDA also provide more detail for the analyst concerned to examine the arms export trends of individual countries. For these reasons, therefore, the bulk of the analysis below is based on statistics produced by ACDA. Nevertheless, it should be noted that all efforts to measure the volume of arms transfers are hampered by the

Table 6.1 Anatomy of a declining market

	1990	1994	% fall
World exports (1994 prices)	$54.3b	$22.1b	59
UK exports (ACDA), 1994 prices)	$5.1b	$3.4b	34
UK exports (MOD 1994/5 prices)	£5.1b	£2.9b	43
Defence trade balance	£4.4b	£1.8b	60
UK defence jobs:			
Exports	145,000	90,000	38
MOD procurement	270,000	175,000	35

Sources: US Arms Control and Disarmament Agency (ACDA), *World Military Expenditures and Arms Transfers 1995* (*WMEAT*), Washington, DC: ACDA 1996; Ministry of Defence, *UK Defence Statistics 1996*, London: HMSO, 1996.

reluctance of national governments to reveal accurate details of what are sensitive transactions; thus any statistics on the arms trade are likely to be less than 100 per cent reliable.

Export trends

As already noted, British officials have not been slow to conclude that government policy has produced a rare economic success story built upon the foundations of competition at home and aggressive marketing abroad. To some extent this is certainly the case: UK export orders have reached record highs in recent years (at least in cash terms) and the MOD estimates that Britain won 19 per cent of the world export market in 1995, making it the world's second largest arms exporter after the USA.[5] As also noted above, however, the MOD's estimates are based on the value of export orders won rather than actual deliveries made and may thus overestimate Britain's share of the market. Nevertheless, even on the basis of statistics produced by ACDA (which measure actual arms deliveries) the UK's share of the global market has risen significantly, from 4 per cent in 1984 to 15 per cent in 1995[6]

However, this impression of export success requires qualification in a number of respects. First, the UK has been winning a larger proportion of a market that has radically diminished in the post-cold war era. Indeed, ACDA estimates the world market shrank by some 72 per cent between 1987 and 1994,[7] and by almost 60 per cent in just the four years since 1990 (see Table 6.1). In some respects this makes the UK's achievement even more impressive, as it has occurred in a market which is now characterised by increased competition for fewer orders (and also the emergence of new competitors from the developing world). It also means, however, that while the UK has been winning a larger slice of the arms market, in real terms British defence exports have actually shrunk by 47 per cent since 1987[8] and by 34 per cent since 1990 (see Table 6.1).

Second, the way in which the arms market has shrunk provides at least a partial explanation for Britain's success in obtaining an ever-increasing share of global defence exports. This is because the most significant declines in defence imports have occurred in regions such as the former Warsaw Pact region, North and Sub-Saharan Africa, Central America and the Caribbean, Southern Asia and South America which do not represent major markets for the UK defence industry. Indeed, between 1992 and 1994 combined arms exports to these markets amounted to just 2 per cent of all UK arms transfers. In contrast, the overall level of imports in Britain's traditionally important markets, the Middle East, USA and NATO Europe (which together accounted for 91 per cent of UK arms transfers between 1992 and 1994) have held up relatively well.[9] Analyses of the UK's uptake of market share in each region from 1981–91 shows that in many areas its position actually weakened. For example, its market share declined over the period in East Asia, Southern Asia, Europe (including NATO Europe since 1987) and Africa. Only in the North American and Middle Eastern regions did Britain's market share actually increase.[10] Moreover, the UK's export success in the latter region is primarily a function of just one very large contract – the Al Yamamah contract with Saudi Arabia. Indeed, Britain's reliance on this project is overwhelming, not only in the Middle East[11] but in general – a reliance reflected in the fact that between 1992 and 1994, UK exports to Saudi Arabia accounted for some $9.4 billion and made up 75 per cent of all British defence exports (see Table 6.2).

The sheer size of this one project also provides further explanation for Britain's success in winning an increasing level of market share. While other defence exporters have lost out in the face of a rapidly shrinking market, the Al Yamamah contract has served to cushion the UK DIB from the worst effects of the decline in the global defence trade. In consequence, it has also served to provide a flattering impression of Britain's overall export performance. An illustration of this can be gained by stripping out Saudi imports from the statistics on the

Table 6.2 Top five recipients of UK arms

Country	Arms purchases 1992–4 $ millions	Percentage of UK exports
Saudi Arabia	9400	75.0
USA	1400	11.0
Malaysia	450	3.6
South Korea	270	2.2
Oman	150	1.2

Source: ACDA, *WMEAT*, Table III.

world arms trade and calculating the UK's share of the remaining global market over the 1992–4 period. Once this is done, Britain's share of the market shrinks from the 15.8 per cent it achieves when the Saudi market is included as part of the world arms trade, to just 5.2 per cent when it is excluded.[12]

Of course, the Al Yamamah programme is a real defence project providing real jobs and in this sense it can be argued that to exclude it from any judgement about Britain's export performance is an artificial exercise. However, the point at issue here is not *whether* the UK has achieved *x* per cent of the global defence market but *how* it has been achieved; and the suggestion is that factors other than the efficiency of the British defence industry have more explanatory value. In this sense, illustrating Britain's dependence on the Saudi market is relevant precisely because there is much to suggest the initial Al Yamamah agreement was less a function of either price competitiveness or equipment performance than it was of other considerations.

First, the opportunity for Britain to obtain the contract only arose as a consequence of action by the US Congress to prevent the sale of top-of-the-range US F15E fighters to the Saudis. This allowed other countries to step in and offer alternatives. Official details of the subsequent negotiations and contract between Britain and Saudi Arabia have never been released, but press reports suggested that up until the last moment the Saudis had decided to opt for the French produced Mirage 2000 on technical grounds, and that by 1985 the French had even won a letter of intent.[13] Only the personal intervention of the British prime minister, additional lobbying in support of the British bid by Ronald Reagan, the US president,[14] and the UK's willingness to incur high commercial expenses secured the deal. For example, according to Ohlson, the final agreement included offset arrangements totalling 35 per cent of the contract and an agreement to buy a number of old British-made planes back from the Saudis.[15] According to Al-Ghrair and Hooper, however, the Al Yamamah deal has an investment target of 25 per cent of the technical sales cost of the programme over 10 years.[16] Nevertheless, even this lower figure will, on the MOD's own estimates, require £1 billion of UK investment into Saudi Arabia.[17] The deal also included a commitment that the English football team would play a friendly match in Riyadh and that the English Football Association would actively promote the game in Saudi Arabia.[18] In addition, the terms of the deal provided for payment in kind through the daily shipment of some 300,000 barrels of oil[19] (now raised to 600,000 in response to falling oil prices[20]). The agreement has also been dogged by reports of large 'commissions' paid by UK defence manufacturers to middlemen involved in negotiating the deals as well as claims of outright bribery of key members of the Saudi Royal family. For example, press reports have variously suggested the team involved in brokering the deal for British manufacturers (which included Mark Thatcher, the ex-prime minister's son) received some £240 million in commissions and that 30 per cent or even 45 per cent of the deal was accounted for in commissions and bribes.[21] Indeed, in 1992, documents were produced in a US court case which suggested that US diplomats had monitored the secret transfer by Rolls-Royce and BAe of as much as $4 billion to a Saudi in order to delay an engine decision related to the Al Yamamah programme.[22]

As is noted below, offset arrangements, payments in kind and even bribery are not exceptional in the defence trade. In this sense the Al Yamamah agreement shows that with high level backing from government the British DIB has been able to exploit the rules of the game as well as, if not better than most of its competitors. What it does not demonstrate, however, is the innate competitiveness of British defence products.

Furthermore, while the value of UK exports has withstood the dramatic decline in the arms trade relatively well, and while the UK has increased its global market share, Britain's overwhelming dependence on the Al Yamamah contract means future success is unduly tied to the continuation of this one programme. On the one hand, this also provides grounds for reassurance. The latest orders secured under stage two of the deal will continue to provide work for the UK aerospace industry in the immediate future,[23] and current defence sales also provide an incentive for the Saudis to continue buying British simply to gain the benefits of compatibility. However, falls in the price of oil coupled with the costs of the Gulf War have led to a large Saudi budget deficit, a slowdown in the economy, and consequent problems in meeting contractual commitments.[24] It seems unlikely, therefore, that future orders will be on the scale of recent years. In addition, falling global demand means Britain's competitors are likely to pursue any new Saudi orders with increased vigour. From this viewpoint, Britain's excessive dependence on the Saudi market does not represent a secure foundation on which to build the long-term future of defence exports. Equally, falling defence spending in the UK's other main markets – the US and Europe – is likely to not only reduce potential sales opportunities *per se*, but also to give encouragement to the protectionist instincts of national procurement agencies, thus further reducing the opportunities for British defence sales. Elsewhere, UK exporters are likely to face increasingly tough competition from international competitors desperate to survive in a shrinking market. Furthermore, if reductions in UK domestic procurement expenditure continue, this may well threaten the critical mass necessary for the British DIB to compete effectively in the overseas market.

The MOD now regularly celebrates the success of Britain's defence trade and officials explain this success in terms of the efficiencies instilled in the UK DIB as a consequence of government initiatives to promote competition at home. In real terms, however, Britain's exports have fallen. Moreover, the defence industry's success in winning an increasing proportion of the arms market is due less to domestic efficiency than to the structure of decline in the international market and the cushioning effects of the Al Yamamah contract. Indeed, when considered on a regional basis, far from being a success story, the UK's export performance has been at best mixed. In consequence, the outlook for Britain's export performance in the long term is not necessarily as rosy as it may at first appear. Continued reductions in the global arms market and doubt over the long-term prospects for future Saudi orders, coupled with the emergence of new rivals in the Third World and increasingly aggressive competition from current ones, cast doubt on the defence industry's ability to sustain current levels of exports and its share of the arms trade. Nevertheless, UK defence exports are likely to remain substantial both in absolute terms and in terms of market share. This is particularly so given the current administration's support for defence exports, support rooted in the assumption that Britain derives distinct economic, military-strategic, and political security benefits from the export of arms to other countries. In reality, however, the security benefits accruing from defence exports are questionable.

Economic security

It is perhaps the economic benefits of defence exports which appear to be the most obvious. According to ACDA, UK defence exports contributed $3.4 billion to Britain's balance of payments in 1994.[25] The latest MOD estimates suggest UK exports stood at £2.9 billion in 1994.[26] According to the ministry, British defence exports sustain an estimated 90,000 jobs which also produce benefits for the Exchequer. Furthermore, the MOD considers the export of defence equipment leads to economies of scale that produce savings for its own procurement budget. In 1992 for example, the department estimated it saved £340 million in lower unit costs as a result of defence exports.[27] The department also benefits from the imposition of export levies and licence fees where it has paid for the development of equipment, although this is sometimes waived or reduced where it is deemed necessary. Currently, the MOD estimates receipts from levies bring in some £30 million a year.[28] In addition, many export orders also involve the provision by the MOD of ammunition, spares, training aids and training courses, which can result in significant financial remuneration for the ministry.[29] In the cases of the Al Yamamah programme and also a recent large contract with Malaysia, the department has also created special units inside the MOD to oversee these contracts for which it charges a management fee. Finally, the ministry calculates defence export orders now account for over 40 per cent of the total output of the UK DIB. Particularly in the light of post-cold war reductions in domestic procurement, such a contribution is considered essential if the critical mass necessary for the preservation of a viable DIB is to be preserved.[30] On the face of it, therefore, it would appear that British defence sales produce clear economic and financial benefits both to the economy as a whole and to the MOD.

However, this view needs to be qualified in a number of ways. For example, as Ron Smith has noted, while individual arms firms probably do profit from defence sales it is less clear whether this is the case for the UK economy as a whole once the various forms of subsidy and support for defence sales are taken into account.[31] Subsidisation begins with the MOD's protectionist approach to the procurement of equipment. Indeed, Keith Hartley has suggested that cost savings of up to 25 per cent could be available to a nation willing to procure from the cheapest supplier on the world market.[32]

Through the Export Credit Guarantee Department (ECGD) the government also provides interest rate subsidies which allow buyers to benefit from cheap loans, and offers insurance cover which guarantees compensation to exporters in the event of a buyer defaulting on payments. In recent years the government has expanded the level of support available to Britain's arms traders from the ECGD. In 1985 for example, a £270 million arms deal with Jordan required the government to provide an interest rate subsidy for the bank loans that financed the arms sales. This involved the MOD transferring a sum of about £500,000 a year to the ECGD for this purpose.[33]

In 1988, the government also announced an additional facility of £1 billion to cover situations where large defence sales could not be accommodated within normal ECGD country limits,[34] and in 1993 it announced the provision of £1.4 billion in extra cover for 12 key markets including Indonesia. This latter increase was reportedly required because a £500 million order for BAe Hawk aircraft had pushed the ECGD over its limit to that country. Not surprisingly, therefore, the proportion of ECGD export guarantees going to defence projects has increased markedly in recent years. In the five years to 1984–5, just under 10 per cent of export credits went to defence. In the five years to 1994–5, 30 per cent of export credits went to defence.[35]

International comparisons of the export credit support given to defence are difficult to make, not least because governments are often reluctant to divulge them. However, one recent study by the US General Accounting Office (GAO) found that just 1 per cent of German export credits went to defence in 1993 (the most recent year for which figures are available) and even France, which is renowned for the support it provides domestic exporters, only committed some 21 per cent of export credits to defence (see Chapter 8, Table 8.1). Of course, the proportion of export credits devoted to defence will vary from year to year depending on both the incidence and scale of defence sales for which credits have been provided. Consequently, the GAO's one year snapshot may not represent an accurate reflection of the level of credit support these two nations provide their defence sectors. However, in the absence of any other figures, there is at least tentative evidence to suggest the UK devotes a higher proportion of its export credits to defence.

Not only does the ECGD provide an effective subsidy for British defence exports, but states sometimes default on payments for defence goods – either because of economic crisis or because of a change in relations brought about, for instance, by war or revolution – and the government (through the ECGD) effectively insures the arms industry against this risk. In this respect it is notable that the Scott Inquiry revealed misgivings in the Treasury over the UK's excessive willingness to provide export credits to arms buyers who did not represent good financial risks. Indeed, officials complained that Treasury ministers opposing ECGD cover for particular arms deals (for example the sale of patrol boats to Oman) were overruled in the rush to secure defence orders.[36]

This was certainly the case with regard to the provision of export credits to Iraq, which subsequently defaulted on the repayment of £940 million worth of loans and credit arrangements underwritten by the ECGD.[37] By February 1996, the ECGD had paid out £696 million on claims related to Iraq, most of it since the Gulf War. Much of this relates to guarantees extended to equipment purchased to shore up Saddam's war machine.[38] Indeed, it is illuminating to chart the evolution of UK policy on export credits to Iraq. Under the terms of a protocol signed with Iraq in 1983 the provision of export credits was to be confined to civil goods. Later, under pressure from the MOD and the Iraqis, first 10 per cent and then 20 per cent of agreed credit provision was made available for defence sales. Furthermore, as the Scott Report details, exports of defence equipment were also funded out of the non-defence allocation, as was the case on an £8.6 million contract for the supply of AMETS equipment to Iraq. Similarly, cover was provided out of the non-defence allocation for a £15–16 million contract which included items with a clear military application (for example, an ejector seat, flight simulators and a human training centrifuge – just these three items alone amounting to almost two-thirds of the value of the contract).[39]

It is also common practice for defence contracts with overseas buyers to include some kind of offset requirement as a condition of purchase. These take various forms but can include requirements to set up local production facilities, to transfer technology to the buying country, to purchase locally produced goods (not necessarily related to the technology/materials being exported), and so on. Given the post-cold war contraction of the defence trade and the consequent buyers' market that now operates it seems likely that the level of offset requirements demanded by customers will grow.

Like many countries the UK officially discourages the use of offsets as they are seen as inimicable to the development of an open, cash-based, multilateral trading system.[40] Despite this official stance, not only does the government publish its own guide for exporters with advice on possible offset requirements and a list of useful contact points, but it has sanctioned the use of offsets in government-to-government defence contracts such as the Al Yamamah contract. Similarly, a recent large contract with Malaysia not only included the provision of substantial amounts of aid from the UK (see below) but also an agreement for the transfer of technology through the British companies involved, assist-ance to Malaysia in specified areas of defence production, and the purchase by the MOD of items produced by the Malaysian defence industry.[41] There have also been reports that the deal included the provision of additional landing slots at Heathrow from British Airways to the Malaysian state airline; British Airways reportedly asked for £90 million in compensation.[42]

Offset requirements are now such an integral part of overseas defence sales that a recent survey of British defence contractors found 62 per cent had been, or were, currently engaged in some form of offset activity.[43] However, while offsets might represent a convenient way of capturing a lucrative defence deal for individual firms, they also imply potential costs to the UK economy overall. In particular, offset require-ments disadvantage small and medium level suppliers by encouraging prime contractors to source certain components from the buyer's market or by encouraging the purchase of subsidised, often low-grade goods, which may then be dumped in the seller's home market. In the US for example, the General Accounting Office has found that US defence companies are commonly offering cash as an incentive for US buyers of non-defence goods to place orders in countries where they have offset commitments.[44] Equally, the beneficial employment effects of defence contracts are mitigated by requirements to set up joint ventures or licensed production in the buyer's country, to source specific com-ponents from the same, or to purchase non-defence goods. Indeed, workers in the US have even gone on strike to protest at the loss of jobs arising from offset deals.[45]

Factors such as technology transfer, licensed production and joint ventures also raise questions about the long-term implications of defence sales. Many buyers specifically include such conditions in arms deals as part of a long-term strategy to develop an indigenous defence industry and to promote general economic development through the importation of key technologies or skills. Moreover, the buyers' market created by the post-cold war downturn in defence sales means importers are able to demand the transfer of ever more up-to-date technology. Thus, today's defence sales are potentially sowing the seeds from which tomorrow's competitors will grow. This, in turn, implies future defence orders will be even harder to come by than at present, further undermining the economic rationale for defence exports.

A further cost arising from some defence contracts stems from the way the UK's aid budget appears to have been used to help secure potential orders. Officially, the use of aid to secure defence orders is against government policy, but in reality a strong correlation exists between the distribution of UK aid and the placing of equipment orders by particular countries. The clearest example of this to date was revealed in the Pergau Dam scandal. In this case the UK government agreed a protocol with Malaysia in 1988 which explicitly linked the provision of aid with a billion pounds arms sale. Subsequently, this formal link was *officially* removed, but some £234 million of aid plus £45.8 million of export credits were nevertheless made available for work on the Pergau Hydro-Electric Project in Malaysia. Aid for the Pergau Project came from an element of the aid budget known as the Aid and Trade Provision (ATP) which provides finance for development projects that result in contracts for UK companies. Arguably, therefore, the provision of aid to Malaysia was in itself a benefit to the British economy as it resulted in the award of contracts to UK companies. However, it should also be noted that a 1992 review of the ATP scheme concluded: 'it is unlikely that the overall benefits of ATP which have accrued to the economy have matched its costs.'[46]

The Pergau Dam case is not an isolated one. Research by the World Development Movement (WDM) has revealed a strong link between arms sales and rises in aid (of between 75 to 189 per cent) to the relatively well-off Third World countries of Oman, Indonesia, Thailand, Jordan and Malaysia. Similar linkages were also identified in relation to

Ecuador and Venezuela, and the study suggested the link between aid and arms sales to low-income countries such as India, Nigeria and Pakistan might also bear further examination.[47] This is not to suggest that all UK aid is linked to arms sales or that all arms sales are linked to the provision of aid. There does, however, appear to be a strong correlation in the case of particular countries.

The benefits available from defence exports are further undermined by the payment of huge commissions to 'middle men' in order to influence the allocation of procurement contracts and/or the straight-forward bribery of government officials. As one defence industry representative has noted: 'there are many countries where, unless the defence minister gets a ten per cent cut of the contract you're not going to get it, and that goes on a lot and that's real bribery and corruption.'[48] Indeed, one British arms dealer told the *Guardian* that Nigeria's generals took up to 70 per cent of the value of an arms deal in commission.[49]

The marketing support provided by the MOD via the Defence Export Services Organisation (DESO) does not come cost free either. The total net cost of the DESO in 1994–5 has been estimated by the MOD at roughly £15 million,[50] although the World Development Movement have suggested the real cost is actually £21 million.[51] In contrast, similar agencies for sectors with far higher exports have much smaller budgets (see Table 6.3). Indeed, while exports of pharmaceuticals (excluding chemicals) and medical equipment were £2 billion higher than those for defence in 1994, the unit responsible for promoting these exports within the Department of Health has just four full-time staff. In comparison, DESO has some 600 staff.[52]

DESO also relies on the UK's defence attachés (DAs) to supply market information and to promote British defence goods. According to the NAO's 1989 report on defence exports, DAs spend roughly a third of their time on such work (although since this report the number of defence attachés has reduced sharply and support for defence sales has become increasingly important). In 1994–5 DAs cost the MOD some £19 million in total.[53] UK defence exporters are also supported by an endless round of ministerial and prime ministerial visits and through the use of naval visits or the detachment of military hardware to defence exhibitions. In one sales promotion effort, four Tornado fighters flew around the world, stopping off at key sales points on the way. In response to questioning in Parliament, the MOD asserted that the cost of this operation could not be calculated without disproportionate effort.

Table 6.3 Export promotion agencies and government funding

Industry	Exports 1994(£b)	Organisation	Government funding (£m)
Food and drink	9.2	Food from Britain	5.25[1]
Construction	7.4	Construction Export Promotion Division	0.35
Pharmaceuticals and medical equipment[2]	4.9	Unit in the International and Industry Division of the Department of Health	4 full-time staff
Clothing and footwear	3.2	None	None
Defence	2.9	DESO	15[3]

Notes: [1] The total budget of Food From Britain was £9.95m, the difference being made up by contributions from industry. MAFF spends a further £1m a year on schemes to further diplomatic relations with non-EC countries and international organisations and to maximise trade and investment opportunities for the UK agro-industry with all countries. [2] Excluding chemical exports. [3] This is the net cost, including sales promotions, inwards missions and certain disposal receipts.

Sources: Department of Health Press Office 13 September 1996; ONS, *Monthly Digest of Statistics*, no. 610, October 1996; Unpublished research by Campaign Against the Arms Trade; Neil Cooper, 'British defence exports: trends, policy and security implications', *Contemporary Security Policy*, vol. 16, no. 2 (August 1995): 230.

It was revealed, however, that just the cost of chartering support aircraft to cover the absent planes amounted to £945,000.[54]

There are also some 130 civil servants based in the DTI's Export Control Organisation who are responsible for issuing export licences, monitoring industry compliance with sanctions and export regulations, and the development of policy on export control issues.[55] It may be argued that to some extent these would be required anyway, even if the UK was not a major defence exporter, but their number would probably be reduced.

This heavy reliance on government support in arms sales promotion shows no sign of lessening. Indeed, given the tighter market conditions of the post-cold war era, the infrastructure of defence promotion may well have to expand if Britain is to maintain its position in the world arms market. It is certainly notable in this respect that the Clinton administration has earmarked $1 billion for the promotion of American military products,[56] and one report from the World Policy Institute has estimated that subsidies for US arms exports amounted to $7.6 billion in 1995.[57]

It should also be noted that equipment made for export often includes a higher proportion of components sourced from cheaper overseas suppliers in order to make it more price competitive in the world market. To the extent that this does occur, the benefits of defence exports both in terms of employment and the maintenance of the defence industrial base are, of course, mitigated. Moreover, there is a significant body of literature which suggests the British DIB has had a negative impact on economic growth by variously depressing investment, diverting scarce R & D resources, and/or by imbuing key economic sectors with a corporate culture antithetical to innovation, low-cost production and competitive marketing.[58] If this is the case, using defence exports to preserve the key position of the defence industry in the UK economy may actually be detrimental to Britain's long-term economic security.

There are, therefore, a number of costs which need to be taken into account when assessing the economic benefits of UK defence exports. The secretive nature of Britain's arms trade means that precise quantification of such costs from public sources is currently impossible. However, the foregoing analysis suggests these costs are substantial, and may even outweigh the advantages that accrue to the British economy from defence exports. Certainly it suggests the economic harvest Britain reaps from its arms trade may not be so substantial that it cannot afford to give it up, particularly if the benefits of defence exports in terms of military and political security are even more questionable.

Military security

In terms of military security the arguments for defence exports appear strong. Defence exports allow economies of scale which reduce equipment costs, thus enabling Britain to field armed forces that carry more or better equipment than might otherwise be the case. It is also argued that in ensuring the preservation of an all-round DIB, arms exports guarantee security of supply for defence equipment. Moreover, exports to allies arguably improve their ability to defend themselves, thus reducing the need for a British military presence/armed involvement in conflict and also making it more likely that stable trading conditions are maintained. It is further suggested that the sale of arms increases the ability of the UK to influence the domestic and foreign policies of client states to the benefit of UK interests.

However, the notion that the preservation of an all-round DIB guarantees security of supply, which in turn guarantees the UK's ability to undertake independent military action is increasingly questionable. First, the political conditions of the post-cold war era, coupled with dramatic reductions in the size of the UK's armed forces, make it virtually inconceivable that Britain would – or could – fight all but the smallest of conflicts independently. Second, as Smith has noted, not only do long lead times make production capacity irrelevant in short duration conflicts but the complex international interdependencies that now exist in the construction of weapons means security of supply is no longer guaranteed by the presence of even a wide-ranging DIB.[59] For example, most major weapons systems are now developed in collaboration with other nations (although production is often sourced domestically). Moreover, even where equipment is ostensibly made in the UK, component parts may well be sourced from overseas. For example, 11 per cent of the Challenger II tank is made abroad – including the fire control computer, the primary sight, and components for the gunnery sight.[60] It should also be noted there is evidence to suggest that capital spending on defence may depress civil exports as it reduces the available goods for export and tends to be concentrated in the more important export sectors such as machinery and transport.[61] Thus, using defence exports to ensure there is a wide-ranging DIB available to serve the needs of the MOD also undermines the balance of payments advantages that accrue from British arms sales. In consequence, not only is the notion of an independent defence production capacity a chimera, but using defence exports to maintain such capacity actually implies a weakening of the UK's economic security.

While defence exports arguably provide security through deterrence for allies, they can equally contribute to action–reaction arms races that not only make conflict more likely, but more devastating when it does occur. Moreover, there is a significant body of academic work which suggests defence expenditure has the potential to depress growth in developing countries, promote inappropriate models of development, and reinforce the power of élites whose position is founded on exploitation, repression and social inequality.[62] Clearly, in countries where such a relationship exists, spending on defence imports has the capacity to exacerbate precisely the kind of tensions likely to produce intra or inter-state conflict. To the extent that such conflicts are exported out – through their effects on the economic, environmental, military or political security of the West – arms exports effectively undermine the UK's security.

When events require direct military intervention, Western forces can find themselves threatened by weapons produced by their own companies. For example, before the Falklands War, the Argentinians were a major customer of the UK defence industry, purchasing Type 42 destroyers, Lynx helicopters, Seacat close range air defence missiles, and armoured cars.[63] Similarly, documents retrieved by UN inspectors after the Gulf War revealed some 30 UK companies had been part of the Iraqi procurement network.[64] One piece of equipment sold to the Iraqis (despite opposition from the MOD's own military advisors) was a radar jamming system made by Plessey. At the Scott Inquiry one witness described how he was visited shortly after the invasion of Kuwait by a Royal Signals Officer to check what sort of equipment Britain had supplied to Baghdad. On being told of the Plessey radar system the officer exclaimed, 'Oh bloody hell ... we have nothing to touch that.'[65] The French had even more problems in the Gulf – their Mirage aircraft were unable to fly because they were indistinguishable from those they had sold to the Iraqis.[66]

Clearly, the possibility that British soldiers might be killed by weapons sold by British defence companies raises serious questions about the nature of the arms trade. Furthermore, the sale of Western weapons to potential adversaries (either directly or indirectly via third parties) risks reducing military advantage and – at the very least – implies the cost of going to war with a customer will be that much higher.

The examples of Western exports to Argentina, Iraq and pre-Khomeini Iran also demonstrate the limitations inherent in using arms sales as a means of influencing the policies of client states. Indeed, where major defence contracts are at stake influence can be a two-way process, inhibiting the seller's willingness to take action against a client for fear of the effects on its own defence business. As will be noted below, this is particularly relevant in the case of British exports to Saudi Arabia, but it would also explain the government's relative insouciance over human rights abuses in Indonesia, for instance, which has recently placed major defence orders with the UK.[67]

The drive to export arms in a contracting market has now led the UK to sign a defence co-operation agreement with the United Arab Emirates (UAE), the UAE having made this a condition of any future defence sales agreement. According to the MOD's own press release on the subject, the agreement 'commits the UK to assist in deterring threats or preventing aggression against the UAE and, in the event of such aggression taking place, implementing appropriate joint military plans.'[68] Thus, the desperate drive to secure export orders is now determining wider strategic policy. Moreover, the same carrot of prospective arms sales has also been dangled in front of the French and the Americans who have negotiated similar defence co-operation agreements with the UAE. There is thus no guarantee that Britain will receive the £5 billion worth of arms orders reportedly on offer. It should also be noted that the UAE has an offset requirement of 60 per cent.[69] This will have to be set against any defence export orders finally obtained.

There have also been occasions when the equipment needs of overseas buyers have been given priority over those of the UK's home forces, to the detriment of military readiness. Most notably, the second stage of the Al Yamamah programme involved the diversion to Saudi Arabia of 20 aircraft originally intended for the RAF and a consequent delay in the build up of the Tornado GR1 reconnaissance force.[70] Given the exigencies of the post-cold war arms market, it seems likely that such occurrences will become more common.

Finally, there is a tension between the need to develop equipment geared to the particular requirements of one's own forces and the needs of exporters to develop weapons that will be attractive in the global market. Certainly in France, equipment is designed to meet the needs of foreign purchasers whose requirements are not necessarily congruent with those of the French military.[71] On balance, the requirements of the UK's own forces are still given priority. However, there is increasing pressure from defence companies to change equipment specifications in order to enhance exportability, and the fierce market conditions of the post-cold war era may well require the MOD to move closer to the French model if the British defence industry is to maintain its position in the export market.

Political security

As Malcolm Rifkind noted when defence secretary:

> national interests are not necessarily, or even often, simply material interests. Indeed, the essential purpose of defence in a free society is to ensure that no external enemy can destroy the institutions and way of life that express that society's moral and political values.[72]

In this sense defence is not simply about the maintenance of military or economic security but ultimately about the maintenance of a society's political security through the preservation of social and political values. In a democracy such as the UK it is not unreasonable to suggest that such values should include openness, democratic accountability and a commitment to the integrity of social and political institutions.

It can be argued that defence exports promote such political security precisely by contributing to the nation's military and economic security. Military security ensures freedom from actual or threatened invasion, thus guaranteeing the physical security of a society's institutions and preventing the enforced imposition of an alternative social and political order. Economic security provides for growth which allows relative freedom from hardship and sustainable levels of welfare. This in turn reduces the potential for dissatisfaction with the economic and political system, and gives individuals a material interest in the preservation of social order as well as norms and institutions perceived to promote material well-being.

However, as the foregoing analyses has suggested, the economic benefits derived from defence exports are questionable and may even be negative. Similarly, the export of arms seems more likely to diminish the UK's military security in the long run rather than reinforce it. At the same time, defence exports themselves actually undermine the UK's political security in a number of ways. This is particularly the case with respect to arms sales to Saudi Arabia, where the British defence industry's overwhelming reliance on the Al Yamamah programme has overlapped with the material, organisational and political interests of key groups in the UK policy-making machinery (for example, the services, MOD, DESO, DTI) effectively to create a condition of dependency *vis-à-vis* Britain's relationship with Saudi Arabia. In consequence, government policy has frequently been dictated by the need to maintain the flow of money for arms coming from the Saudis. In a number of instances the by-product has been an erosion in public accountability and the integrity of government institutions. For example:

- Allegations that the Al Yamamah contract was only secured after the bribery of high-ranking Saudi officials were investigated by the National Audit Office only for publication of the report to be shelved due to concern over Saudi reaction at a time when stage two of the Al Yamamah programme was still under discussion.
- In another case, details of a dispute with the Saudis over payment for land leased from them during the Gulf War were removed from the public record of a hearing of the Public Accounts Committee at the behest of the MOD – again because of concern at the possible reaction of Britain's largest defence customer.[73]
- It was also made clear to the Foreign Affairs Committee that 'the overseas sensitivities' of two major buyers of UK arms were factors that the MOD had to 'watch very carefully' when it appointed a new head of the Defence Export Services Organisation in 1989.[74] It seems probable that one of the two countries concerned was Saudi Arabia, although concern for the sensitivities of these customers meant the MOD refused to name them in public (despite the influence they had had on the appointment of a British public official).
- One report in the press suggested that 'under Foreign Office over-sight' BBC news reporting on Saudi Arabia is 'handled with extreme sensitivity' given the size of the Al Yamamah programme,[75] and journalists who have worked in Saudi Arabia report being asked by British diplomats to bear in mind the number of jobs dependent on Saudi business when reporting news from the state.[76]
- Britain initially refused asylum to a prominent Saudi dissident (Dr Mas'ari) on the grounds that he had spent a month in the Republic of Yemen where he had the opportunity to apply for asylum. However, Dr Mas'ari argued he would not be safe if returned to the Yemen and his proposed expulsion was blocked by an independent adjudicator.[77]
- In January 1996 the government then announced that Dr Mas'ari was to be deported to Dominica. Newspaper reports made it clear the government had been pressurised into this decision both by the Saudis and by major UK defence companies such as British Aero-space and Vickers who considered that important defence contracts would be at stake if Dr Mas'ari remained in the UK. This was

underlined by the Home Office minister, Ann Widdecombe, who justified the expulsion by arguing, 'We have close trade relations with a friendly state who have been the subject of very consistent criticisms from Mr Mas'ari and we have got enormous export considerations, British job considerations and we have therefore tried to find a solution which satisfied both sides.'[78] Asked in one interview whether the British government was surrendering the principle of free speech, Ann Widdecombe replied, 'I don't think we have surrendered that principle. Mr Mas'ari can say whatever he likes – in Dominica.'[79]

- In order to persuade Dominica to take Dr Mas'ari, the government promised that UK aid to Dominica would be increased from £500,000 in 1994–5 to £2 million in each of the following two years.[80] This of course represented yet another subsidy for British arms exports.

- On 5 March 1996 Dr Mas'ari was successful in his appeal against deportation to Dominica. The judge found that Michael Howard, the home secretary, had failed to establish that Dr Mas'ari would be safe in Dominica and had no right to refuse his application for political asylum in Britain. The judge's ruling suggested that an attempt had been made to circumvent the UN Convention on Refugees for diplomatic and trade reasons.[81]

- On 15 March, the prime minister announced the government was looking at introducing new laws to crack down on foreign activists to ensure they do not use Britain as a haven from which to promote violence or foster dissent. He stated, 'It may be that the time has come to look at the activities not only of those who actively conspire to commit terrorist acts but also those who from safe havens abroad foster dissent elsewhere in a way which creates a climate in which terrorism can flourish.'[82]

- On 21 March, Virginia Bottomley (the national heritage secretary) announced moves to close a legal loophole which allowed any organisation to make satellite broadcasts from Britain to non-European countries. Under the terms of the prescription order, the Independent Television Commission will have to license any satellite service from Britain to non-European countries. According to press reports at the time, the change meant foreign governments would be able to complain about a service's broadcasts from Britain. The *Guardian* noted: 'it is understood the Home Office was concerned about rumours that Mohammed al-Mas'ari, the Saudi Arabian dissident ...

was preparing to broadcast views critical of the Saudi regime to the Middle East.'[83]

- In July, prior to a visit to Saudi Arabia by the foreign secretary, Malcolm Rifkind, it was reported that the law was to be changed so that asylum would be denied to individuals engaged in inciting or directly helping terrorism. It was also announced that Britain was to propose a change in the UN Convention on Refugees so that anyone aiding and abetting terrorism would not be entitled to claim asylum. According to the *Guardian*, 'British ministers admitted that the attempt was prompted by concern expressed by Saudi Arabia and fear of losing arms export deals.'[84] Officials of the UN High Commissioner for Refugees expressed concern that the definition of those covered by the proposed new UN convention could be so wide as to affect those refugees with genuine cases.[85]

Thus, in a variety of ways, the concern to appease a major arms client has had a significant influence on both domestic and foreign policy.

The concern to promote defence exports has corroded the integrity of government in other ways. As already noted, for instance, a recent study by the World Development Movement has identified a strong correlation between the distribution of aid to particular countries and the allocation of defence contracts from those countries. This is despite the fact that it has been the declared policy of successive governments that overseas development aid should be provided neither for the purchase of military equipment nor as a condition of defence sales.[86] It is also despite the fact that current policy emphasises the use of aid to promote good government and political reform, including reductions in excessive military expenditure.[87] Indeed, in the case of the Pergau Dam scandal, government aid to Malaysia was challenged in the courts and ruled illegal on the grounds that it did not promote the development of the country's economy as required by law.[88]

As the proceedings of the Scott Inquiry have so clearly revealed, the government also broke its own guidelines on the sale of defence equipment to Iraq and Iran during the 1980s. In December 1984 the government adopted guidelines restricting the supply of defence equipment to both sides of the Iran–Iraq War. In particular, the guidelines noted the UK would 'not in future, approve orders for any defence equipment which, in our view, would significantly enhance the capability of either side to prolong or exacerbate the conflict.'[89] Despite the introduction of these guidelines Britain continued to supply military equipment to both Iran and Iraq. In the case of Iraq, the list of products licensed for export between 1987 and 1990 includes aircraft, air defence simulators, armoured vehicles and spares, artillery fire control, depleted uranium, explosive detonators, explosives, fast assault craft, jet engines and parts, laser rangefinder, mortar locating radar and an automatic vehicle location system.[90] One lone voice holding out against the flow of arms to Iraq was that of Lt.-Col. Glazebrook, the MOD official responsible for ensuring sales abroad did not endanger the UK military. In a 1989 report headed 'British assistance to the emerging Iraqi arms industry' he noted that 'UK Ltd is helping Iraq, often unwittingly, but sometimes not, to set up a major indigenous arms industry.' Britain's contribution to Iraq, he recorded, included setting up a major research and development facility to make weapons, machinery to make gun barrels and shells, and a national electronics manufacturing complex. Echoing the language of the 1984 guidelines, he concluded that the exports represented 'a very significant enhancement to the ability of Iraq to manufacture its own arms.' Glazebrook recommended a tightening of the export guidelines; instead, officials quietly buried the report and the flow of defence equipment continued.[91] Indeed, MOD officials at the Scott Inquiry estimated that UK defence exports to Iraq amounted to some $222 million between 1985 and 1990. However, this figure did not include either exports redirected to Iraq via third party countries such as Jordan, or dual-use equipment such as machine tools. As the Matrix Churchill affair has revealed, the UK was Iraq's leading supplier of machine tools, selling $93 million worth between 1987 and 1989 alone.[92] Moreover, this was done in the knowledge that such equipment was destined for use in military production. Indeed, on one occasion the government was aware that machine tools destined for Iraq could well be used in the development of Saddam's nuclear weapons programme, yet the then Foreign Office minister, William Waldegrave, was still prepared to sanction their export, justifying it with the comment: 'screwdrivers are also required to make H-bombs'.[93] After the Gulf War UN inspectors subsequently confirmed that Matrix Churchill lathes had indeed been used in the Iraqi nuclear programme.

Not content with supplying weapons directly to the Iraqis, the government also sanctioned arms export sales to Jordan and Saudi Arabia in the knowledge that equipment was being re-routed through these countries to Saddam Hussein. Indeed, it was so well known that Jordan was fronting as an arms buyer for Iraq that officials nicknamed the country 'Jorq'.[94] For example, the British knew that some of the equipment sold to Jordan as part of a £270 million defence deal struck in the mid-1980s was being sold on to Iraq to update 200 British Chieftain tanks captured from the Iranians.[95] As part of this same deal the Jordanians received an interest rate subsidy from the government amounting to some £500,000 a year. It is also notable that in 1984, when the arms sale was being negotiated, British aid to Jordan more than doubled. Thus, not only did the British government connive with the Jordanians in breaking the UK's own arms embargo, but it provided aid and a subsidy to do it. Indeed, even six weeks after Saddam's invasion of Kuwait, the government still approved the export of 5,000 artillery shells (produced by Royal Ordnance) despite the fact they were likely to be redirected to Iraq.[96]

In December 1988 the Howe guidelines were amended so that they now read along the following lines: 'We should not in future approve orders for any defence equipment which, in our view, would be of direct and significant assistance to either country in the conduct of offensive operations.'[97] Parliament, however, was not informed. Indeed, a succession of ministers led Parliament to believe that the 1984 guidelines (which had been made public in 1985) were still in operation. For instance, on 21 April 1989 the prime minister, Margaret Thatcher, told MPs: 'the government have not changed their policy on defence sales to Iraq' and went on to note that 'applications for export licences continue to be considered on a case-by-case basis according to the guidelines as announced in the House by the foreign secretary on 29 October 1985 and in the light of developments in the peace negotiations with Iran.'[98] Moreover, when independent action by customs officers led to charges against Matrix Churchill executives for breaching the UK's official arms embargo, the government denied its own complicity in the Matrix exports and attempted to prevent the defendants gaining access to official papers which proved they acted with government support. Indeed, it was so concerned not to reveal the extent of government support for exports to Iraq that it even withheld crucial papers from Customs' senior prosecution counsel, Alan Moses. These included a GCHQ intelligence report dated October 1989 which linked Matrix Churchill to Iraq's military build-up and specifically referred to contracts cited in the prosecution indictment. In evidence to the Scott

Inquiry Moses stated, 'I can't understand why on earth I didn't know about this ... I don't think I would have gone on with the prosecution if I had.'[99] Thus, not only did the government break its own arms export guidelines and lie to Parliament about their operation but it was prepared to see innocent men jailed in order to cover up the extent of its own corruption.

It should also be noted the UK has committed itself to the EU's common criteria for arms transfers, as well as criteria agreed by the Permanent Five in 1991 and the Principles Governing Arms Transfers agreed at the CSCE in November 1993. The criteria set out in these documents, and the UK's own guidelines governing the export of arms, variously include the requirement to avoid transfers likely to prolong or exacerbate armed conflict, increase tension or introduce destabilising military capabilities in a region. They also include the requirement to take into account the human rights record of a potential recipient state and the potential for equipment sold to be used for internal repression. However, these criteria appear to be honoured more in the breach than in the observance. It is difficult to see how, for example, the export of arms to states in the Middle East such as Saudi Arabia, Jordan and Oman can be equated with the former category of requirements. Equally, it is hard to see the UK's concern to target the Asia-Pacific market as anything other than a contribution to a regional arms build-up which is fuelling tensions in the area.

Similarly, the emphasis given to human rights considerations in UK defence exports is rather low; indeed, it has been estimated that 68 per cent of UK arms transfers are to regimes with poor records on human rights.[100] A recent television documentary has also aired statements by defence company representatives asserting they had supplied electro-shock batons to Saudi Arabia. Moreover, the government subsequently had to pay £55,000 in libel damages to the producer of the programme after ministers at the DTI suggested the allegations were contrived.[101] Throughout the 1980s the UK continued to supply Iraq with military equipment, including materials necessary for chemical and nuclear weapons production, despite its appalling human rights record and its use of chemical weapons against both the Iranians and its own Kurdish population. Similarly, Indonesia's continued annexation of East Timor and appalling human rights abuses by the Suharto regime have not prevented Britain assiduously courting defence trade with the country. In contrast, Indonesia's abuse of human rights has persuaded the US to stop the sale of live arms to the country, and Portugal, Sweden and Italy operate self-imposed arms embargoes.[102]

While the UK pays lip-service to concerns about human rights and regional arms races, the reality is quite different. Not only is Britain one of the world's major exporters but UK officials have explicitly set out a goal of acquiring $8 billion of new arms orders each year.[103] This desperate scramble for sales in a declining market has left little room for concern about the gassing of Kurds or the implications of regional arms races. Nor has it left room for concern about the failure of the British state to live up to its commitments in the international arena.

Summary

Far from promoting a virtuous circle of benefits based upon the efficiency of the British defence industry and enjoyed by all, UK defence exports arguably promote a vicious circle of disadvantage from which only the arms traders benefit. Certainly the UK's position in the league table of the world's arms exporters is less a function of efficiency instilled through competition at home, and more a function of the structure of decline in the global arms market, the cushioning effects of the Al Yamamah contract and the aggressive marketing of British weapons abroad. Moreover, while the value of Britain's arms trade is certainly significant, the prospects for future arms orders are not so promising, and the economic benefits derived from current sales are eroded by the need to maintain an extensive marketing apparatus as well as the use of bribes, offsets, aid and subsidised credit to ensure that potential customers buy British. In both military and political security terms the advantages that accrue from defence exports are more than questionable, while the more competitive environment of the post-cold war arms market suggests that the costs of defence exports to Britain in economic, military and political terms may actually rise in the years ahead.

7

Inefficiency in procurement

So far, the concern of this book has principally been with an examination of the MOD's policy towards the arms trade since 1979, in particular its policies on competition, collaboration and defence exports. What remains to be considered is the extent to which these policies have resulted in greater efficiency – what the MOD terms 'value for money' – in the acquisition of weapons. Clearly, the concept of efficiency or value for money is ultimately a subjective one which turns on a host of value judgements. Thus, while efficiency in weapons procurement is easy to grasp as a goal, in reality it is a rather illusive concept which is difficult to pin down. With these qualifications in mind, however, the aim of this chapter is to consider the MOD's claims for introducing greater efficiency in procurement against a number of different criteria. First, the success of its competition policy in holding down the costs of the initial contract, coupled with the benefits of protectionism and maintenance of a wide-ranging defence industrial base. Second, the extent to which cost increases over and above the initial contract price have been controlled. Third, the success or otherwise of the MOD in delivering weapons on schedule. Fourth and finally, the effectiveness of the equipment acquired when measured against the original performance envisaged for it.

The savings from competition and the benefits of protectionism

As already noted in Chapter 4, the MOD has claimed savings of a billion pounds a year as a result of its competition policy. However, the extent to which real savings have been achieved is debatable. This is particularly so given the selective nature of the savings reported by the

ministry, the costs of administering competition, the delay induced by
the competitive process and the fact that most, if not all, the annual
£400 million costs of bidding incurred by industry are passed back to
the ministry. This is to say nothing of the rise in recorded fraud that
has occurred since the competition initiative was introduced, and the
deleterious effect on reliability and maintainability that competition is
alleged to have had, particularly in its early years.

Moreover, notwithstanding certain overseas acquisitions, the competition policy has, in reality, been overlaid with a heavy dollop of
protectionism, with all but 10 per cent of MOD equipment being
procured from domestic producers. As already noted in earlier chapters,
the potential savings from open competition in Europe have been
estimated at 8–17 per cent, and potential savings from full international
competition have been estimated at up to 25 per cent. Even if it is
accepted that the ministry has operated open competition in some cases,
and that UK companies have responded to domestic competition by
sourcing more sub-components from cheaper overseas suppliers (see
below), it is not unreasonable to suggest that a significant proportion of
the annual £9 billion procurement budget could be saved if protectionism were to be abandoned.

Of course, it is often countered that buying British provides wider
national economic benefits which more than offset any savings from
overseas procurement. For example, it is argued that domestic procurement results in a healthier balance of payments, job creation, and
higher receipts to the Treasury from the taxes paid by the additional
defence workers employed to do the jobs generated by protectionism.
However, this argument is problematic on a number of grounds. First,
any consideration of the advantages and disadvantages of international
competition has to take into account the opportunity costs involved –
the potential economic and social benefits that could be derived from
employing the money saved on other forms of public expenditure, for
example health or education. Moreover, as already noted in Chapter 6,
there is much evidence to suggest that the British DIB has ultimately
had a negative effect on growth by depressing investment, diverting
scarce R&D resources and by promoting inefficiency in key sectors of
the UK economy.

Furthermore, both the balance of payments and employment benefits
derived from the defence industry are actually in decline. For example,
the numbers employed both directly and indirectly as a result of dom-

estic procurement expenditure have been in long-term decline as a consequence of cuts in expenditure and improvements in productivity. This was the case even in the early 1980s when procurement expenditure experienced substantial growth. Indeed, since 1980 the number of domestically generated defence industrial jobs has fallen by 40 per cent to 175,000 (amounting to one job for every £51,428 of expenditure).[1] On past experience, even if procurement expenditure were to experience a small rise (which seems unlikely in the short term at least), employment in the defence sector will continue to decline as developments in technology increase productivity.

Obtaining reliable figures on Britain's defence balance of payments is made problematical by the fact that the categories used to define defence imports and exports have undergone a certain amount of revision. From 1993, radio, radar and optical equipment were omitted from the statistics, and in 1995 the estimates of aerospace equipment exports from 1988 onwards were revised upwards as a result of methodological changes in the estimates of additional military exports provided to the ministry by the Society of British Aerospace Companies (SBAC). For example, under the revised figures, aerospace exports in 1991 doubled from £807 million to £1,626 million and for 1992 they went from £811 million to £1,588 million.[2] In addition to changes in the definition of defence equipment, it should be noted that while the defence export figures include estimates of additional exports provided by the SBAC, no estimate of additional imports is provided by the Society. However, to the extent that comparisons over time are useful, it is notable that though the defence trade still records a substantial balance of payments surplus (of £1.8 billion) there has, in real terms, been a 60 per cent fall in this surplus since 1990. The extent of the fall is such that changes in the definition of defence equipment seem unlikely to explain it. Indeed, it is equally possible that the changes, coupled with the absence of any estimate of additional imports from the SBAC, actually mask a larger fall. Instead, the reduction in the defence balance of payments surplus is probably best explained by the fall in defence exports resulting from the contraction in the global arms market and an increase in the volume of defence imports. Given that the proportion of the MOD's expenditure devoted to overseas procurement has remained stubbornly fixed at around 10 per cent of a declining procurement budget, the increase in defence imports seems best explained by two factors. First, the increasing internationalisation of the defence market, and, second, the fact that companies are responding to both a shrinking overseas market and the ministry's domestic competition policy by sourcing more sub-components from cheaper overseas suppliers. Given these factors, the fall in the defence balance of payments may well continue.

Of course, the figures given above do not take into account the additional monies that would have to go abroad if protectionism were abandoned, or the possible loss of export revenue consequent upon any reduction in the UK DIB following the application of such a policy. It could be argued, therefore, that if these are factored into the calculations then the benefits of protectionism are self-evidently substantial. However, this ignores the fact that the dramatic fall in the global arms trade has created a buyers' market in which purchasers such as the MOD can demand generous offset deals, sometimes amounting to over 100 per cent of the value of the equipment acquired. As was noted in Chapter 6, such deals take a variety of forms but can include requirements to set up local production facilities, to transfer technology to the purchasing country, or to purchase locally produced goods (not necessarily from the defence sector). Indeed, where it does purchase abroad, the MOD already seeks offsets on purchases over £10 million and, despite its relatively low level of expenditure on overseas procurement, these offset deals have generated £4–5 billion worth of work in the past ten years. Offsets can also generate additional work on future export orders acquired by the supplier company. For example, having established a relationship with Lockheed in the 1960s, Marshals of Cambridge has attracted work from Hercules operators in more than 30 countries as well as significant US orders for the conversion of TriStars to commercial freighters.[3] Even if one accepts that requiring overseas companies to offer offset deals may involve some amelioration of the cost advantages derived from international competition, it still seems likely that offsets can offer the ministry the opportunity to combine job creation with substantial savings in procurement expenditure.

As already noted, the last ten years have witnessed a dramatic increase in defence imports which, in real terms, have risen by over three times their value in the mid-1980s – a phenomenon which is at least partly explained by the fact that UK companies may be sourcing more sub-components from cheaper overseas suppliers. If this is the case, and if the rise in defence imports continues its upward trend, to some extent at least the UK procurement budget will be purchasing substantial levels of overseas defence equipment without extracting the kind of concessions on price and offsets that the MOD's role as a major arms buyer would enable it to obtain on major equipment orders. Consequently, the application of competition with protectionism may be doubly disadvantaging the UK: first by raising the costs of equipment procured, and second by reducing the likelihood and/or scale of offsets achievable against what is a dramatically rising level of defence imports.

Of course, it is argued that international competition implies the erosion of a domestic defence industrial base, the maintenance of which is essential if the UK is to retain its ability to engage in independent military action to preserve national interests. It is also claimed that overseas procurement involves a Faustian bargain which brings one-off savings that are ultimately offset by dependence on an overseas monopoly supplier for spares and updates. Both of these arguments, however, are specious. In the latter case, the MOD is just as likely to find itself locked into a monopoly supplier at home as it is abroad; in the former, the UK has already abandoned the industrial capability to produce key elements of defence equipment, not the least of which being its nuclear missiles. In addition, as the rising levels of defence imports testify, the internationalisation of the defence market means that even equipment ostensibly purchased in the UK has significant levels of foreign sub-components incorporated in it. As the MOD itself has noted: 'international interdependency for defence equipment is a fact for all nations ... and most of our complex equipment includes at least some components from overseas.'[4] Moroever, as was noted in Chapter 5, the preservation of a wide-ranging defence industrial base in the UK has only been achieved at the expense of undue dependence on key arms buyers such as Saudi Arabia, Indonesia and Malaysia. Furthermore, the rising costs of defence equipment coupled with cuts in the defence budget have meant that, irrespective of the breadth of its DIB (which is by no means self-sufficient), reductions in front-line forces have led to a situation in which the UK's ability to undertake independent military action is already severely curtailed. For example, prior to the Falklands War, the UK had a destroyer and frigate force of 59; today it has a force of just 35, with the number of ships actually available to go to sea at short notice being much lower.[5] And the situation is unlikely to improve in the future. Equipment costs are rising by an average of 10 per cent per annum so that weapons costs actually double every 7.25 years.[6] As each year goes by it becomes even less conceivable that the UK could field an all-round capability army able to take independent action. For example, Kirkpatrick has noted that the UK would only be able to afford a successor to the Eurofighter in 2025 if the procurement budget were doubled, if developments in technology halve the cost of aircraft development, and if the number of nations collaborating on the new fighter were to be enlarged. As he comments, 'it is virtually impossible that several fantastically-favourable developments will occur simultaneously, and without such a miraculous conjunction the UK will be unable to afford a viable force of combat aircraft.'[7] Indeed, he argues that even off-the-shelf procurement from the US will only delay the need to make hard decisions over whether to abandon certain military capabilities and to integrate military forces and procurement with that of other nations.

Thus, the notion of military independence has become a perpetually receding chimera, the pursuit of which has effectively turned the UK into the lap-dog of its major arms buyers. A rational defence procurement strategy is not one that pays lip-service to the need for interdependence while pursuing a policy at odds with reality. The MOD needs to free itself from any illusions about maintaining security of supply and take advantage of the cost benefits that can be derived from abandoning a protectionist procurement policy. As already noted, this could result in savings of up to 25 per cent. Of course, some international competition does take place already, UK companies are increasingly buying sub-components from overseas anyway, and an offset strategy might ameliorate some of the cost advantages of overseas procurement. Furthermore, estimates of cost savings are likely to be most relevant for the 30 per cent of the procurement budget spent on major equipment projects. Even allowing for all these factors, it is not unreasonable to suggest that the UK could save some 15 per cent of the major equipment budget, or roughly £430 million per annum, by purchasing from the cheapest source available – and without any overall negative effect on the national economy.

Control of cost growth on projects

In addition to the savings claimed for its competition policy the ministry has also argued that its increased use of fixed- and firm price contracts has protected it against any cost increases that do occur on such contracts as it is the companies that are required pick up the bill for any rise in price. However, the evidence for the ministry's claim is debatable.

For example, a survey of defence projects undertaken by Schofield in 1995 found several cases where, contrary to the MOD's assertion, it was not indemnified from cost increases on fixed- and firm price contracts and made compensatory payments. In other examples, he suggested that the scale of the increases, taking into account revisions on quantities ordered, indicates that there were additional payments by the MOD on what were originally fixed-price contracts.[8] The ALARM (air launched anti-radiation missile) project was hailed as the first example of the success of fixed-price contracts, yet the original £200 million contract had to be renegotiated in 1986 (adding at least another £200 million to costs) because of major problems with the engine developed by the then state-owned Royal Ordnance. Similarly, although all four batches of the Type 23 frigate have been placed under fixed-price contracts, the programme has suffered from a £400 million cost overrun and it would seem that the ministry has made extra, post-fixed-price payments to the contractor. Other examples cited by Schofield of fixed- or firm price projects where post-contract payments may have been made include the Type 2400 submarine, the Warrior, Starstreak, LAW 80, and TOGS (Thermal Observation Gunnery Sight). Clearly, therefore, whether it be due to deficiencies in the original contract or the ministry's role in bringing about cost increase, the MOD has not been able completely to protect itself from the phenomenon of cost overrun on projects.

It could, of course, be argued that the use of fixed- and firm price contracts has at least allowed the MOD severely to curtail its exposure to any cost overruns that do occur and that this, combined with the incentive that such contracts provide for firms to complete to cost in the first place, has led to greater control of the cost growth on projects borne by the ministry. Moreover, at first glance the evidence appears to support this view. For instance, as noted in Chapter 1, studies by the NAO and the ministry in the mid-1980s recorded average cost increases of 91 per cent and 66 per cent respectively. In comparison, the 1994 Major Projects Report (MPR 94) undertaken by the NAO examined 25 major projects, which together accounted for roughly 30 per cent of the annual procurement budget, and found average costs (to the MOD) were projected to decrease by 5.3 per cent compared with original estimates.[9] However, on closer inspection the ministry's record on controlling costs has not been as good as these figures would suggest. This is for a number of reasons that are discussed in detail below.

First, the figures are skewed by the very large forecast cost decrease of £3.4 billion for the (non-competitive) Trident programme – cost savings that are more apparent than real. For example, the NAO have noted that the cost underrun on Trident should be interpreted with care as a large percentage of it relates to the ministry's assumptions about inflation and the effect of exchange rate variations on the cost of those elements of the programme procured from the US.[10] In addition, a third of the reported savings (£1.1 billion) have been achieved as a result of the ministry's subsequent decision to process missiles in the US, rather than from any inherent efficiency in the procurement process. Furthermore, the end of the cold war has seen the MOD reduce the number of warheads to be carried by each of the four Trident submarines from 128 to 96, providing opportunities for additional savings on plutonium and other materials.[11] The Defence Committee have also noted that substantial cost overruns on some elements of the programme have been met from allocations set aside in the original estimates for contingencies, and that the scale of the original contingency suggested 'a pessimistic – if realistic – assessment of the accuracy of the original estimates'.[12] It would seem that, given the political sensitivity of the Trident programme, the ministry built in a particularly large margin of error to its cost estimates to avoid potential charges of profligacy on what is a high profile and contentious project. Moreover, the costings on the Trident programme do not take full account of overruns on some associated building programmes, most notably at Faslane and Aldermaston, only part of which is attributed directly to Trident. It is also the case that if the savings resulting from the decision to process missiles in the US are excluded, in real terms (and at a constant exchange rate of $1.55), the overall costs of the UK element of the programme have actually risen by some £339 million. Conversely, on the US element of the programme costs have fallen by over 40 per cent, primarily as a result of reductions in the cost of the Trident missile.[13] To the extent that the UK has benefited from these savings it has done so because of a buy-abroad procurement strategy which (of necessity) emphasised purchase from the most capable supplier rather than preference for the domestic defence industry. This is in contrast to the approach adopted on conventional procurement where the bias is reversed. Thus, given all these factors, the extent to which the Trident programme has or has not been efficiently managed, and the extent to which it is representative of the MOD's general approach to conventional weapons procurement, is debatable to say the least.

Table 7.1 Cost increases on major projects

	£ million	Percentage increase
Total cost increase (all major projects)	599	1.1
Total cost increase (excluding Trident)	4,247	11.4

Source: The Committee of Public Accounts, *Ministry of Defence: Major Projects Report 1994*, Minutes of evidence, Session 1994–5, HC 487-I, London: HMSO 1995, p. 19, q. 35.

A second major area of doubt centres on the fact that the NAO's figures relate only to the *approved* equipment programme and so do not include forecast cost variances for elements of expenditure on a programme(s) which have not yet been formally approved. For example, MPR 94 records a cost increase of just £1.1 billion for the Eurofighter. However, the real cost increase on the programme, including those elements not yet formally approved, currently stands at £2.2 billion. Taking this into account, forecast costs on the MOD's major projects are significantly higher than those given in MPR 94. Indeed, if Trident is excluded from the calculations, for the reasons given above, then the projected cost increase on all the ministry's major projects actually stands at some £4.2 billion (see Table 7.1).

Clearly, in absolute terms this represents a substantial level of inefficiency. Indeed, to place this figure in some perspective, it is roughly equal to the whole of the MOD's major equipment budget for 1996–7[14] and double the cost of *all* the UN's peacekeeping operations in 1995 (see Table 7.3). Even on these latter figures, however, the level of cost control on projects would appear to have improved markedly, with average cost increases falling from the 60–90 per cent recorded in the mid-1980s down to 11.4 per cent today.

Once again though, the headline figures are deceptive. First, the average cost increase of 11.4 per cent contains within it some large cost overruns such as that for the Tornado mid-life update which has increased in cost by some 50 per cent.[15] Second, it may well be that lower levels of cost overrun simply reflect the fact that companies working under fixed-price and incentive contracts have inflated initial cost estimates as an insurance against unexpected development problems, and in an attempt to obtain higher profits. Certainly, in one example, 60 per cent of the contract value was revealed to be contingency.[16] Clearly, if this is the case, then lower levels of cost increase may not reflect greater efficiency in procurement but simply a more realistic assessment of potential cost escalation on the part of contractors. Apparent improvements in efficiency as a result of greater cost control may also be masking significant levels of profit that have been achieved on particular programmes which could have been completed at far lower cost to the taxpayer. For the MOD, this latter form of inefficiency may be of less concern than spiralling programme costs which, unlike company profits, are transparent and inevitably lead to criticisms from Parliament and the press.

Nevertheless, it seems clear that the ministry has afforded cost control on projects a particular priority. Arguably, however, this is less a reflection of efficiency in procurement than it is of a change in the ministry's priorities in the weapons procurement process. In the past the emphasis was placed on meeting the operational requirement (OR), that is the capabilities and performance specified for the equipment; today the emphasis is much more on meeting cost targets, even if this means reducing equipment capability or numbers. For example, analysis by the NAO found that forecast overruns were much higher for projects in the development stage compared to those that had entered production, and concluded that: 'forecast cost overruns in the development phase are sometimes offset by reducing the requirement either by cutting the numbers to be purchased or by reducing equipment capability.'[17] In the case of the Tornado mid-life update the number of aircraft to be upgraded was reduced and certain equipments deleted in order to curb the level of cost growth. Similarly, a £209 million overrun in development on the EH101 Merlin helicopter prompted the ministry to examine de-scoping options to bring the price down. Indeed, almost 50 per cent (by value) of the cost reductions identified by the NAO in 1994 were accounted for either by reductions in numbers or by changes to the specification of equipment. The NAO's results are supported by Schofield, who found that 12 out of 23 projects he examined had experienced cut-backs and that, while savings had occurred on projects, this was largely a function of reductions in numbers and delays in the placing of contracts.[18]

Of course, reductions in numbers have not only been prompted by the concern to reign in cost overruns but also by falling defence budgets and the *Options for Change* defence review. For example, the Warrior project recorded an underspend of £128 million as a result of a post-Options cut in production quantities from 1,048 to 789.[19] However, the extent to which cuts in numbers have been determined by rising development costs, falling defence expenditure, changes in the strategic environment, or a combination of these factors is difficult to determine with any accuracy. For instance, while the MOD have cited *Options for Change* as a major factor in the downward revision of procurement plans, Schofield's study questioned the extent to which it had determined cuts in programmes and argued that, given the time-scales involved, the decision to cut many of the projects he had considered must have been made prior to Options.

Irrespective of the motive for cuts in numbers, the effect is to flatter the statistics on overall cost growth on projects. At the same time, however, such reductions also lead to increases in the unit cost (in other words the cost per tank, plane or ship acquired) of equipment. This was a trend noted by the NAO in its study on defence procurement in the 1990s where it concluded that, while reductions in numbers led to a decrease in overall cost, 'the unit cost of equipment has generally increased as a result of production overheads, learning curve costs and development costs being spread over a smaller base.'[20] For instance, though costs on the Warrior project cited above may have fallen, the cut in production quantities led to a 14 per cent increase in the unit cost of the equipment.[21] Furthermore, where the ministry has reduced orders for equipment it has sometimes found itself confronted with claims for compensation from contractors, as indeed was the case on the Warrior contract.[22] It is not clear whether these offsetting contractual claims are factored into the calculation of cost variation on projects.

Slippage

The analysis of cost increase on projects does not include all the additional costs incurred as a result of delay, or what is termed slippage, in the completion of projects. This is particularly significant as it is clear that the ministry is increasingly responding to limitations on its budget by either delaying or stretching out programmes. Indeed, as can be seen from Table 7.2, the average delay for a major project now stands at over three years, and the percentage of projects over two years late has risen to over 60 per cent compared with 35 per cent in 1989. Moreover, MPR

Table 7.2 The percentage of major projects behind schedule

	1986[1]	1989[1]	1990[2]	1991[3]	1992[4]	1993[5]	1994[6]
Projects behind schedule (%)	59	56	75	83	–	87	95
Average slippage (years)	–	–	1.8	2.6	–	2.7	3.1
Projects more than 2 years late (%)	–	35	31	39	–	52	66

Notes: [1] Derived from figures in Neil Cooper, 'MOD Weapons Procurement Policy 1979–1991', PhD thesis, University of Kent, 1992, p. 515. [2] Figures calculated from Major Projects Statement (MPS) 1990 in Committee of Public Accounts, *The 1990 Statement on Major Defence Projects and the 1989 Summary of Post-Costing Activity*, Tenth Report, Session 1992–3, HC 143, London: HMSO, 1992, pp. 22–4. This excludes a number of projects for which actual months slippage was classified, thus giving a total sample of 16 projects. [3] Figures calculated from MPS 1991, HC 121. This excludes one project for which actual slippage was classified giving a total sample of 23 projects. [4] No major project statement was published for this year. [5] Figures calculated from MPS 1993, HC 356, p. 4, table 2 and p. 12, paras. 3.9–3.10. This excludes 1 project for which actual slippage was classified and 1 project which was cancelled, giving a total sample of 25 projects. [6] Figures calculated from MPs 1994, HC 436, pp. 41–120 and p. 8, para. 2.15. This excludes a number of projects for which actual slippage was classified, giving a total sample of 21 projects.

94 found that while technical difficulties are the largest single source of slippage, between them, delays in procurement and budgetary constraints account for 40 per cent of all slippage, and an earlier study by the NAO found that 14 out of 37 projects had been delayed as a result of budgetary pressures.[23]

For the ministry there are obvious advantages in delaying projects. First, the services are ultimately able to obtain prestigious equipment, even if the need to accommodate them within a limited budget means that expenditure has to be delayed or eked out over a longer number of years. Second, simply delaying or stretching out programmes is far easier to defend than cancelling some projects outright. However, in the long term this strategy is not cost-effective. For example, the NAO have noted that the cost to industry of keeping project teams on ice while existing orders are confirmed and/or new orders announced is often passed on to the MOD in the form of higher prices.[24] Indeed, one contractor has estimated that delays led to a 30 per cent increase in the development costs of a project. Similarly, stretching out programmes is also uneconomical. For example, one US study estimated that a 50 per cent reduction in annual production rates compared with the basic rate would increase real unit costs by a median figure of over 20 per cent.[25] Even Peter Levene, when chief of defence procurement, acknowledged that slipping programmes to the right did not represent the best use of resources and could cost the taxpayer more money in the long run.[26]

Where slippage results in extra cost to the project itself, this is added to the calculation of cost increase; however, currently any associated costs incurred as a result of delay are not. Delay in the introduction of new equipment often involves running on older, less capable equipment which has higher maintenance costs. This has occurred on the Euro-fighter programme where a two-year slippage has required the ministry to extend the lives of Jaguar and Tornado F3 aircraft beyond their original out-of-service dates. Consequently, the Department will have to pay for fatigue modifications and upgrades to these aircraft which would otherwise not have been necessary. The MOD have estimated the additional costs of retaining the aircraft in-service at £104 million.[27] These costs are not, however, included in the estimates of cost increase on the Eurofighter project. Similarly, a slippage of four years on the Bowman project has required the department to retain its Clansman radios for longer than planned. This has involved additional expenditure of £200 million.[28]

Unfortunately the ministry does not, as yet, produce systematic estimates for the associated costs of slippage. Moreover, the costs involved on each programme will depend on both the scale of slippage and the particular costs of running on equipment the project is designed to replace. It is, therefore, difficult to produce a reliable estimate of the total associated costs of slippage across all the MOD's equipment programmes. However, even if the costs cited above are assumed to have been highlighted because they are exceptionally large, given that over 60 per cent of major equipment projects are over two years late, it seems reasonable to suggest that the associated costs of slippage across all the MOD's equipment programmes is, at the very least, double the combined published costs of slippage on the Eurofighter and Bowman – in other words, some £600 million and quite probably more.

The effectiveness of equipment

A further yardstick against which to measure the success of the ministry's approach to weapons procurement is the effectiveness of the equipment it produces. As with much in defence procurement, however, there are difficulties involved in measuring this. First, much of the detail of equipment performance (both of national and comparable overseas equipment) is subject to official secrecy. Second, the question of what an equipment's performance should be measured against is itself debatable. For instance, should it be measured against the performance of a previous generation of equipment, the performance of comparable equipment held by other forces, or the original performance required of the equipment when first specified? Even if this question is settled, it is still difficult to produce a set of objectively quantifiable criteria which would allow measurement of performance.

However, while the question of how objectively to measure the effectiveness of equipment is open to debate, it does seem clear that, in a number of cases, inefficiency in the procurement process has had a negative impact on the level of performance *originally envisaged* for equipment. This occurs in a number of ways. As noted above, poor cost control in the early stages of projects has resulted in cuts in either equipment performance or numbers – or both. Delay in the production of equipment also impacts on the operational effectiveness of the services as well. In part, this is because equipment simply does not come on-stream when planned. For example, the Defence Committee has criticised the delay of over six years on the Phoenix remotely piloted vehicle and has noted that the capability which would have been available if the project had run to time 'is being sorely missed by our forces in the former Yugoslavia, as it was in the Gulf.'[29] It is also in part due to a knock-on effect, because delay on one project can affect the capability of other equipment. For example, while the Type 23 frigate has been operating at sea since 1990, slippage on another programme means that it is doing so without a fully working version of the command system intended for it, and will continue to do so until 1998. In consequence, while it is possible to fire individual weapons, it has not been possible to co-ordinate the firing of weapons in the manner originally envisaged. According to the chief of defence procurement this means the MOD 'cannot put them [the Type 23s] into circumstances of higher danger' as such an undertaking could not be achieved with sufficient safety,[30] or, as the NAO have put it, 'the deployment of Type 23 frigates without the first three phases of software of the Type 23 Command System carries significant military risk.'[31] Not surprisingly perhaps, the Type 23s have been kept well away from conflict environments – they were neither sent to the Adriatic during the conflict in Bosnia, nor used in the Armilla Patrol in the Gulf.

The absence, until 1998, of a fully functioning version of its intended command system is not the only problem the Type 23 suffers from; it still does not have the EH101 Merlin helicopter originally intended for it. This will not now be available until 1998, and it will be a further two years before the Type 23 receives the Mark II version of the helicopter which fully meets the requirement for the ship. The slippage on EH101 (which should have been deployed on the Type 23s by 1993) has meant the Sea King helicopter has had to be kept in service for longer than originally planned. Consequently, this required an increase of three metres in the vessel's length and commensurable increases in the cost of the ship.[32] Despite these changes, however, there are still problems. For example, the Type 23 was designed to accept the EH101, where the undercarriage is towards the front of the aircraft; on the Sea King, however, it is towards the rear and thus brings the aircraft up too close to the superstructure of the ship for safe operation. In consequence, as one defence official has noted, 'landing and normal operations are not possible without a major redesign of the ship.'[33] Not surprisingly perhaps, the MOD have noted that 'the long-term operational capability of a T23 would be severely affected without Merlin.'[34] The inadequacies of the Type 23 have also necessitated running on older, less capable and more manpower intensive (therefore more costly) Type 22s. All in all, taking into account the fact that it is operating with an incomplete command system and is still awaiting the helicopter intended for it, it is difficult not to conclude that the Type 23 represents a floating military joke perpetrated by the vagaries of a procurement system that would embarrass a second-hand car salesman.

Thus, for a variety of reasons, inefficiency in procurement is having a negative impact on the capability originally envisaged for the UK's front-line forces, whether as a consequence of cuts in numbers or capability, or whether as a result of delay in bringing equipment into service.

Summary

To summarise the argument outlined in this chapter, it is not at all clear that the MOD's reforms have actually improved the efficiency of the weapons procurement process. The claimed savings on competition are offset by a variety of factors and the supposed indemnity to cost increase afforded by fixed-price contracts often turns out to be illusory. Moreover, in reality, competition policy has been ameliorated by the pursuit of a broadly protectionist procurement strategy which has involved substantial costs to the defence budget compared with purchasing from the least-cost source of supply. At the very least, purchasing on the open market would probably generate savings of £430 million per year in defence procurement (see Table 7.3). Furthermore, the ministry's success in reigning in cost growth on projects is more apparent than real. Projected cost increases on major conventional projects stand at over £4 billion, and even this figure underestimates the true scale of inefficiency in procurement as the ministry have increasingly opted to control cost growth by cutting equipment numbers or performance. In addition, the associated costs of slippage on weapons projects is not factored into the calculations of cost increase. At the very least, this can be said to add a further £600 million, and quite probably more, to the MOD's procurement bill. Moreover, as noted in Chapter 4, the ministry's mechanisms for preventing and detecting fraud verge on an inducement to criminal activity. Given the weakness of these mechanisms the level of reported fraud is, in all likelihood, substantially below that which is committed. However, the current level of fraud under investigation stands at £22 million, although not all of this relates to procurement fraud and some of it may eventually be clawed back by the ministry. Nevertheless, given the weakness of the ministry's detection mechanism it seems reasonable to assume that the cost of both undetected and unredeemed procurement fraud is, at the very least, equal to the value of fraud currently under investigation by the ministry – in other words £22 million, and quite probably substantially more. In addition, the MOD itself has noted potential savings of £250 million per year from improvements in reliability and maintainability.

Clearly, for various reasons some of the figures given above (and in Table 7.3) are rough estimates of the real costs of inefficiency. However, if anything, such estimates have erred on the side of caution and the costs of inefficiency are likely to be larger rather than smaller. In total,

Table 7.3 Inefficiencies in procurement

Inefficiency	Cost (£m)	Comparative costs
Projected cost increase on all major conventional projects[1]	4,247	Total cost of *all* UN peacekeeping operations in 1995 (£2,000m)[4]
(Eurofighter cost increase)	2,200	UK aid budget 1996–7 (2,155m)[5]
Protectionism[2]	430 (per yr)	FCO budget 1996–7[5] (£1,111m)
Slippage[3]	620	Estimated annual running costs for a permanent UN Military Force of 10,000 (£366m)[6]
Poor reliability and maintainability	250 (per yr)	UK Foreign Office budget for peacekeeping 1995–6 (£252m)[7]
Fraud	22	UK subscription to UN regular budget 1994–5 (£35m)[8]
Total cost of inefficiency in procurement	5,569	UN human development target for health (includes complete immunisation of all children; reduction in under- fives mortality by half; elimination of severe malnutrition and a 50% reduction in moderate malnutrition) (£5–7000m)[9]

Notes: [1] Excludes Trident. [2] This assumes a saving of roughly 15 per cent on the major procurement budget that could be derived from proper international competition. [3] This is a rough estimate based on recorded slippage costs of three projects (Eurofighter, Bowman, Tucano) which together amounted to £310 million. Given that 60 per cent of all major equipment projects are more than 2 years late, the estimated cost of £620 million for slippage (i.e. double the cost of slippage on the three projects noted) is probably a conservative one. [4] David Hannay, 'Paying for the UN: a suitable case for treatment', *The World Today*, vol. 52, no. 6 (June 1996): 161. [5] Foreign Affairs Committee, *Public Expenditure: Spending Plans of the Foreign and Commonwealth Office and the Overseas Development Administration*, Second Report, Session 1995–96, HC 370-I, Vol. 1, London: HMSO, 1996, p. xvi, para. 34. [6] Stephen P. Kinloch, 'Utopian or pragmatic? a UN volunteer military force', in M. Pugh (ed.), *The UN, Peace and Force*, London: Frank Cass, 1997 (forthcoming). [7] *Foreign and Commonwealth Office including Overseas Development Administration: 1996 Departmental Report – The Government's Expenditure Plans 1996–7 to 1998–9*, London: HMSO, Cm. 3203, p. 59, Table 24. [8] Ibid., Table 21, p. 55. The UN Regular Budget is used to finance all of the UN's core activities and programmes other than specific peacekeeping operations, namely the UN's main decision-making bodies, and activities relating to peace and security, disarmament, legal issues, outer space, economic development, social and humanitarian affairs, human rights, refugees, environment, science and technology, regional co-operation, trade and development, drug control, crime issues and human settlements. [9] UNDP *Human Development Report 1994*, Oxford: OUP, 1994, p. 77.

therefore, the cost of inefficiency in weapons procurement currently amounts to over £5 billion, and may well be more. Clearly, the opportunity cost of such inefficiency is substantial. Even if only a portion were to be saved, it would release substantial sums of money which could either be spent on more defence equipment or diverted to alternative forms of government expenditure such as health and education, or tax cuts. Alternatively, it could be spent on non-military forms of security expenditure (see Table 7.3) which, it may be argued, would be more effective in promoting both the UK's national interests and global security than any additional expenditures on defence equipment.

8

Conclusion

The failure of reform

The Thatcher Government of 1979 inherited a procurement system that was still broadly characterised by cost-plus contracts, gold-plating, poor reliability and the absence of competition. At the same time, a combination of escalating weapons costs and the introduction of cash limits conspired to create a crisis in defence expenditure which led to a succession of overspends on the defence budget. This was most pronounced in the 1980–1 financial year when a potential overspend of over half a billion pounds was only avoided by an increase in the cash limit and cuts in defence. In addition, a series of high profile cost overruns – most notably on the Nimrod AEW, which was ultimately cancelled – further demonstrated the failings of the procurement system. That the system was in crisis was not in doubt. However, weapons procurement had been in almost constant crisis since the end of the Second World War, and to some extent the response to the problem was the traditional one adopted by successive administrations – cuts in defence and reform of the weapons procurement system. The former manifested itself in the defence review of 1981. However, this was ultimately undermined by the impact of the Falklands War which resulted in the revision of many of the proposed cuts – at a cost of some £2.4 billion to the defence budget. Consequently, the pressure to reform defence procurement was even more pronounced. However, the direction that procurement reform took (in theory if not always in practice) was ultimately influenced by the ideals of Thatcherism, with its emphasis on the free market, competition, value for money and privatisation. On the issue of arms exports, policy was also influenced by the Thatcherite vision of Britain as 'UK plc', trading its wares abroad.

At the heart of procurement reform was the adoption of competition in the allocation of defence contracts and the move from cost-plus to fixed- and firm price contracts. Although not a central element in the reform of weapons acquisition, policy towards the arms trade also included an emphasis on maximising defence exports in order to achieve economies of scale (and thus savings on domestic procurement), maintain the defence industrial base and generate greater economic return from the huge outlay on defence equipment.

The government have claimed success for the new reforms, arguing that competition has generated savings of £1 billion a year, that fixed-price contracts have protected the MOD from cost increases on projects and that its reforms have improved the efficiency of Britain's defence industry, making it more competitive in the global arms market. The reality, however, is less comforting.

On the issue of arms exports, the UK's growing market share is partly a reflection of the fact the arms purchases have declined less dramatically in the UK's traditional markets than they have in the arms market in general, and is partly due to the effects of one large arms deal – the Al Yamamah contract with Saudi Arabia. Indeed, apart from the Middle East and the USA, the UK's market share in most regions of the world has been at best broadly static and at worst in decline. Moreover, the extent to which the British economy – as opposed to individual arms contractors – gains from the UK's defence export trade is debatable. The defence industry is underpinned by a vast array of subsidies, ranging from protectionism in domestic procurement, export credits, offsets, and marketing support from the MOD. In contrast other sections of British industry, such as construction, receive nowhere near the same level of support for exports. Thus, the extent to which, and indeed whether, defence exports result in a net gain to the economy is debatable.

At the same time, the increasing dependence of the UK DIB on defence exports, combined with the secrecy that traditionally surrounds defence deals, has encouraged a culture of corruption in British government. The most notable examples have been the arms to Iraq and Pergau Dam scandals, where the government broke its own regulations in order to maximise defence sales. But the government has also persistently flouted its own declared commitment to take human rights considerations into account when considering arms exports. In addition, Britain's overwhelming dependence on Saudi defence sales has led to the banning of one public report, the deletion of items in others, and the persecution of a Saudi dissident with a recognised right to claim asylum.

Furthermore, the claimed efficiencies introduced into defence procurement are more apparent than real. In reality, cost growth on the ministry's major weapons projects (accounting for roughly 30 per cent of the procurement budget) currently stands at £4 billion, continued protectionism adds some £430 million a year, and when factors such as poor R&M, fraud, and slippage are also factored into the equation, the cost of inefficiency in procurement stands at over £5 billion. In theory at least, therefore, there are significant savings that could be achieved from the operation of a more efficient procurement system, savings which could be spent either on more weapons or on a combination of domestic economic regeneration and international security. In terms of international security, for example, the cost *increase* on the Eurofighter project alone is equal to *all* the UN's expenditure on peacekeeping in 1995 (see Chapter 7, Table 7.3).

Of course, it is one thing to identify potential savings from greater efficiency in the procurement process, but realising such savings is an altogether different matter. Indeed, some commentators have referred to the futility of reform in the weapons acquisition process and have pointed to a cycle of reform which, at best, only changes the problems inherent in the procurement process rather than eliminating inefficiency. This can be seen in the US system which has moved from cost-plus to competition and, of late, back to cost-plus, without managing to solve the problem of waste in weapons acquisitions.[1] A similar phenomenon can be seen in the UK where the MOD has moved from the cost-plus preferred contractor approach of the 1970s, to competition in the 1980s and is now, in the 1990s, beginning to moderate its competition policy. Yet despite such changes, inefficiency in procurement remains pervasive.

The very nature of the weapons acquisition process makes it difficult to legislate against phenomena such as cost growth, delay and gold-plating. Modern militaries require weapons which operate at the boundaries of technology but are capable of surviving both extremes of climate and the attentions of a teenage squaddie in the midst of battle; they require weapons which operate at the highest possible level of performance, yet have longer life-cycles. Arguably, such demands on weapons technology almost inevitably mean that problems are likely to arise in the development of projects.

Furthermore, the British procurement system (like those in other countries) is characterised by a community of vested interests – buyers, sellers and politicians – which the introduction of competition has only partially alleviated. Ultimately, the MOD wants its high-tech equipment (whatever the price) and a thriving defence industry, the firms want their contracts, and the politicians want to announce fat defence contracts for domestic firms. At the end of day, there is a greater commonality of interests between these actors than there is divergence. On top of this, the defence industry is the ultimate insider group, with regular contact at all levels between it and ministry officials. Indeed, the MOD concludes some 56,000 contracts a year with industry, and its relationship is particularly close with its major contractors. For example, British Aerospace alone concludes some 2,000 contracts a year with the ministry, and the top 5 contractors account for 31 per cent of MOD business.[2] There is also a steady interchange of personnel from MOD to industry, further strengthening the links between them; for example as noted in Chapter 4, in the last ten years almost 5,000 applications to join the defence industry have been approved by the ministry. On top of this, there are a variety of official forums where industry can present its case to the MOD. These include the National Defence Industries Council, the chief of defence procurement's meetings with the trade associations, the systems controllers' conferences with industry, and an annual Defence Export Services Organisation symposium. In recent years these have also been augmented by an expanded programme of visits to industry and meetings with industrialists on the part of ministers and senior officials.[3]

Clearly, given the closeness of the relationship between the MOD and industry, other avenues of influence are really only so much icing on the military-industrial cake. However, it should also be noted that in the two years to 1995, the Conservative Party received almost £1 million from those firms paid £5 million or more by the MOD in 1995–6. Indeed, three of the companies paid over £100 million by the MOD (Hunting plc, Rolls-Royce and GKN) donated over £180,000 between them.[4] These figures are probably less significant than they might appear, both because of the already close relationship between industry and MOD, and because many companies have substantial civil interests they might wish to promote through political donations to the Conservatives. Moreover, the extent to which donations to the Conservative Party can influence MOD procurement policy is, of course, debatable.

Nevertheless, they do demonstrate the diversity of influence that military-industrial interests can bring to bear on decision makers.

Thus, the structure of relations between government and industry are so close, even after the introduction of competition, that it arguably undermines any attempt at efficient procurement. In addition, the very nature of the weapons acquisition process is such that cost growth and delay are, on one view at least, almost an inevitable feature of the system. Nevertheless, despite these qualifications, what is notable about inefficiency in the procurement system is that much of it derives from a simple failure to apply principles that have long been recognised as necessary to reduce the incidence of inefficient procurement. For example, three-quarters of the cost variation identified by the NAO in MPR 94 was attributed to underestimation of costs at the outset.[5] As was noted in Chapter 1, this is a phenomenon that was commented on by the Rayner Report 25 years ago, noted in 1979 by the then chief of defence procurement, noted again in 1988 by the MOD's own *Learning from Experience* report, and yet still remains a persistent feature of procurement practice. The ministry's latest solution has been to introduce a system of three-point estimating for future project submissions, which will translate identified risks on a project into upper, middle and lower cost estimates. Arguably, this process may serve to concentrate minds in the MOD on the potential for cost escalation. However, officials are supposed to have been taking this into account in the past anyway. Moreover, at the end of the day, just one of these estimates will have to be used for the purpose of drawing up contracts with firms and for the planning of long-term expenditure. Perhaps crucially, the incentive to depress initial cost estimates in order to get a project accepted will remain. Furthermore, the ministry's past failure to rectify this problem does not bode well for the future – in terms of its aim to improve procurement, the MOD seems to be forever setting off but rarely arriving at its destination.

Similarly, failure to follow the Downey procurement procedures outlined in Chapter 1 has long been recognised as a cause of subsequent technical and cost problems. Despite this, an NAO report in 1996 found that out of a sample of 28 projects which had begun full development since 1985, over half had missed out a stage of the Downey cycle and many of these subsequently encountered unforeseen technical difficulties in development. The Downey Report also argued that the investigation required to provide an adequate basis on which to proceed to full development might involve expenditure of up to 15 per cent of the estimated development cost of a project, the Rayner Report actually recommended a figure of 15–25 per cent – a level of funding with which *Learning from Experience* concurred. Despite this, the NAO's 1996 report still found average funding of below 10 per cent, and noted a correlation between the level of funding in the early stages of projects and the incidence of subsequent technical problems in development.[6]

Inefficiency in procurement is also a product of the MOD's refusal to abandon procurement strategies which are self-evidently costly, whether it be the emphasis on protectionism, which raises costs and hampers the development of an open European market in defence; the practice of slipping programmes to the right as a response to budgetary pressure; or the failure to implement effective strategies to detect and deter fraud. Indeed, on this latter issue, it is notable that while the DHSS set up a telephone hot-line in August 1996 to encourage whistle-blowers to reveal instances of benefit fraud, the MOD has still not set up an independent hot-line for defence company employees to reveal fraud on weapons contracts worth billions of pounds. Instead, it prefers to carry on with a system which does not even claw back the interest earned on excessive profits when they are discovered.

Even where the ministry has made progress in reforming the procurement system, questions still remain about the effectiveness of its reforms. Cost-plus contracts may have been virtually eliminated, but the use of fixed-price contracts may simply encourage firms to include high levels of contingency in their price estimates. Where projects do go over-budget, the complexity of the procurement process and the contracts themselves often means the ministry is still not protected from the financial consequences of cost growth. Competition on new contracts may now be relatively high but the bidding costs of firms are passed on in the next contract, post-competitive amendments allow firms to claw back profits, and there is a notable correlation between the introduction of competition and a rise in recorded fraud (despite the weakness of the department's fraud detection procedures). Moreover, the introduction of competition has also given rise to concern about its effects on the long-term reliability and maintainability of equipment. In response to these concerns the MOD has introduced a range of measures to improve R&M, and the breadth and depth of these initiatives probably represents the brightest spot on the ministry's procurement horizon. Even here, however, problems remain – as noted in Chapter 4, there is a continuing shortage of R&M officers (and those in post are often inexperienced), there is no one agency responsible for R&M input throughout an equipment's life, and the ministry has been notably reluctant to build in financial rewards for contractors who achieve high levels of R&M. Moreover, the fruits of the department's R&M reforms will only be seen in the long term and, given the continuing tendency for R&M requirements to be the first to be cut in the face of other pressures, it could well turn out to be a fairly rotten harvest.

The military security bias

However, perhaps the most costly form of procurement inefficiency does not relate to the MOD's pursuit of flawed acquisition strategies or its failure to follow its own recommended procedures. An efficient procurement system should start by procuring only the weapons and equipment necessary for the optimum promotion of national security and a proportionate contribution to the maintenance of global security. In the case of the UK, however, the policy-making paradigms imposed by the legacy of Empire, the tradition of high defence expenditure, the obsession with maintaining a nuclear deterrent, and the power of the military-industrial lobby have produced a structural imbalance in the relative weight attached to military as opposed to non-military means of furthering national and global security. Thus, as can be seen in Table 8.1, despite substantial cuts to the defence budget in recent years, the UK has continued its tradition of spending relatively more of its GDP on defence than its European allies. Indeed, if one excludes Greece and Turkey (which, because of their particular security concerns, spend proportionately more on defence), the average percentage of GDP spent on defence in NATO Europe is even less than that given in Table 8.1, coming down to just 2.1 per cent, compared with a UK figure of 3.1 per cent. Of Britain's main European allies, only France has spent similar levels of GDP on defence, and it has now announced substantial cuts in its defence budget.

Much has been made by both industry and the Defence Committee of the fact that government funding for defence R&D declined by 25 per cent between 1985 and 1992 while in France and Germany it rose.[7] However, the decline in defence R&D in the UK has occurred against the backdrop of an overall decline in all government expenditure (civil and defence) on R&D. Moreover, even taking into account the increase

Table 8.1 The UK's relative commitment to defence and non-military security in comparison with other European states

	UK	France	Germany	Italy	NATO Europe/EU[1]
% of GDP to defence (1995)[2]	3.1	3.1	1.7	1.9	2.4
% of government R&D to defence (1993)[3]	42.5	33.5	8.5	8.5	19.7
% of export credits to defence industry (1993)[4]	48.0	21.0	1.0	NA	NA
Overseas development aid as a % of defence expenditure (1992)[5]	8.0	19.0	16.0	17.0	31.0
Number of overseas diplomats (1995)[6]	2,472	4,851	3,551	2,833	NA

Notes: [1] The figure for the percentage of GDP committed to defence expenditure is for NATO Europe. The figure for the percentage of government R&D expenditure committed to defence is for the 12 member states of the EU as at 1993. The figure for the percentage of overseas development aid is an average for all 15 current members of the EU including Austria, Finland and Sweden who officially became members in 1995. Excluding these three states the average is 17%. [2] Ministry of Defence, *Statement on the Defence Estimates 1996*, Cm 3223, London: HMSO 1996, p. 50, fig. 9.A. [3] Eurostat and CSO, *UK Business in Europe: A Statistical Comparison*, London: HMSO, 1995, p. 134, table 33.3. [4] US General Accounting Office, *Export Finance: Comparative Analysis of US and European Union Export Credit Agencies*, GAO/GCD-96-1, p. 9, Table 3, note b. [5] UNDP, *Human Development Report, 1995*, Oxford: Oxford University Press, 1995, p. 206, Table 31. [6] Foreign Affairs Committee, *Public Expenditure: Spending Plans of the Foreign and Commonwealth Office and the Overseas Development Administration 1996–7 to 1998–9*, Second Report, Session 1995–6, HC 370-I, London: HMSO, 1996, p. x, table I.

in defence R&D in France and Germany, the UK still spends a larger proportion of government-funded R&D on defence. Similarly, the proportion of export credits going to the UK's defence industry is significantly higher than that for either France or Germany. In contrast, non-military security promotion does not receive the same priority from UK policy makers. For example, Britain commits the lowest proportion of overseas aid relative to defence expenditure of any state in the EU and has fewer overseas diplomats than either France, Germany or Italy (see Table 8.1).

The structural and paradigmatic bias in favour of military security programmes has not only resulted in a relatively high tolerance of inefficiency in the *process* of weapons acquisition but also in decisions to acquire weapons whose utility, particularly in the post-cold war era, is questionable. Of particular note in this context are the Eurofighter 2000 and the Trident nuclear missile.

The former was conceived in the days of the cold war and has been designed to enhance the RAF's air superiority role with the aim of counteracting the threat from Soviet combat aircraft. However, in the post-cold war era it is debatable whether there is any rationale (other than inertia) for the continuation of the project. The final cost of the programme is currently expected to be £15 billion (over £250 for every man, woman and child in the UK) and at the peak of production, expenditure is likely to consume 20 per cent of the procurement budget potentially displacing other equipment programmes more appropriate to the actual operations of the armed forces. Yet despite this, the Eurofighter programme continues.

Much the same criticisms can be made of Trident. Even when the original decision to procure Trident was made in the early 1980s, the missile's utility was questionable and the dramatic increase in nuclear capability it represented seemed, quite literally, like overkill. With the end of the cold war, the attempts to justify Trident seem increasingly specious. Russia is no longer deemed an enemy of the UK and the two countries have agreed not to target their nuclear weapons at each other. Yet Trident is still justified primarily as an insurance policy against a recidivist Russian state, even though its armed forces are now severely depleted and cannot even effectively prosecute a war against the guerrillas in Chechnya. Occasionally, officials also refer to the newly conceived rationale for Trident as a deterrent against rogue Third World regimes.[8] However, almost in the same breath they tend to retreat from this notion as they come up against the harsh reality that prescribing such a role presents a number of problems for British policy. First, Trident's role in this capacity is limited by Britain's commitment at the UN not to use nuclear weapons against non-nuclear powers. Second, it also undermines the already shaky logic upon which Britain justifies its retention of nuclear weapons while arguing against their acquisition by non-nuclear states. This justification is based on the notion that Britain has developed a stable deterrence relationship with Russia which makes nuclear deterrence both safe and workable, whereas the acquisition of nuclear weapons by non-nuclear states would create new deterrence relationships which, by definition, would not be stable and therefore unsafe. Not only does this implicitly concede the UK should not have developed a nuclear deterrent in the first place, but, as MOD officials recognise, it makes it even more difficult to justify Trident as an effective and safe deterrent against Third World leaders who, as one defence official has noted, may have value systems and strategic conceptions the UK does not understand.[9]

Despite Trident's apparent position as one of the better managed equipment projects, Dunleavy has included it in his list of British policy disasters. This is on the basis that it is now redundant, a state of affairs he argues was foreseeable from the programme's inception and certainly prior to the years of peak expenditure which occurred between 1990 and 1994.[10] The initial acquisition cost of Trident is currently estimated at over £12 billion and critics have put the overall cost at £30 billion when running, maintenance and de-commissioning costs are taken into account. The opportunity costs of maintaining a nuclear deterrent are, therefore, substantial. But despite a succession of defence reviews since the decision to procure it, the project has remained inviolate and continues to be the centrepiece of Britain's procurement programme.

Thus, despite the ending of the cold war and despite cuts to the defence budget, the MOD has managed to maintain defence spending at relatively high levels as well as retaining both prestigious weapons programmes of dubious utility and the military commitments they service. Ironically, however, this may not be the best manner in which to promote UK and international security. First, the UK's front-line military commitments and high profile weapons projects have been preserved at a price. As Sue Willett has noted:

> Major commitments have been maintained and prestigious pro-
> grammes saved from the axe. But stocks and spares have been reduced
> to a minimum, inventories have been cut-back, [and] manpower re-
> duced. ... What has taken place is a face saving exercise, which main-
> tains the illusion of military power and continuity but has resulted in
> UK forces being less effective than they could be if resources were
> less thinly spread and more concentrated on specific tasks and func-
> tions.[11]

This was best illustrated in the *Front Line First* Review initiated after the 1993 budget statement presaged a £750 million cut in the MOD's budget for 1996-7. The ministry's response was to ring-fence front-line forces on the dubious grounds that a distinction could be made between cuts in support services and what the defence secretary referred to as the UK's 'fighting effectiveness'. In consequence, signifcant cuts were made in the holdings of spares, support manpower was cut by 19,000, and rationalisation of many support activities was proposed. Yet, as Ron Smith has noted, platforms without the spares and facilities needed to make them effective, and cuts in maintenance and munitions 'combine to produce a real military capability which is only a fraction of the nominal battle order.'[12] Indeed, to put this is in perspective, some 70 per cent of RAF personnel deployed in the Gulf were actually logistics specialists and just under half the total strength of the 1st Armoured Division was made up of logistics and support personnel. As David Greenwood has observed, the number of unserviceable vehicles, and the lack of spares and ordnance, meant that the successes of the UK's forces in the Gulf could not have been achieved– or only at a much higher cost in casualties – if the operation had been a 'come as you are engagement'.[13] This is a constraint on defence policy that practice since the Gulf War has served only to aggravate.

Second, the military-security paradigm that predominates in British foreign and defence policy circles assumes that the retention of high defence expenditure and wide-ranging military forces are the best way to defend British citizens at home, and promote peace and conflict resolution abroad. This is not at all obvious. In the post-cold war era, the UK itself is now in one of the safest parts of one of the safest continents in the world. Indeed, Chalmers has estimated that the forces required for uniquely national requirements (including support of the civil power in Northern Ireland and the defence of the Falklands) probably account for no more than 15–20 per cent of defence spending.[14] Of course, as a member of the international community Britain has a responsibility to make a reasonable contribution to any peacekeeping and peace enforcement activities mandated by the UN. But in such circumstances, both the straitened nature of the UK's military forces and the benefits of multinational action mean the UK will always be participating as part of a coalition. This neither requires Britain to maintain relatively higher levels of defence commitment than its European partners nor an army which offers everything, but does none of it well.

Moreover, the main threat to international security in the post-cold war era arises from the breakdown of states, as a result of ethnic antagonism or economic collapse, and the promotion of terrorism by radical states. Such threats to international security are not easily amenable to traditional military solutions, and even where such solutions are invoked, the international community – as demonstrated in Somalia, Rwanda and Bosnia – often has insufficient will to pursue them at an early enough stage and with the necessary commitment.

The UK (and indeed the world community in general) needs to ask itself what balance of security promotion gives the best return on investment in a post-cold war world. Is it a balance of priorities which is heavily skewed towards military security solutions, in a world where the roots of conflict lie in economic deprivation and resource depletion; where conflicts no longer have clearly demarcated battle lines but are traced by following the intra-communal clash of neighbours; and where the 'CNN factor' paralyses military options that risk soldiers' lives and politicians' poll ratings? Alternatively, is it better promoted by abandoning the chimera of an all-round defence capability; by cutting defence spending and cold war equipment projects, and by diverting the resources released both to the promotion of domestic regeneration and international security?

Unfortunately, the military-security paradigm that dominates policy making in the UK emphasises the former approach and consequently conceives the promotion of peace as best furthered by the extraction of 'more bang for ever more bucks', rather than more security per pound. Thus, little consideration is given to whether the £180 million cost of two Merlin helicopters gives a return in security equal to the estimated £200 million it costs to provide basic village-level water supplies to ten million people,[15] or whether the £30 billion cost of Trident does more to eliminate conflict and promote the conditions for trade than the estimated £20–27 billion cost of meeting the UN's development targets for education, health, population control *and* universal access to safe drinking water.[16] Such considerations have lost out to a combination of the military-industrial lobby and blinkered inertia.

Thus, not only is the procurement process marked by inefficiency costs of over £5 billion and the production of weapons which are late in delivery and often fail to match up to their original specification, but the prevalence of a military-security paradigm in British policy making has preserved an undue commitment to relatively high levels of defence expenditure, cold war equipment programmes and an all-round defence capability. Ironically, however, the logic of weapons costs which effectively double every 7.25 years has meant that high-tech weapons projects have been preserved only by depleting military support functions – and consequently eroding the ability of the UK's forces to make an effective contribution to international action. Moreover, unless there is some radical improvement in the efficiency of the procurement system, which on past form seems unlikely, these same cost trends will have to be accommodated by cuts in the UK's military commitments and a strategy of role specialisation. This will almost inevitably come about but, on present form, it will not be a planned and structured reshaping of UK military forces. Rather it is likely to be forced by circumstance, and achieved reluctantly, in an *ad hoc* and incremental manner.

Of course, it could be argued that the logic of cost growth in procurement actually implies that what the UK needs is a reversal of past defence cuts in order to restore the armed forces to their former glory. Not only would this be simply an exercise in delaying the inevitable, but it misunderstands the main threats to Britain's security as it enters the new millennium. For the UK, the threat is no longer invasion but relative economic decline; and for the world community, it is not Russian expansionism but the implosion of states as a consequence of ethnic hatred and grinding poverty – problems that are immune to solution by gun and bomb, and are often exacerbated by them. What this analysis mandates then, is a more sensible restructuring of spending on Britain's security which involves less not more expenditure on military security, and the promotion of other forms of security at home and abroad. This may seem a long way from a discussion of inefficiency in weapons procurement policy, but eliminating inefficiency is not solely about tackling the causes of cost growth or slippage in equipment programmes. Ultimately, it has to be about ensuring the right balance between the different forms of security expenditure, and the acquisition of equipment relevant to the security environment of the post-cold war era. It is the sad truth that the UK is still spending too large a proportion of its scarce resources on acquiring weapons which are delivered late, over-budget and frequently reduced in capability – and for which there is often no need.

Notes

Introduction

1. Ministry of Defence, *Value for Money in Defence Equipment Procurement*, Defence Open Government Document 83/01, London: MOD, 1983.
2. Ibid., p. 3.
3. Committee of Public Accounts, *Initiatives in Defence Procurement*, Forty-first Report, Session 1990–1, HC 246, London: HMSO, Minutes of evidence, p. 6, q. 2657; Jonathan Aitken, 'Defence procurement: past, present and future', *RUSI Journal* (February 1994): 41.

1. The cost-plus, bottomless bucket gravy train

1. *The Government Organisation for Defence Procurement and Civil Aerospace*, London: HMSO, Cmnd 4641 (presented to Parliament April 1971), p. 3. para. 1.
2. Ibid.
3. R.M. Hastie-Smith, 'The tin wedding. A study of the evolution of the Ministry of Defence 1964–74', *Seaford House Papers* (1974): 34–5. Also personal interview with ex-MOD official, 1 February 1991.
4. *Official Report of the House of Commons*, May 24–June 11, Session 1970–1, vol. 818, London: HMSO, 27 May 1971, col. 709.
5. Michael Howard, *The Central Organisation of Defence*, London: RUSI, 1970, p. 28. For a similar list of problems also see A.J.R. Groom, *British Thinking About Nuclear Weapons*, London: Frances Pinter (Publishers), 1974, pp. 546–7.
6. *Official Report of the House of Commons*, April 28–May 9, Session 1974–5, vol. 890, London: HMSO, 25 April 1975, col. 397.
7. Geoffrey Williams et al., *Crisis in Procurement: A Case Study of the TSR-2*. London: RUSI, 1969, p. 31.
8. Ibid., p. 7.
9. F.E. Tyndall (Air Commodore), 'Project management for defence equipment', *Weapons Procurement, Defence Management and International Collaboration. A Series of Six Lectures Delivered at the University of Southampton*, London: RUSI, 1972, p. 14.
10. The 1961 White Paper also emphasised the importance of ensuring that defence R&D was 'efficiently and economically carried out.' See A.J.R. Groom, *British Thinking About Nuclear Weapons*, p. 548, see note 5.
11. House of Commons Defence Committee, *Ministry of Defence Organisation and Procurement*, Second Report, Session 1981–2, HC 22-II. London: HMSO, 16

June 1982, p. xxvii. Also see *First Report of the Inquiry into the Pricing of Ministry of Aviation Contracts*, London: HMSO, Cmnd 2428 (presented to Parliament July 1964).

12. F.E. Tyndall, 'Project management for defence equipment', see note 9.

13. Sir Frank Cooper (ex-Permanent Secretary, MOD), personal interview, 26 May 1989.

14. R.M. Hastie-Smith, *Seaford House Papers*, p. 35, see note 3.

15. *The Government Organisation for Defence Procurement and Civil Aerospace*, p. 18 and p. 46, see note 1.

16. John Bayliss, *British Defence Policy: Striking the Right Balance*. Houndsmill, Basingstoke, Hampshire and London: Macmillan, 1989, pp. 15–16. Also see Michael Dockrill, *British Defence Since 1945*, Oxford: Basil Blackwell, 1988, p. 107.

17. R.M. Hastie-Smith, *Seaford House Papers*, p. 35, see note 3.

18. House of Commons Defence Committee, *Ministry of Defence Organisation and Procurement*, Second Report, Session 1981–2, HC 22-I, London: HMSO, 16 June 1982, p. xxvi, para. 52.

19. *The Government Organisation for Defence Procurement and Civil Aerospace*, p. 23, see note 1.

20. Ministry of Defence, *Statement of the Defence Estimates 1980*, London: HMSO, Cmnd 7826, 1980, p. 24.

21. Personal interview with MOD representative, 12 July 1988.

22. Sir Michael Carey, 'A lecture given at RUSI, 17 October 1973', *RUSI Journal* (March 1974): 21.

23. Trevor Taylor and Keith Hayward, *The UK Defence Industrial Base: Development and Future Policy Options*, London, Oxford, Washington: Brassey's Defence Publishers, 1989, p. 100. Also see John Lovering, *The Restructuring of the Defence Industries and the Role of the State*, Working Paper 59, Bristol: University of Bristol (School for Advanced Urban Studies), 1986, pp. 10–12.

24. Lawrence Freedman, *Arms Production in the UK: Problems and Prospects*, London, Royal Institute for International Affairs, 1978, p. 2.

25. *The Government Organisation for Defence Procurement and Civil Aerospace*, p. 23, see note 1.

26. Sir Frank Cooper, personal interview, see note 13.

27. Vallin Pollen Research and Planning Unit, *Report into Defence Procurement Issues*, p. 92, see note 20.

28. Ibid., p. 7.

29. Ibid., p. 20.

30. This is not to say that long-term considerations are not taken into account in the present approach. Rather there appears to be a difference of emphasis.

31. *The Government Organisation for Defence Procurement and Civil Aerospace*, p. 23, see note 1.

32. J.M. Legge, 'Management of the equipment programme', *Weapons Procurement, Defence Management and International Collaboration: A Series of Six Lectures Delivered at the University of Southampton*, London: RUSI, 1972, p. 13.

33. Expenditure Committee (Defence and External Affairs Sub-Committee), *Defence Policy After the Review: Industry and Employment*, Session 1974–5, HC 431-ix. London: HMSO, 10 November 1975, Minutes of evidence, p. 208, q. 765.

34. Sir Frank Cooper, personal interview, see note 13. Also see Vallin Pollen Research and Planning Unit, *Report into Defence Procurement Issues*, p. 82, see note 20.

35. House of Commons Defence Committee, *Statement on the Defence Estimates 1988*, Seventh Report, Session 1987–8, HC 495, London: HMSO, 28 June 1988, p. xix, para. 2.46. Also see Lawrence Freedman, *Arms Production in the UK*, p. 1, see note 24.

36. Ron Smith and Jacques Fontanel, 'Weapons production versus imports', Ian Bellany and Tim Huxley (eds), *New Conventional Weapons and Western Defence*, London: Frank Cass, 1987, p. 69.

37. Committee of Public Accounts, *Matters Relating to the MOD*, Sixteenth Report, Session 1979–80, HC 648, London: HMSO, 16 June 1980, p. xiv, para. 24.

38. Ibid.

39. Ibid., p. xv, para. 27.

40. Ibid., p. xv, para. 26.

41. House of Commons Defence Committee, *Ministry of Defence Organisation and Procurement*, pp. 276–7, q. 1352, see note 18. Also see comments made by Dr Gilbert in House of Commons Defence Committee, *The Sting Ray Lightweight Torpedo*, Third Report, Session 1980–1, HC 218, London: HMSO, 13 May 1981, Minutes of evidence, p. 38, q. 221.

42. Parliament, *Official Report of the House of Commons*, 8 February–9 February, Session 1970–1, vol. 811, London: HMSO, 8 February 1971, col. 58.

43. House of Commons Defence Committee, *Ministry of Defence Organisation and Procurement*, p. 318, q. 1582, see note 18.

44. David Greenwood, *Budgeting for Defence*, London: RUSI, 1972, p. 73.

45. Ibid. Also see *Statement on the Defence Estimates 1972*. London: HMSO, Cmnd 4891, p. 6, para. 46.

46. Expenditure Committee (Defence and External Affairs Sub-committee), *Defence Expenditure 1973–74*, Eighth Report, Session 1973–4, HC 169, London: HMSO, 7 February 1974, p. viii, para. 6.

47. John Marriot, 'The defence industry – the industry', *NATO's 15 Nations* (April–May 1976): 31.

48. John Lovering, *The Restructuring of the Defence Industry and the Role of the State*, p. 15, see note 23. Also see Angus Rae, 'The organisation of defence procurement and production in the UK', *Aberdeen Studies in Defence Economics*, 13 (December 1979): 28–9.

49. Nicole Ball and Milton Leitenberg (eds), *The Structure of the Defence Industry*, Beckenham, Kent: Croom Helm Ltd., 1983, p. 352, appendix 1, table 11.5.

50. T. Truman, 'The British defence industry – the challenge of the eighties', *Seaford House Papers* (1980): 12.

51. Keith Hartley, *A Market For Aircraft: A Critique and Proposal for Radical Reconstruction of British Government Procurement Policy*, Hobart Paper 57, London: Institute of Economic Affairs, 1974, p. 25.

52. P. Isaac and K. Cartney quoted in Roger Hutton, 'Technical innovation in the UK defence sector: three companies observed', in Ian Bellany and Tim Huxley (eds), *New Conventional Weapons and Western Defence*, London: Frank Cass, 1987, p. 14.

53. ESRC/SPSG Defence Science and Technology Policy Team, *Future Relations Between Defence and Civil Science and Technology*, SPSG Review Paper 2, London: Science Policy Support Group, March 1991, p. 20.

54. National Audit Office, *Ministry of Defence: Control and Management of the*

Development of Major Equipment, Report by the Comptroller and Auditor General, Session 1985–6, HC 568, London: HMSO, 22 July 1986. p. 23, para. 6.

55. F.E. Tyndall (Air Commodore), 'Project management for defence equipment', *Weapons Procurement, Defence Management and International Collaboration. A Series of Six Lectures Delivered at a Seminar at the University of Southampton*, London: RUSI, 1972, p. 17, see note 9.

56. For example out of a sample of 81 US military programmes conducted between 1950 and 1980, only 10 per cent took place within the original cost estimate. To obtain a 50/50 chance of success estimates would have needed increasing by 148 per cent. Sir Frank Cooper. 'Resources for defence – AD 2000', *Defence Attache 2* (1987): 31–2. Also Gansler has suggested that historically, programme cost growth in the USA has averaged between 50 and 100 per cent of the original cost estimate of each weapons system. Jacques S. Gansler, 'Building reform in weapons acquisition', in William P. Synder and James Brown (eds), *Defense Policy in the Reagan Administration*, Washington DC: National Defense University Press, 1988, p. 373.

57. Paul Laurent, 'The costs of defence', in Stuart Croft (ed.), *British Security Policy: The Thatcher Years and the End of the Cold War*, London: HarperCollins Academic, 1991, p. 97. Also see National Audit Office, *MOD: Control and Management of the Development of Major Equipment*, appendix 4, Nimrod: Mission System Avionics, pp. 28–9, see note 54. Steve Broadbent, 'Nimrod – the hunter killed', *Jane's Aviation Review* (1987): 28–33. Dan Boyle, 'UK AEW Nimrod system looks like being first in Europe', *International Defense Review* (3/1979): 372–6. *Financial Times*, 6 March 1985.

58. House of Commons Defence Committee, *MOD Organisation and Procurement*, pp. 439–44, see note 11. A further example would of course be that of the Chevaline programme which rose in cost from the £250 million estimate given to the Cabinet in 1974 to the £1000 million announced by the Defence Secretary in 1980. Lawrence Freedman, *Britain and Nuclear Weapons*, London, Basingstoke: Macmillan, 1980, pp. 52–5.

59. National Audit Office, *MOD: Control and Management of the Development of Major Equipment*, p. 10, see note 54.

60. Ministry of Defence, *Learning from Experience. A Report on the Arrangements for Managing Major Projects in the Procurement Executive*, London: HMSO, 1988, p. 7.

61. Ministry of Defence, *Review of Operational Requirements Procedure*, MAN S (ORG) Report No. 455, Defence Open Government Document 82/22, London: MOD, May 1982. p. 38.

62. Ibid., p. 41.

63. Ibid., p. 23 and annexe B, p. 1.

64. Committee of Public Accounts, *Production Costs of Defence Equipment*, Twenty-third Report, Session 1985–6, HC 56, London: HMSO, 28 April 1986, p. 35, appendix 4. Also see National Audit Office, *MOD: Control and Management of the Development of Major Equipment*, p. 14, see note 54. Also see Ministry of Defence, *Learning from Experience*, p. 13, see note 60. One notable example of this was that of the programme to develop the mission system avionics for the Nimrod AEW where operational urgency induced MOD to opt for a compressed and overlapping development and production programme. Estimates of the cost of completion of the MSA indicated that it would have required a real cost increase of 101 per cent to meet the

minimum initial operating capability. National Audit Office, *MOD: Control and Management of the Development of Major Equipment*, appendix 4, see note 54.

65. House of Commons Defence Committee, *MOD Organisation and Procurement*, memorandum by the MOD, p. 331, see note 11. Also see National Audit Office, *MOD: Control and Management of the Development of Major Equipment*, p. 14, see note 54.

66. Ministry of Defence, *Learning from Experience*, p. 10, see note 60.

67. Ibid.

68. National Audit Office, *MOD: Control and Management of the Development of Major Equipment*, p. 14, see note 54.

69. Ministry of Defence, *Learning from Experience*, p. 15, see note 60. Also see National Audit Office, *MOD: Control and Management of the Development of Major Equipment*, p. 2, see note 54.

70. Ministry of Defence, *Learning from Experience*, p. 13, see note 60.

71. House of Commons Defence Committee, *MOD Organisation and Procurement*, memorandum by the MOD, p. 331, see note 11.

72. Committee of Public Accounts, *Matters Relating to the MOD*, Sixteenth Report, Session 1979–80, HC 648, London: HMSO, 16 June 1980, Minutes of evidence, p. 56, q. 2683. Also see National Audit Office, *MOD: Control and Management of the Development of Major Equipment*, p. 41, see note 54.

73. Sir Frank Cooper, personal interview, see note 13. Also see *The Government Orgainisation for Defence Procurement and Civil Aerospace*, pp. 20–1, see note 1.

74. Geoffrey Williams et al., *Crisis in Procurement*, see note 7.

75. Sir Michael Cary, 'A lecture given at RUSI, 17 October 1973', *RUSI Journal* (March 1974): 20.

76. Keith Hartley, *A Market for Aircraft*, p. 37, see note 51. Also see John Simpson, 'The political and parliamentary implications of transnational defence procurement', *Weapons Procurement, Defence Management and International Collaboration. A Series of Six Lectures Delivered at a Seminar at the University of Southampton*, London: RUSI, 1972, p. 29.

77. Ministry of Defence, *Statement on the Defence Estimates 1985*, London: HMSO, Cmnd 9430-II, p. 14.

78. Committee of Public Accounts, *Matters Relating to the MOD*, Sixth Report, Session 1978–9, HC 328, London: HMSO, 2 April 1979, pp. xviii–xix, paras 40–1. Examples of late pricing would be:

1. The Harrier aircraft, where 6 of the first 9 airframe follow-on contracts worth some £55 million were not priced until more than 60 per cent of the costs had been incurred. The last three contracts were priced when some 70 per cent of the costs had been incurred.

2. The Sea Harrier, where pricing negotiations were still proceeding in 1978 on two contracts placed in 1975 for development of this version and production of the first batch, delivery of which was programmed to commence in mid-1979. Committee of Public Accounts, *Matters Relating to the MOD*, Session 1978–9, HC 328, London: HMSO, 2 April 1979, Minutes of evidence, pp. xix–xx, para. 44.

79. Committee of Public Accounts, *Production Costs of Defence Equipment*, p. xxxiii, see note 64.

80. House of Commons Defence Committee, *MOD Organisation and Procurement*, Minutes of evidence, p. 373, see note 11.

81. Ministry of Defence, *Learning from Experience*, p. 7, see note 60. Also personal

interview with ex-member of the Procurement Executive, 1 November 1988; Vallin Pollen Research and Planning Unit, *Report on Research into Defence Procurement Issues II*, see note 20.

82. Ibid., p. 13, see note 20.

83. House of Commons Defence Committee, *The Procurement of Major Defence Equipment*, Fifth Report, Session 1987–8, HC 431, London: HMSO, 14 June 1988, p. xxviii, para. 110. Also see National Audit Office, *MOD: Control and Management of the Development of Major Equipment*, p. 15, see note 54.

84. House of Commons Defence Committee, *The Procurement of Major Defence Equipment*, p. xxvi, para. 102, see note 83.

85. Vallin Pollen Research and Planning Unit, *Report on Research into Defence Procurement Issues II*, p. 19, see note 20.

86. J.M. Legge, 'Management of the equipment programme', p. 12, see note 32.

87. House of Commons Defence Committee, *The Procurement of Major Defence Equipment*, p. xxxi, para. 125, see note 83.

88. National Audit Office, *Ministry of Defence: Reliability and Maintainability of Defence Equipment*, Report by the Comptroller and Auditor General, Session 1988–9, HC 173, London: HMSO, 1 February 1989, p. 1.

89. Ibid., p. 8.

90. Ibid.

91. Ibid.

92. House of Commons Defence Committee, *The Procurement of Major Defence Equipment*, p. xxxi, para. 134, see note 83.

93. Ibid., para. 131.

94. Ibid.

95. *The Government Organisation for Defence Procurement and Civil Aerospace*, p. 37, para. 78, see note 1.

96. House of Commons Defence Committee, *The Procurement of Major Defence Equipment*, minutes of evidence (note by MOD), p. 21, see note 83.

97. Vallin Pollen Research and Planning Unit, *Report on Research into Defence Procurement Issues*, p. 63, see note 20.

98. Ibid. Also see ibid., p. 25.

99. National Audit Office, *MOD: Reliability and Maintainability of Defence Equipment*, p. 3, see note 88.

100. Ibid., p. 12.

101. Ibid., p. 8.

102. Ibid., p. 2.

103. Personal interview with a representative of the defence industry, 9 September 1989.

104. Ministry of Defence, *Learning from Experience*, p. 38, see note 60.

2. Rising costs and finite budgets

1. Personal interview with MOD representative, 12 July 1988. Also Vallin Pollen Research and Planning Unit, *Report on Research into Defence Procurement Issues II*, London: Vallin Pollen and Consensus Research, March 1986, p. 4.

2. Personal interview with member of the Defence Committee, 6 June 1989. Also personal interview with Procurement official, 13 September 1990.

3. Sir Frank Cooper, personal interview, 10 August 1990.

4. J. Bayliss, *British Defence Policy: Striking the Right Balance*, Houndsmill, Basingstoke, Hampshire and London: Macmillan, 1989, appendix 1, p. 139.

5. Personal interview with ex-MOD official, 26 May 1989.

6. Ibid.

7. Neil Cooper, 'MOD weapons procurement policy 1979–1991', PhD thesis, University of Kent, 1992, pp. 96–7.

8. D. Smith, 'The political economy of British defence policy', in M. Shaw (ed.), *War, State and Society*, Basingstoke and London: Macmillan, 1984, p. 204.

9. *The Economist*, 9 March 1977.

10. Ministry of Defence, *Statement on the Defence Estimates 1984*, London: HMSO, Cmnd 9227-I, p. 16.

11. M. Chalmers, 'British defence spending in the 1980s', *A.D.I.U Report*, 3, vol. 6 (May–June 1984): 3, table 2.

12. T. Benn, *Office Without Power: Diaries 1968–72*, London, Sydney: Hutchinson, 1988, p. 100. Also see Sir R. Verdon Smith, 'The need for a closer relationship between defence and industry', *RUSI Journal* (March 1971): 16.

13. Ministry of Defence, *Statement on the Defence Estimates 1972*, London: HMSO, Cmnd 4891, p. 6.

14. Ministry of Defence, *Report of the Steering Group on the Functions of R & D Establishments*, Defence Open Government Document 80/35, London: MOD, June 1980 (Chair Lord Strathcona), p. 15 and p. 2.

15. A. Rae, 'The organisation of defence procurement and production in the UK', *Aberdeen Studies in Defence Economics*, 13 (December 1979): 24.

16. L. Freedman, *Arms Production in the United Kingdom: Problems and Prospects*, London: The Royal Institute of International Affairs, 1978, p. 9. Also see *Review of the Framework for Government R&D*, London: HMSO, 1979, Cmnd 5046, p. 8, para. 18.

17. Personal interview, see note 3.

18. House of Commons Defence Committee, *Ministry of Defence Organisation and Procurement*, Second Report, Session 1981–2, HC 22-II, London: HMSO, 16 June 1982. Minutes of evidence (memorandum by the Plessey Co. Ltd.), p. 422, para. 3.2.

19. Personal interview, see note 3.

20. Expenditure Committee (the Defence and External Affairs Sub-committee), *Defence Expenditure*, Eighth Report, Session 1973–4, HC 169, London: HMSO, 7 February 1974, p. xiii, para. 24.

21. Committee of Public Accounts, *Matters Relating to the MOD*, Sixth Report, Session 1978–9, HC 328, London: HMSO, 2 April 1979, p. xviii, para. 39.

22. Ibid.

23. Neil Cooper, 'MOD weapons procurement policy', appendix 2, see note 7.

24. Committee of Public Accounts, *Production Costs of Defence Equipment*, Twenty-third Report, Session 1985–6, HC 56, London: HMSO, 28 April 1986, Appendix 4.

25. Personal interview with then member of the Defence Committee, 16 December 1989.

26. T. Truman, 'The British defence industry – the challenge of the eighties', *Seaford House Papers* (1980): 12.

27. Neil Cooper, 'MOD weapons procurement policy', appendix 2, see note 7.

28. Personal interview, see note 5.

29. Personal interview, see note 25.

30. See annual statistics for defence RPE in House of Commons Defence Committee, *Statement on the Defence Estimates 1989*, Fourth Report, Session 1988–9, HC 383, London: HMSO, 7 June 1989. Minutes of evidence (letter from the private secretary to the Secretary of State for Defence to the Clerk of the Committee enclosing a memorandum updating evidence given in Session 1987–8), p. 46, a. 6.

31. M. Wright, *Public Spending Decisions*, London, Boston: George Allen & Unwin, 1980, p. 101.

32. P. Riddell, *The Thatcher Government*, Oxford, New York: Basil Blackwell, 1987, p. 120. Also on this point see M. Levitt, 'The economics of procurement: national economic pressures and the defence budget', *A Report on the Proceedings of a One Day BOW Group Conference*, London: London Press Centre, 1986, p. 17.

33. I.P. Wilson, 'Britain's defence programme: some personal observations on equipment procurement policy, practice and mythology', *Seaford House Papers* (1985): 94.

34. Committee of Public Accounts, *Matters Relating to the MOD*, Third Report, Session 1980–1, HC 125, London: HMSO, 30 April 1981, p. 18, q. 114.

35. Ministry of Defence, *The Study of Control of Expenditure 1981*, Defence Open Government Document 81/01, London: MOD, 1981, p. 2, para. 5.

36. Committee of Public Accounts, *Matters Relating to the MOD*, p. 17, q. 111–12, see note 34.

37. *Financial Times*, 22 February 1983, see also note 34.

38. House of Commons Defence Committee, *MOD Organisation and Procurement*, Second Report, Session 1981–2, HC 22-I, London: HMSO, 16 June 1982, p. xxi, para. 38.

39. House of Commons Defence Committee, *Defence Commitments and Resources and the Defence Estimates 1985–86*, Third Report, Session 1984–5, HC 37-II, London: HMSO, 23 May 1985. Minutes of evidence (memo from MOD – 'Defence Commitments and Resources' submitted on 27 July 1984), p. 14, a. 25.

40. Ministry of Defence, *Statement on the Defence Estimates 1987*, London: HMSO, Cmnd 101–1, p. 44, para. 504.

41. Personal interview with MOD representative, 6 October 1995.

42. House of Commons Defence Committee, *Statement on the Defence Estimates 1995*, Ninth Report, Session 1994–5, HC 572, London: HMSO, 18 July 1995, p. viii, para. 7

43. For example the French Mirage F1 which entered service in the 1970s cost five times more (in real terms) than the first indigenously produced French jet fighter after World War Two. E.A. Kolodziej, *Making and Marketing Arms: The French Experience and its Implications for the International System*, Princeton, NJ: Princeton University Press, 1987, p. 141. In 1955 the US Department of Defense spent approximately $7 billion (at 1982 prices) to procure 1,400 military aircraft; by 1982 it was spending $14 billion a year for approximately 200. J.S. Gansler, *Affording Defense*, Cambridge, MA; London, England: MIT Press, 1989, p. 7.

44. In comparison, in 1982 the US Congressional Budget Office estimated real defence growth at 4.4 per cent, with higher figures for projects with emerging technology (ET) and the French indicated a figure of plus 5 per cent – Sir Frank Cooper, *Defence Procurement*, 1984 (paper given to the author by Sir Frank Cooper),

p. 2. and Sir Frank Cooper, 'Resources for defence – AD 2000', *Defence Attache*, 2 (1987): 31.

45. Ministry of Defence, *Statement on the Defence Estimates 1982*, London: HMSO, Cmnd 8529–1, p. 27, para. 402–3.

46. Ibid., p. 27, para. 402.

47. Ibid., p. 27, para. 406.

48. '"Economic constraints and British defence", Speech by Secretary of State for Defence, John Nott at IISS (excerpts)', *Survival*, 2, vol. xxiv (March–April 1982): 89–90. Also Malcolm Chalmers noted in 1985 that the real terms cost of producing 385 Tornados would be greater than the cost of 21,000 Spitfires made before and during World War Two. M. Chalmers, *Military Spending and British Decline*, London: Pluto Press, 1985 p. 23–4.

49. *Official Report of the House of Commons*, July 18–July 29, Session 1983–4, vol. 46, London: HMSO, 20 July 1983, col. 397.

50. Ministry of Defence, *Statement on the Defence Estimates 1988*, London: HMSO, Cm 344–1, p. 44, para. 1.

51. Ministry of Defence, *Value for Money in Defence Equipment Procurement*, Defence Open Government Document 83/01, London: MOD, October 1983, para. 4.

52. House of Commons Defence Committee, *Defence Cuts and Defence Estimates: Minutes of Evidence Taken by the Committee on 11 and 18 March 1981 and Appendix*, Session 1980–1, HC 223, London: HMSO, 11 and 18 March 1981. Minutes of evidence (memo submitted by the MOD, 'Winter supplementary estimates'), p. 3, para. 1.

53. House of Commons Defence Committee, *Ministry of Defence Organisation and Procurement*, pp. 118–19, q. 525, see note 18.

54. Ministry of Defence, *The Study of Control of Expenditure 1981*, p. 2, para. 7, see note 35.

55. This was legitimised by the Winter supplementary defence estimates presented to Parliament on 2 December 1980, see note 52.

56. Ibid., p. 3, para. 2.

57. The £203 million provided for the full additional cost of the armed forces pay award of £54 million and an extra £200 million determined, according to the MOD, 'in the light of current international considerations and the priority attached to the defence programme'. The resultant increase of £254 million was abated by £50 million in respect of overspending by MOD on the previous year's cash limit. After some other minor adjustments, therefore, this left a net increase to the defence budget of £203 million. The extra £50 million for the armed forces pay award was actually allocated to the equipment vote (Vote 2) rather than to Vote 1, where money for pay normally goes. Thus all of this extra £203 million ended up being allocated to the procurement budget. Ibid., pp. 3–4.

58. House of Commons Defence Committee, *Ministry of Defence Organisation and Procurement*, p. 119, see note 18.

59. The ban applied to extra-mural research and development, to purchases of capital equipment and goods, to purchases of land and to new construction, to purchases of spares, stocks and reserves and to new services, see note 52.

60. Ibid.

61. House of Commons Defence Committee, *Ministry of Defence Organisation and Procurement*, p. 19, see note 18. Also see *Financial Times*, 5 February 1982.

62. Ministry of Defence, *The Study of Control of Expenditure 1981*, p. 2, see note 35.

63. *Financial Times*, see note 61.

64. *Official Report of the House of Commons*, 3 November 1980, Session 1980–1, vol. 991, London: HMSO, 22 October–7 November, col. 475.

65. Ministry of Defence, *The Study of Control of Expenditure 1981*, p. 3, para. 8, see note 35.

66. House of Commons Defence Committee, *Defence Cuts and Defence Estimates: Minutes of Evidence*, p. 4, see note 52.

67. House of Commons Defence Committee, *Ministry of Defence Organisation and Procurement*, p. xxxviii, para. 95, see note 18.

68. Committee of Public Accounts, *Profit Formula for Non-competitive Government Contracts*, Twenty-fifth Report, Session 1984–5, HC 390, London: HMSO, 15 July 1985, Minutes of evidence (Peter Levene), p. 2, q. 2006.

69. This has been calculated on the basis of figures given in ibid., appendices to the minutes of evidence, p. 16.

70. House of Commons Defence Committee, *Ministry of Defence Organisation and Procurement*, p. 39, see note 18.

71. Ministry of Defence, *The Study of Control of Expenditure 1981*, p. 6, para. 19, see note 35.

72. Ibid., p. 9, para. 27.

73. *Official Report of the House of Commons*, see note 64.

74. House of Commons Defence Committee, *Defence Cuts and Defence Estimates: Minutes of Evidence*, p. 4, see note 52. The figure for pay and price increases and the figures for faster progress on orders and faster billing exceed the final total of £277.5 million because £30.8 million was abated as a result of savings in other areas.

75. Personal interview with ex-defence procurement official, 1 February 1991.

76. Ministry of Defence, *The Study of Control of Expenditure 1981*, p. 9, para. 27, see note 35. Also see Ministry of Defence, *Statement on the Defence Estimates 1982*, London: HMSO, Cmnd 8529–1, p. 29, para. 419. However, one MOD representative qualified this to a certain extent when he told the Defence Committee: 'We [the MOD] are now planning to move as near as possible to the aim of a 2.5% block adjustment in 1982–83. Land systems usually stand out as different from the other two because the programme is different; it is an amalgam of a large number of rather smaller programmes and the control of a programme of that kind does present slightly different problems from those of the other Controllers. Therefore we have taken the view that a rather larger block adjustment is appropriate in that area.' House of Commons Defence Committee, *Ministry of Defence Organisation and Procurement*, p. 127, see note 18.

77. House of Commons Defence Committee, *Ministry of Defence Organisation and Procurement*, p. 122, see note 18.

78. Ibid., p. 136.

79. House of Commons Defence Committee, *Defence Cuts and Defence Estimates: Minutes of Evidence*, p. 33, q. 78, see note 52.

80. House of Commons Defence Committee, *Ministry of Defence Organisation and Procurement*, p. 138, see note 18.

81. Jordan and Sons Surveys Ltd., Industry Commentary by J.O.G. Paton (Miltrain Ltd.), *Jordans – the British Defence Industry 1983*, London: Jordan & Sons Surveys, p. xiv.

82. *Guardian*, 24 June 1981.

83. *Guardian*, 26 September 1980.

84. *Daily Telegraph*, 26 September 1980.

85. *The Times*, 4 November 1980.

86. For example Bruce George (MP) of the Defence Committee somewhat caustically observed that: 'if one thinks that the main purpose of the military is the distribution of metal and weapons in the general direction of the enemy this surely is impaired if the personnel responsible for that (A) do not have the right equipment and (B) do not have the right fuel and the resources.' House of Commons Defence Committee, *Ministry of Defence Organisation and Procurement*, p. 120, see note 18.

87. Francis Pym quoted in K. Harris, *Thatcher*, London: Wiedenfield & Nicolson, 1988, p. 115.

88. D. Greenwood, 'Setting defence priorities', *A.D.I.U. Report*, 3, vol. 3 (May–June 1981): 3.

89. House of Commons Defence Committee, *Ministry of Defence Organisation and Procurement*, pp. 131–2, see note 18.

90. House of Commons Defence Committee, *Defence Commitments and Resources and the Defence Estimates 1985–86*, p. 1, para. 4, see note 39.

91. *The United Kingdom Defence Programme: The Way Forward*, London: HMSO, Cmnd 8288 (presented to Parliament on June 1981), p. 3, para. 2.

92. Ibid., p. 4, para. 4.

93. *Financial Times*, 19 May 1981.

94. *Daily Telegraph*, 19 June 1981.

95. *Daily Telegraph*, 19 May 1981.

96. *The United Kingdom Defence Programme: The Way Forward*, p. 10, para. 29, see note 91. Also see *Financial Times*, 15 December 1982; 'Pounds, shillings and pence', *Analysis*, transcript of a programme broadcast on Radio 4, 25 June 1985.

97. *The United Kingdom Defence Programme: The Way Forward*, p. 10, para. 27, see note 91. Also see P. Byrd (ed.), *British Defence Policy Under Thatcher*, Oxford, New York: Philip Allan Publishing/St. Martin's Press, 1988, p. 173.

98. *The Times*, 29 June 1981. Also see J. Critchley, 'Can Nott defend defence against the Treasury?', *Daily Telegraph*, 27 January 1982.

99. *The Falklands Campaign: The Lessons*, London: HMSO, Cmnd 8758 (presented to Parliament December 1982), pp. 32–4.

100. *Financial Times*, 15 December 1982.

101. Ibid.

102. Ministry of Defence, *Statement on the Defence Estimates 1985*, London: HMSO, Cmnd 9430–1, p. 25, para. 435.

103. Ibid., p. 25.

104. House of Commons Defence Committee, *The Future Size and Role of the Royal Navy's Surface Fleet*, Sixth Report, Session 1987–8, HC 309, London: HMSO, 21 June 1988, p. xxxvi, para. 137. Also see House of Commons Defence Committee, *The Future Size and Role of the Royal Navy's Surface Fleet: Government Response to the Sixth Report from the Defence Committee, Session 1987–88, HC 309*, London: HMSO, Cm 443, p. 2, para. 7.

105. House of Commons Defence Committee, *The Future Size and Role of the Royal Navy's Surface Fleet*, Minutes of evidence, p. 48, q. 457, see note 104.

106. Ibid., p. xxx, note 3.

107. K. Harris, *Thatcher*, p. 129, see note 87.

108. Personal interview, see note 23. Also see *Daily Telegraph*, 19 June 1981.

109. *The Falklands Campaign: The Lessons*, p. 33, para. 308, see note 99.

110. Ibid., para. 309.

111. Ibid.

112. Ibid., p. 34, para. 311.

113. Ibid., pp. 34–5, para. 311.

114. *Financial Times*, 21 October 1982.

115. House of Commons Defence Committee, *Statement on the Defence Estimates 1988*, Seventh Report, Session 1987–8, HC 495, London: HMSO, 28 June 1988, p. vii. Also see *Financial Times*, 7 November 1986.

116. *Financial Times*, 29 October 1982.

117. N. Cooper, 'MOD Weapons Procurement Policy 1979–1991', appendix 7, see note 7.

118. 'Pounds, shillings and pence', *Analysis*, see note 96.

119. *The Times*, 13 December 1984.

120. J. Bayliss, 'Evolution of British defence policy 1945–86', in M. Edmonds (ed.), *The Defence Equation, British Military Systems Policy Planning and Performance Since 1945*, London, Oxford: Brassey's Defence Publishers, 1986, p. 32.

121. *Jane's Defence Weekly*, 10 November 1984. Also see *The Times*, 17 December 1984; *Guardian*, 29 December 1984.

122. House of Commons Defence Committee, *Defence Commitments and Resources and the Defence Estimates 1985–86*, p. xxiv, see note 39.

123. Chalmers, 'British defence spending in the 1980s', p. 2, see note 11.

124. 'Pounds, shillings and pence', *Analysis*, see note 96. Also on this point see Michael Heseltine in *Official Report of the House of Commons*, 12 June 1985, Session 1984–5, vol. 80, London: HMSO, 3 June–14 June, col. 912. *The Times*, 17 February 1984.

125. Personal interview, see note 3. Also see House of Commons Defence Committee, *Defence Commitments and Resources*, Minutes of evidence, p. 24, para. 37, see note 39.

126. House of Commons Defence Committee, *Defence Commitments and Resources*, Minutes of evidence, pp. xxxiii–xxxiv, para. 86, see note 39.

127. *The Times*, 13 May 1986. Also see *The Financial Times*, 28 April 1986.

128. *Official Report of the House of Commons*, 30 June 1986, Session 1985–6, vol. 100, London: HMSO, June 23–July 4, col. 713.

129. Ministry of Defence, *Statement on the Defence Estimates 1986*, London: HMSO, Cmnd 9763–1, p. 46, para. 515.

130. House of Commons Defence Committee, *Statement on the Defence Estimates 1989*, p. xix, para. 56, see note 30.

131. House of Commons Defence Committee, *Defence Commitments and Resources and the Defence Estimates 1985–86*, p. 213 para. 1363, see note 39.

132. K. Hartley, 'The affordability of air systems', in P. Sabin (ed.), *The Future of United Kingdom Air Power*, London: Brassey's Defence Publishers, 1988, p. 108.

133. *Britain's Army for the 90s*, London: HMSO, July 1991.

134. House of Commons Defence Committee, *Britain's Army for the 90s: Commitments and Resources*, Second Report, Session 1992–3, HC 306, London: HMSO, 14 Jan. 1993, p. xxi, para. 4; *Independent*, 14 October 1991.

135. D. Greenwood, 'Expenditure and management', in P. Byrd (ed.), *British Defence Policy: Thatcher and Beyond*, London: Philip Allan, 1991, pp. 58–9.

136. House of Commons Defence Committee, *Statement on the Defence Estimates 1994*, Sixth Report, Session 1994, HC 68, London: HMSO, 22 June 1994, p. iv, para. 20; N. Cooper, 'Front Line First', in *Parliamentary Brief*, vol. 2, no. 8, May–June 1994, p. 28.

137. House of Commons Defence Committee, *Statement on the Defence Estimates 1995*, Ninth Report, Session 1994–5, HC 572, London: HMSO, 18 July 1995, p. vii, para. 5.

138. Ministry of Defence, *Front Line First: The Defence Costs Study*, London: HMSO, 1994, T. Dodd, *Front Line First: The Defence Costs Study*, House of Commons Library, Research Paper 94/101, Oct. 1994.

139. Michael Biddis, 'Thatcherism: concept and interpretations', in Kenneth Minogue and Michael Biddis (eds), *Thatcherism: Personality and Politics*, London: Macmillan, 1987, p. xvi.

140. Jonathon Michie, *The Economic Legacy 1979–1992*, London: Academic Press, 1992, p. 96.

141. Peter Riddell, *The Thatcher Government*, Oxford: Basil Blackwell, 1987, p. 221; *Guardian*, 12 January 1981.

142. Personal interview with former MOD official, 26 May 1989.

143. *On the Record*, interview with Michael Heseltine, BBC 1, 18 Nov. 1990.

144. *Guardian*, 1 May 1985.

145. 'Big spenders inside the MOD', *Business and Government*, April/May 1989, p. 15.

146. Paul Dunne and Ron Smith, 'Thatcherism and the UK Defence Industry', see note 140.

3. Competition with limits

1. Catherine J. Goldsmith, 'Interview: Lord Trefgarne, British Minister of State for Defence Procurement', *Defence and Diplomacy*, (July–August 1989): 15; Peter Levene, lecture, 'Competition and collaboration: UK defence procurement policy', London: RUSI, 25 February 1987.

2. National Audit Office, *Ministry of Defence: Initiatives in Defence Procurement*, Report by the Comptroller and Auditor General, Session 1990–1, HC 189, London: HMSO, February 1991, p. 3, para. 7.

3. Ministry of Defence, *Departmental Report by the Ministry of Defence: The Government's Expenditure Plans 1993/94 to 1995/96*, Cm 2201, London: HMSO, February 1993, p. 14, para. 31.

4. *Financial Times*, 21 March 1984.

5. Committee of Public Accounts, *Ministry of Defence: The Profit Formula*, Fifty-second Report, Session 1987–8, HC 503, London: HMSO, 14 November 1988, Minutes of evidence, p. 8.

6. Ministry of Defence, *Departmental Report by the Ministry of Defence, The Government's Expenditure Plans 1991–92 to 1993–94*, London: HMSO, Cm 1501, p. 17, para. 47.

7. National Audit Office, Report by the Comptroller and Auditor General, *Ministry of Defence: Defence Procurement in the 1990s*, London: HMSO, HC 390, May 1994, p. 19, para. 3.18.

8. Ministry of Defence, *Statement on the Defence Estimates: Britain's Defence for the 90s*, London: HMSO, July 1991, Cm 1559-I, p. 72, para. 7.

9. Ministry of Defence, *UK Defence Statistics: 1995 Edition*, London: HMSO, 1995, p. 15, Table 1.14; Ministry of Defence, *Statement on the Defence Estimates 1985*, London: HMSO, Cmnd 9430-II, p. 14.

10. National Audit Office, p. 18, para. 3.10, see note 5.

11. Letter from the MOD, December 1993.

12. For discussion of these trends see W. Walker and P. Gummett, 'Britain and the European armaments market', *International Affairs*, no. 3, vol. 65 (Summer 1989), pp. 426–7; Andrew Moravcsik, 'The European armaments industry at the cross-roads', *Survival*, no. 1, vol. XXXIII (January/February 1990), pp. 65–85.

13. Committee of Public Accounts, *Initiatives in Defence Procurement*, Forty-first Report, Session 1990–1, HC 246, London: HMSO, 16 October 1991, Minutes of evidence, p. 5, para. 2652.

14. *The Times*, 24 January 1990; *Financial Times*, 25 January 1990; *Sunday Times*, 28 January 1990.

15. *The Times*, 25 July 1986; *Financial Times*, 25 July 1986.

16. Personal interview with a representative of the defence industry, 11 October 1990.

17. Personal interview with a representative of the defence industry, 11 September 1990.

18. National Audit Office, *Ministry of Defence: Defence Procurement in the 1990s*, p. 18, para. 3.13, see note 7.

19. House of Commons Defence Committee and the Trade and Industry Committee, *Aspects of Defence Procurement and Industrial Policy*, First Report, Session 1995–6, HC 61, 62, London: HMSO, 23 November 1995, p. xxxiv, para. 90.

20. Ibid., p. xxxv, para. 90.

21. *Guardian*, 'UK refuses to aid missile marriage', 13 June 1995.

22. Monopolies and Mergers Commission, *British Aerospace Plc and Thomson-CSF SA: A Report on the Proposed Merger*, London: HMSO, January 1991, C. 1416, pp. 27–9; *Observer*, 3 March 1991; *Guardian*, 31 January 1991.

23. RUSI, 'The FLA: still flying into adversity', *Newsbrief*, vol. 15, no. 3, March 1995, pp. 17–19.

24. Telephone interview, May 1991.

25. William Walker and Phillip Gummett, p. 423, note 7; see note 12.

26. *Daily Telegraph*, 24 May 1995; *Observer*, 25 June 1995.

27. William Walker and Phillip Gummett, p. 422, see note 12.

28. Monopolies and Mergers Commission, *The General Electric Company Plc: A Report on the Proposed Merger*, London: HMSO, August 1986, Cm 9867, p. 62, para. 7.16 and pp. 68–70.

29. Monopolies and Mergers Commission, *British Aerospace Plc and Thompson-CSF SA: A Report on the Proposed Merger*, p. 15, Table 3.1 and p. 17, para. 3.19, see note 22.

30. Monopolies and Mergers Commission, *The General Electric Company Plc, Siemens AG and The Plessey Company Plc: A Report on the Proposed Merger*, London: HMSO, April 1989, Cm 676, p. 23, Table 3.2.

31. Keith Hartley and Nick Hooper, *Study of the Value of the Defence Industry to the UK Economy: A Statistical Analysis for DTI, MoD, SBAC and DMA*, London:

DTI, 1995, p. 33. Also on this point, see House of Commons Defence Committee, *Statement on the Defence Estimates 1990*, Eighth Report, Session 1989–90, HC 388, London: HMSO, 6 June 1990, Minutes of evidence, p. 46, answer 11 (c).

32. Monopolies and Mergers Commission, *The General Electric Company Plc: A Report on the Proposed Merger*, p. 45, Table 5.11, see note 28; Monopolies and Mergers Commission, *The General Electric Company Plc, Siemens AG and The Plessey Company Plc*, p. 24, Table 3.3, see note 30.

33. Committee of Public Accounts, *Initiatives in Defence Procurement*, Minutes of evidence, p. 4, q. 2651, see note 13.

34. House of Commons Defence Committee, *Ministry of Defence Organisation and Procurement*, Second Report, Session 1981–2, HC 22-II, London: HMSO, 16 June 1982, Minutes of Evidence, p. 33, q. 39.

35. Ron Smith and Jacques Fontanel, 'Weapons production versus exports', in Ian Bellany and Tim Huxley (eds), *New Conventional Weapons and Western Defence*, London: Frank Cass, 1987, p. 69.

36. Quoted in I.P. Wilson, 'Britain's defence programme: some personal observations on equipment procurement policy, practice and mythology', *Seaford House Papers* (1985): 100.

37. Lord Trefgarne, 'The government view', in London Press Centre, *A Report on the Proceedings of A One Day BOW Group Conference*, London: London Press Centre, 1986, p. 8.

38. House of Commons Defence Committee, *The Appointment and Objectives of the Chief of Defence Procurement*, Fifth report, Session 1984–5, HC 430, London: HMSO, 10 July 1985, Minutes of evidence, p. 114, q. 111.

39. House of Commons Defence Committee, *Statement on the Defence Estimates, 1988*, Seventh Report, Session 1987–8, HC 495, London: HMSO, 28 June 1988, p. xix, para. 2.46.

40. Telephone interview, December 1995.

41. Ibid.

42. Personal interview with MOD official, September 1990.

43. John Lovering, *The Restructuring of the Defence Industries and the Role of The State*, Working Paper 59, Bristol: University of Bristol (School for Advanced Urban Studies), 1986, p. 32.

44. House of Commons Defence Committee, *Statement on the Defence Estimates 1989*, Fourth Report, Session 1988–9, HC 383, London: HMSO, 7 June 1989, pp. xvi–xvii.

45. RUSI, *Newsbrief*, vol. 9, no. 8 (August 1989): 64. Also see *Financial Times*, 4 June 1990; *Independent*, 27 June 1988.

46. *Observer*, 27 January 1991.

47. Richard Ware, *Replacing the Chieftain Tank*, Research Note 428, London: House of Commons Library, 8 December 1988, p. 6.

48. Committee of Public Accounts, *Matters Relating to the MOD*, Third Report, Session 1980–1, HC 125, London: HMSO, 30 April 1981, p. xix, para. 50.

49. *Independent*, 10 March 1995.

50. National Audit Office, *Ministry of Defence: Defence Procurement in the 1990s*, p. 15, para. 2.20, see note 7.

51. 'Big spenders inside the MOD: an interview with Peter Levene and Lord Trefgarne', *Business and Government* (April/May 1989): 15.

52. Personal interview with a senior procurement official of the MOD, January 1991.

53. Keith Hartley, 'Efficiency, industry and alternative weapons procurement policies', in Christian Schmidt (ed.), *The Economics of Military Expenditure: Military Expenditures, Economic Growth and Fluctuations*, Hampshire and London: Macmillan, 1987, p. 284.

54. Stuart Croft, 'The Westland helicopter crisis: implications for the British defence industry', *Defence Analysis*, vol. 3, no. 4 (1987): 301.

55. Monopolies and Mergers Commission, *The General Electric Company Plc*, p. 65, see note 28

56. Philip Gummett, *The Future of the European Armaments Capability*, paper presented at the ECPR Paris Conference, September 1995; House of Commons Defence Committee and the Trade and Industry Committee, *Aspects of Defence Procurement and Industrial Policy*, see note 19.

57. House of Commons Defence Committee and Trade and Industry Committee, *Aspects of Defence Procurement and Industrial Policy*, Minutes of evidence, Session 1994–5, HC 333-iv, p. 76, q. 320.

58. Ibid., p. 84–5, q. 349.

59. Ibid., p. 85, q. 350.

60. *Independent*, 2 July 1988.

61 'Roger Freeman; British defense procurement minister', *Defense News*, 18 June 1995, p. 70.

4. The costs and effectiveness of competition

1. Ministry of Defence, *Statement on the Defence Estimates 1984*, London: HMSO, Cmnd 9227-I, p. 17, para. 237.

2. House of Commons Defence Committee, *The Appointment and Objectives of the Chief of Defence Procurement*, Fifth Report, Session 1984–5, HC 430, London: HMSO, 10 July 1985, Minutes of evidence, p. 13, para. 104.

3. House of Commons Defence Committee, *Statement on the Defence Estimates 1988*, Seventh Report, Session 1987–8, HC 495, London: HMSO, 28 June 1988, p. xv, para. 2.33.

4. House of Commons Defence Committee, *Statement on the Defence Estimates 1989*, Fourth Report, Session 1988–9, HC 383, London: HMSO, 7 June 1989, p. xi, para. 27.

5. Ministry of Defence, *Statement on the Defence Estimates 1984*, p. 17, para. 237, see note 1; *Guardian*, 31 March 1988; National Audit Office, *Ministry of Defence: Defence Procurement in the 1990s*, HC 390, London: HMSO, 20 May 1994, p. 16, para. 3.2.

6. Personal interview with a representative of the MOD, March 1991.

7. House of Commons Defence Committee, *The Appointment and Objectives of the Chief of Defence Procurement*, p. xv, para. 2.34, see note 2.

8. Ministry of Defence, *Statement on the Defence Estimates 1988*, London: HMSO, Cm 344-I. 1988.

9. Ibid.

10. *Official Report of the House of Commons*, 30 June 1986, Session 1985–6, vol. 100, London: HMSO, June 23–July 4, col. 714.

11. *The Times*, 4 January 1988.

12. House of Commons Defence Committee, *The Procurement of the Tucano*

Trainer Aircraft, Eighth Report, Session 1988–9, HC 372, London: HMSO, 12 July 1989, pp. v–xv.

13. Steven Schofield, 'The Levene reforms: an evaluation', *Defense Analysis*, no. 2, vol. 11 (1995): 155.

14. Ibid.

15. House of Commons Defence Committee and Trade and Industry Committee, *Aspects of Defence Procurement and Industrial Policy*, First Report, Session 1995–6, HC 61, 62, London: HMSO, 23 November 1995, pxxxi, para. 82.

16. *Government Reply to the First Reports from the Defence and Trade and Industry Committees Session 1995–96 On Aspects of Defence Procurement and Industrial Policy*, Session 1995–6, HC 209, 210, London: HMSO, 7 February 1996, p. iv, para. 7.

17. House of Commons Defence Committee and Trade and Industry Committee, *Aspects of Defence Procurement and Industrial Policy*, p. xxvi, para. 82, see note 15.

18. National Audit Office, *Ministry of Defence: Defence Procurement in the 1990s*, p. 19, para. 3.15, see note 5.

19. Vallin Pollen Research and Planning Unit, *Report on Research into Defence Procurement Issues*, vol. II, London: Vallin Pollen and Consensus Research, March 1986, p. 16.

20. Merton J. Peck and Frederick M. Scherer, *The Weapons Acquisition Process: An Economic Analysis*, Boston: Harvard University, 1962, p. 405.

21. Telephone interview with MOD representative, May 1991.

22. Personal interview with MOD representative, August 1990.

23. Ministry of Defence, *Learning from Experience: A Report on the Arrangements for Managing Major Projects in the Procurement Executive*, London: HMSO, 1988, p. 19, para. 40.

24. National Audit Office, *Ministry of Defence: Defence Procurement in the 1990s*, p. 19, para. 3.15, see note 5.

25. *Financial Times*, 13 November 1986.

26. House of Commons Defence Committee, *Statement on the Defence Estimates 1984*, First Report, Session 1983–4, HC 436, London: HMSO, 22 May 1984, p. xi, para. 41.

27. Interview with MOD representative, March 1991.

28. Catherine J. Goldsmith, 'Interview with Lord Trefgarne', *Defence and Diplomacy* (July–August 1989): 18.

29. Personal interview with former minister of state for defence procurement, January 1991.

30. A company response to structured questions for R.N. Cooper, *MOD Weapons Procurement Policy 1979–1991*, PhD thesis, University of Kent at Canturbury, 1992.

31. Briefing for MPs from a defence trade association, undated.

32. Personal interview with representative of the defence industry, September 1990.

33. Personal interview with representative of the defence industry, October 1990.

34. Ibid.

35. Personal interview with MOD representative, see note 22.

36. House of Commons Defence Committee, *The Reliability and Maintainability of Defence Equipment*, Fourth Report, Session 1989–90, HC 40, London: HMSO, 14 March 1990, Minutes of evidence, p. 7, q. 65.

37. National Audit Office, *Ministry of Defence: Developments in the Reliability and*

Maintainability of Defence Equipment, HC 690, London: HMSO, November 1994, p. 12, para. 35.

38. House of Commons Defence Committee, *The Reliability and Maintainability of Defence Equipment*, see note 36; Committee of Public Accounts, *Reliability and Maintainability of Defence Equipment*, Thirty-first Report, Session 1988–9, HC 206, London: HMSO, 3 July 1989; National Audit Office, *Ministry of Defence: Reliability and Maintainability of Defence Equipment*, HC 173, London: HMSO, 1 February 1989.

39. Peter Levene, 'Obtaining value for money', in Philip Sabin (ed.), *The Future of United Kingdom Air Power*, London: Brassey's Defence Publishers, 1988, p. 131.

40. Letter from MOD, 7 June 1991.

41. National Audit Office, *Ministry of Defence: Initiatives in Defence Procurement*, HC 189, London: HMSO, 6 February 1991, p. 8, para. 20.

42. National Audit Office, *Ministry of Defence: Reliability and Maintainability of Defence Equipment*, p. 2, para. 5, see note 38.

43. National Audit Office, *Ministry of Defence: Developments in the Reliability and Maintainability of Defence Equipment*, p. 3, para. 9, see note 37.

44. Ministry of Defence, *Departmental Report by the Ministry of Defence: The Government's Expenditure Plans 1995/96 to 1997/98*, Cm 2801, London: HMSO, 1995, p. 26, table 9.

45. House of Commons Defence Committee, *The Reliability and Maintainability of Defence Equipment*, pp. xvii–xviii, para. 56, see note 36.

46. Personal interview with MOD representative, see note 22.

47. Admiral Sir Lindsay Bryson, 'How should the Services adapt to economic constraints?', in London Press Centre, *Defence Procurement 1986: A Report on the Proceedings of a One Day BOW Group Conference 1986*, London: London Press Centre, May 1986, p. 25.

48. Personal interview with MOD representative, September 1990.

49. House of Commons Defence Committee, *The Reliability and Maintainability of Defence Equipment*, Minutes of evidence, p. 96, a. 9, see note 36.

50. National Audit Office, *Ministry of Defence: Developments in the Reliability and Maintainability of Defence Equipment*, see note 37.

51. Ibid., appendix 3, p. 40.

52. House of Commons Defence Committee, *The Reliability and Maintainability of Defence Equipment*, Minutes of evidence, p.15, see note 36.

53. National Audit Office, *Ministry of Defence: Developments in the Reliability and Maintainability of Defence Equipment*, pp. 6–7, para 19–21, see note 37.

54. House of Commons Defence Committee, *The Reliability and Maintainability of Defence Equipment*, p. xiv, para. 41, see note 36.

55. House of Commons Defence Committee, *Market Testing and Contracting Out of Defence Support Functions*, Thirteenth Report, Session 1994–5, HC 426, London: HMSO, 1 November 1995.

56. House of Commons Defence Committee, *The Reliability and Maintainability of Defence Equipment*, Minutes of evidence, p. 110, a. 5, see note 36.

57. Personal interview with representative of the defence industry, October 1990.

58. National Audit Office, *Ministry of Defence: Developments in the Reliability and Maintainability of Defence Equipment*, pp. 14–15, see note 37.

59. House of Commons Defence Committee, *The Reliability and Maintainability of Defence Equipment*, Minutes of evidence, p. 115, a. 2, see note 36.

60. Committee of Public Accounts, *Matters Relating to the MOD*, Sixteenth Report, Session 1979–80, HC 648, London: HMSO, 16 June 1980, Minutes of evidence, pp. 50–2.

61. National Audit Office, *Ministry of Defence: Reliability and Maintainability of Defence Equipment*, p. 24, paras. 5.13–14, see note 38.

62. Personal interview with a representative of the defence industry, September 1989.

63. National Audit Office, *Ministry of Defence: Initiatives in Defence Procurement*, p. 10, para. 26, see note 41.

64. Steven Schofield, 'The Levene reforms: an evaluation', *Defence Analysis*: 160, see note 13.

65. National Audit Office, *Ministry of Defence: Defence Procurement in the 1990s*, p. 25, para. 4.13, see note 5.

66. D. Francis Pace, *Negotiation and Management of Defense Contracts* , New York: Wiley Interscience, 1970, p. 183.

67. Personal interview with a representative of the defence industry, September 1990.

68. National Audit Office, *Ministry of Defence: Defence Procurement in the 1990s*, p. 25, paras 4.12–14, see note 5.

69. National Audit Office, *Ministry of Defence: Major Projects Report 1993*, HC 356, London: HMSO, 29 April 1994, p. 14, para. 3.15.

70. National Audit Office, *Ministry of Defence: Defence Procurement in the 1990s*, p. 20, para. 3.19, see note 5.

71. House of Commons Defence Committee, *Defence Procurement: Certain Projects and Accounting for Inflation*, Tenth Report, Session 1993–4, HC 512, London: HMSO, 29 September 1994, p. xii, para. 25.

72. Ibid., p. xv, para. 41.

73. Committee of Public Accounts, *Ministry of Defence: Fraud in Defence Procurement*, Forty-sixth Report, Session 1994–5, HC 365, London: HMSO, 1 November 1995, pp. xi–xii.

74. For details of all three corruption cases see: National Audit Office, *Ministry of Defence: The Risk of Fraud in Defence Procurement*, Session 1994–5, HC 258, London: HMSO, 10 March 1995; Committee of Public Accounts, *Ministry of Defence: Fraud in Defence Procurement*, see note 73.

75. *Guardian*, 16 February 1994.

76. Letter to Mr Derek Fatchett MP from MOD, 8 February 1995.

77. Letter to Mr Derek Fatchett MP from MOD, 1 December 1994.

78. *Guardian*, 27 February 1995.

79. Public Concern at Work, *Blowing the Whistle on Defence Procurement*, London: Public Concern at Work, 1995, p. 7.

80. Ibid., p. 18.

81. Ibid., p. 9; Committee of Public Accounts, *Production Costs of Defence Equipment*, Twenty-third Report, Session 1985–86, HC 56, London: HMSO, 28 April 1986, Minutes of evidence, pp. 1–4.

82. Personal interview with representative of the defence industry, see note 33.

83. National Audit Office, *Ministry of Defence: Design and Procurement of Warships*, Session 1984–5, HC 423, London: HMSO, 5 June 1985, p. 16, para. 5.3.

84. Review Board for Government Contracts, *Report on the 1995 Annual Review*

of the Profit Formula for Non-Competitive Government Contracts March 1995, London: HMSO, 1995, p. 21.

85. House of Commons Defence Committee, *Staffing Levels in the Procurement Executive*, Second Report, Session 1988–9, HC 269, London: HMSO, 23 May 1989, p. viii, para. 10.

86. House of Commons Defence Committee, *The Reliability and Maintainability of Defence Equipment*, Minutes of evidence, p. 33, a. A, see note 36.

87. Committee of Public Accounts, *Initiatives in Defence Procurement*, Forty-first Report, Session 1990–1, HC 246, London: HMSO, 16 October 1991, p. vi, para. 4.

88. D. Francis Pace, *Negotiation and Management of Defense Contracts*, p. 366, see note 66.

89. Personal interview with representative of the defence industry, see note 33.

90. Public Concern at Work, *Blowing the Whistle on Defence Procurement*, p. 26, see note 79.

91. Committee of Public Accounts, *Ministry of Defence: Procurement Irregularities*, Thirty-fifth Report, Session 1987–8, HC 450, London: HMSO, 4 July 1988, Minutes of evidence, p. 17.

92. Committee of Public Accounts, *Production Costs of Defence Equipment*, p. x, para. 31, see note 81.

93. Telephone interview with MOD representative, June 1991.

94. Committee of Public Accounts, *Production Costs of Defence Equipment*, Minutes of Evidence, p. 2, see note 81.

95. *The Times*, 18 May 1988.

96. Committee of Public Accounts, *Ministry of Defence: The Profit Formula*, Fifty-second Report, Session 1987–8, HC 503, London: HMSO, 14 November 1988, Minutes of evidence, p. 7, q. 4790.

97. National Audit Office, *Ministry of Defence: The Risk of Fraud in Defence Procurement*, p. 27, para. 4.4, see note 74.

98. Committee of Public Accounts, *Ministry of Defence: Procurement Irregularities*, Minutes of evidence, p. 10, q. 1241, see note 91.

99. Ibid.

100. Committee of Public Accounts, *Ministry of Defence: The Profit Formula*, Minutes of evidence, p. 2, para. 5, see note 96.

101. Public Concern at Work, *Blowing the Whistle on Defence Procurement*, p. 31, see note 79.

102. Committee of Public Accounts, *Ministry of Defence: Procurement Irregularities*, Minutes of Evidence, p. 1, para. 4, see note 91.

103. Ibid., p. v, para. 3.

104. National Audit Office, *Ministry of Defence: The Risk of Fraud in Defence Procurement*, p. 7, para. 1.6, see note 74.

5. The cost of non-Europe

1. Commission of the European Communities, *The Challenges Facing the European Defence-Related Industry, A Contribution for Action at European Level*, Com (96) 10, The Commission, Brussels, 24.1.96, p. 5, para. 2.1.1.

2. House of Commons Defence Committee and Trade and Industry Committee,

Aspects of Defence Procurement and Industrial Policy, First Report, Session 1995–6, HC 61, 62, London: HMSO, 1995, p. xiii, para. 24.

3. Commission of the European Communities, *The Challenges Facing the European Defence-related Industry*, p. 8, para. 2.1.3, see note 1.

4. Todd Sandler and Keith Hartley, *The Economics of Defense*, Cambridge: Cambridge University Press, 1995, p. 235.

5. House of Commons Defence Committee and Trade and Industry Committee, *Aspects of Defence Procurement and Industrial Policy: Minutes of Evidence, Tuesday 23 May 1995*, Session 1994–5, HC 333-iv, London: HMSO, 1995, p. 87, q. 358.

6. National Audit Office, *Ministry of Defence: Eurofighter 2000*, Report by the Comptroller and Auditor General, Session 1994–5, HC 724, London: HMSO, 11 August 1995, pp. 6–7, para. 2.30.

7. House of Commons Defence Committee and Trade and Industry Committee, *Aspects of Defence Procurement and Industrial Policy*, p. xvi, para. 32, see note 2.

8. National Audit Office, *Ministry of Defence: Eurofighter 2000*, see note 6.

9. Todd Sandler and Keith Hartley, *The Economics of Defense*, pp. 224–32, see note 4.

10. House of Commons Defence Committee and Trade and Industry Committee, *Aspects of Defence Procurement and Industrial Policy*, p. xiv, para. 27, see note 2.

11. Martyn Bittleston, 'Co-operation or competition? Defence procurement options for the 1990s', *Adelphi Papers* no. 250, Spring 1990, London: Brassey's for the IISS, pp. 12–13.

12. Todd Sandler and Keith Hartley, *The Economics of Defense*, p. 277, see note 4.

13. Paul Cornish, *The Arms Trade and Europe*, Chatham House Papers, London: Pinter, 1995, p. 15.

14. Juliet Lodge, 'European Community security policy: rhetoric or reality?', in Michael C. Pugh (ed.), *European security – towards 2000*, Manchester: Manchester University Press, 1992, pp. 50–1.

15. Todd Sandler and Keith Hartley, *The Economics of Defense*, pp. 228–9, see note 4.

16. See Philip Gummett, 'The future of the European armaments capability', Paper given at the ECPR Conference, Paris, 1995, p. 6, note 1.

17. Ibid. p. 6.

18. Paul Cornish, *The Arms Trade and Europe*, p. 19, see note 13.

19. See Neil Nugent, *The Government and Politics of the European Community*, 2nd edn, Basingstoke and London: Macmillan, 1991, pp. 404–5.

20. Anond Menon, Anthony Forster and William Wallace, 'A common European defence', *Survival*, vol. 34, no. 3, Autumn 1992, pp. 98–118.

21. House of Commons Defence Committee, *Western European Union*, Fourth Report, Session 1995–6, HC 105, London: HMSO, 8 May 1996, Minutes of evidence, pp. 4–5.

22. House of Commons Defence Committee and Trade and Industry Committee, *Aspects of Defence Procurement and Industrial Policy: Minutes of Evidence*, p. 70, see note 5.

23. Cited in Philip Gummett, 'The future of European armaments capability', p. 7, see note 16.

24. *Financial Times*, 12 January 1996; House of Commons Defence Committee and Trade and Industry Committee, *Aspects of Defence Procurement and Industrial Policy*, p. xv, paras 29–31, see note 2.

25. Commission of the European Communities, *The Challenges Facing the European Defence-related Industry*, see note 1.

26. Ibid., p. 4.

27. Monopolies and Mergers Commission, *British Aerospace Public Limited Company and VSEL plc: A report on the proposed merger*, London: HMSO, May 1995, Cm 2851, table 3.2, p. 28; Keith Hartley and Nick Hooper, *Study of the Value of the Defence Industry to the UK Economy: A Statistical Analysis for DTI, MOD, SBAC and DMA*, London: Department of Trade and Industry, 1995, p. 64.

28. *Financial Times*, 25 October 1995.

29. RUSI, 'Restructuring of French defence industries: a catalyst for consolidation of the European defence sector', *Newsbrief*, vol. 16, no. 9 (April 1996): 26; *Guardian*, 22 February 1996.

30. Commission of the European Communities, *The Challenges Facing European Defence-related Industry*, p. 3, see note 1.

31. Philip Gummett, 'The future of the European armaments capability', p. 5, see note 16.

32. Keith Hayward and Trevor Taylor, 'Governmental control of internationalised defence industrial concerns in Europe'. Paper given at the ECPR Conference, Paris, 1995, p. 3.

33. Philip Gummett, 'The future of the European armaments capability', p. 5, see note 16.

34. Commission of the European Communities, *The Challenges Facing the European defence-related Industry*, p. 6, see note 1.

35. Ibid., p. 7 and table 3, p. 32.

36. Keith Hartley, 'Economic premise and resource availability', in G.A.S.C. Wilson, *British Security 2010: Proceedings of a Conference held at Church House, Westminster November 1995* [no publisher, n.d., 1996], p. 231.

37. Trevor Taylor, *European Defence Co-operation*, Chatham House Papers 24, London: RIIA and Routledge and Kegan Paul, 1984, p. 60.

38. House of Commons Defence Committee, *The Appointment and Objectives of the Chief of Defence Procurement*, Fifth Report, Session 1984–5, HC 430, London: HMSO, 10 July 1985, Minutes of evidence, p. 27.

39. *Financial Times*, 8 October 1984.

40. Stuart Croft, 'The Westland Helicopter Crisis: Implications for the British Defence Industry', *Defence Analysis*, vol. 3, no. 4 (1987): 291–303.

41. National Audit Office, *Ministry of Defence: Collaborative Projects*, Report by the Comptroller and Auditor General, Session 1990–1, HC 247, London: HMSO, 26 February 1991, pp. 13–14.

42. Ibid.

43. House of Commons Defence Committee and Trade and Industry Committee, *Aspects of Defence Procurement and Industrial Policy: Minutes of Evidence*, p. 71, see note 5.

44. House of Commons Defence Committee and Trade and Industry Committee, *Aspects of Defence Procurement and Industrial Policy*, p. xiv, para. 26, see note 2.

45. House of Commons Defence Committee, *The Procurement of the Multiple Launch Rocket System and the Phoenix Remotely Piloted Vehicle*, Second Report, Session 1990–1, HC 49, London: HMSO, 1 March 1991, pp. viii–ix, para. 16.

46. House of Commons Defence Committee, *The Procurement of the EH101 Heli-*

copters and the Light Attack Helicopter, Third Report, Session 1989–90, HC 145, London: HMSO, 17 January 1990.

47. Stuart Croft and David H. Dunn, 'The impact of the defence budget on arms control policy', in Mark Hoffman (ed.), *UK Arms Control in the 1990s*, London: Manchester University Press, 1990, p. 58; *Independent*, 26 February 1987.

48. Personal interview with MOD representative, August 1990.

49. National Audit Office, *Ministry of Defence: Collaborative Projects*, p. 20, para. 4.15, see note 41.

50. Trevor Taylor, 'Defence industries in international relations', *Review of International Studies*, vol. 16, no. 1 (January 1990): 62.

51. *Guardian*, 13 June 1995.

52. House of Commons Defence Committee and Trade and Industry Committee, *Aspects of Defence Procurement and Industrial Policy*, p. xvii, para. 3, see note 2; *Defense News*, 12 June 1995, p. 70.

53. Personal interview, see note 48.

54. *Financial Times*, 26 January 1996.

55. Tom Dodd, *Europe – The Next Phase: The New European Community Structure for Foreign Affairs and Defence*, Research Note No 92/44, House of Commons Library, 15 May 1992, p. 2.

56. Philip Gummett, 'The future of the European armaments capability', p. 7, see note 16.

57. *Financial Times*, 27 February 1996; Paul Cornish, *The Arms Trade and Europe*, pp. 56–7, see note 13.

58. House of Commons Defence Committee and Trade and Industry Committee, *Aspects of Defence Procurement and Industrial Policy: Minutes of Evidence*, p. 86, q. 354, see note 5.

59. Dick Evans, 'European defence consolidation – challenge and opportunity', *RUSI Journal* (February 1996): 15.

60. *Government Reply to the First Reports from the Defence and Trade and Industry Committees Session 1995–96 on Aspects of Defence Procurement and Industrial Policy*, Session 1995–6, HC 209, 210, London: HMSO, 7 February 1996, p. viii, para. 30.

61. Ministry of Defence, *Statement on the Defence Estimates 1996*, London: HMSO, Cm 3223, 1996, table 10, pp. 66–7.

62. House of Commons Defence Committee and Trade and Industry Committee, *Aspects of Defence Procurement and Industrial Policy*, p. xiv, see note 2.

63. Commission of the European Communities, *The Challenges Facing European Defence-related Industry*, Annex, table 4, p. 32, see note 1.

64. Ibid.

65. House of Commons Defence Committee and Trade and Industry Committee, *Aspects of Defence Procurement and Industrial Policy: Minutes of Evidence*, p. 74, para. 2, see note 5.

6. The cost of British arms exports

1. MOD press release, *Intimate Government–Industry Teamwork Wins Britain Huge Defence Orders*, London: MOD, 11 November 1996.

2. Sir Alan Thomas, 'Attacked from all sides: the UK 20 per cent in the arms market?', *RUSI Journal* (February 1994): 43.

3. Jonathan Aitken, 'Defence procurement: past, present and future', *RUSI Journal* (February 1994): 41.

4. For a discussion on the merits of SIPRI and ACDA figures see Frank Blackaby and Thomas Ohlson, 'Military expenditure and the arms trade: problems of the data', in Christian Schmidt (ed.), *The Economics of Military Expenditures: Military Expenditures, Economic Growth and Fluctuations*, London: Macmillan, 1987.

5. MOD press release, see note 1.

6. US Arms Control and Disarmament Agency (ACDA), *World Military Expenditures and Arms Transfers 1995*, Washington DC: ACDA, 1996, p. 16, Table 6.

7. Ibid., p. 103, Table II.

8. Ibid., p. 149, Table II.

9. Ibid., p. 10, Table 4, and pp. 153–7, Table III.

10. Neil Cooper, 'British defence exports: trends, policy and security implications', *Contemporary Security Policy*, vol. 16, no. 2 (August 1995), pp. 219–39.

11. Exports to Saudi Arabia accounted for 98 per cent of all UK defence exports to the region between 1992 and 1994. Calculated from statistics given in ACDA, *World Military Expenditures and Arms Transfers 1995*, p. 155, Table III, see note 6.

12. Ibid., pp. 153–7, Table III.

13. *Guardian*, 'Tornado Rip-Off', 19 March 1989; *Guardian*, 'Mystery of the millions amassed by secretive son of Thatcher', 10 October 1994.

14. *Sunday Times*, 'An opportunist on a gravy train: how Thatcher made his millions', 9 October 1994.

15. Thomas Ohlson, *Arms Transfer Limitations and Third World Security*, Oxford: SIPRI and Oxford University Press, 1988, p. 138.

16. Abdullah M. Al-Ghrair and Nick Hooper, 'Saudi Arabia and offsets', in Stephen Martin (ed.), *The Economics of Offsets: Defence Procurement and Countertrade*, Amsterdam, Harwood Academic Publishers, 1996, p. 233.

17. Ministry of Defence, *Al Yamamah Offset*, London: MOD (undated), p. 1.

18. Joanna Spears, 'Britain and conventional arms transfer restraint', in Mark Hoffman (ed.), *UK Arms Control in the 1990s*, Manchester: Manchester University Press, 1990, p. 178.

19. Kleinwort Grieveson Investment Research, *Defence Bulletin I*, Kleinwort Grieveson, September 1986, p. 7.

20. *Financial Times*, 'Arms sales emerge from desert mirage', 30–31 January 1993.

21. *Guardian*, 'Thatcher was warned says MP', 11 October 1994.

22. Although even by defence industry standards this does seem a rather incredible sum. *Independent*, 'MPs may investigate Saudi arms sales bribery claims', 11 May 1992.

23. *Jane's Defence Weekly*, 'Getting a slice of the action', 13 February 1994, pp. 38–41.

24. *International Herald Tribune*, 'Saudis inform US firms of cash crunch', 8 January 1994.

25. ACDA, *World Military Expenditures and Arms Transfers 1995*, p. 149, Table II, see note 6.

26. Ministry of Defence, *UK Defence Statistics, 1996*, London: HMSO, p. 21, Table 1.1.

27. National Audit Office, Report by the Comptroller and Auditor General, *Ministry of Defence: Defence Procurement in the 1990s*, London: HMSO, 1994, p. 33, para. 5.23.

28. Personal interview, 1996.

29. Lawrence Freedman, *Arms Production in the UK: Problems and Prospects*, London: Royal Institute of International Affairs, 1978, p. 29.

30. Foreign Affairs Committee, *Public Expenditure: Pergau Hydro-Electric Project, Malaysia, the Aid and Trade Provision and Related Matters*, vol. II. Third Report, Session 1993–4, HC 271-II, London: HMSO, 1994, Minutes of evidence, p. 326.

31. Scilla Elworthy and Paul Ingram (eds), *International Control of the Arms Trade*, Oxford Research Group, Current Decisions Report, no. 8, 1992, pp. 12–15.

32. Keith Hartley, 'Aerospace: the political economy of an industry', in H.W. de Jong (ed.), *The Structure of European Industry*, 2nd edn, Dordrecht, The Netherlands: Kluwer Academic Publishers, 1988.

33. *The Economist*, 'Giving arms a hand', 5 November 1994, pp. 32–3.

34. National Audit Office, Report by the Comptroller and Auditor General, *Ministry of Defence: Support for Defence Exports*, HC 303, London: HMSO, 10 April 1989, p. 30, para. 4.8.

35. House of Commons Defence Committee and House of Commons Trade and Industry Committee, *Aspects of Defence Procurement and Industrial Policy*, Memoranda, Session 1994–5, HC 333, London: HMSO, p. 103.

36. World Development Movement, *Gunrunners Gold: How the Public's Money Finances Arms Sales*, London: WDM, 1995, pp. 19–34.

37. *Independent*, 'Taxpayers face £940 million credit bill', 13 November 1992.

38. *Official Report*, written answers, col. 337, 26 February 1996, vol. 272, no. 57, London: HMSO.

39. Sir Richard Scott, *Report of the Inquiry into the Export of Defence Equipment and Dual-Use Goods to Iraq and Related* Prosecutions, vol. 1, London: HMSO, 1996, pp. 236–57; also see John Sweeney, *Trading with the Enemy: Britain's Arming of Iraq*, London: Pan Books, 1993, p. 133.

40. Overseas Trade Services, Projects and Export Policy Division, *Countertrade: A Guide for Exporters 1993/94 Edition*, Stratford on Avon: DTI Export Publications, 1994, p. 1.

41. Foreign Affairs Committee, *Public Expenditure: Pergau Hydro-Electric Project*, p. 15, see note 30.

42. *The Economist*, 'The curse of Pergau', 5 March 1994, p. 30.

43. Ronald Mathews, 'Butter for guns: the growth of under-the-counter trade', *The World Today*, vol. 48, no. 5, May 1992, pp. 87–90.

44. *Wall Street Journal Europe*, 28–29 January, 1994.

45. *Arms Sales Monitor*, no. 31, (5 December 1995): 7.

46. Foreign Affairs Committee, *Public Expenditure: Pergau Hydro-Electric Project*, vol. I, p. xlvi, para. 114, see note 30.

47. Ibid., vol. II, pp. 112–31.

48. Personal interview with a defence industry representative, March 1993.

49. *Guardian*, 13 November 1995.

50. Letter to Bruce George MP from MOD, 7 October 1994.

51. World Development Movement, *Gunrunners Gold*, p.12, see note 36.

52. MOD press release, *Intimate Government–Industry/Teamwork*, see note 1.

53. Letter to Bruce George MP, see note 50.

54. World Development Movement, *Gunrunners Gold*, p. 13, see note 36.

55. Charles Drace-Francis, 'From policies to specific decisions', in Trevor Taylor

and Imai Ryuukichi (eds), *Security Challenges for Japan and Europe in a Post-Cold War World. Vol. III – The Defence Trade: Demand, Supply and Control*, London: Royal Institute of International Affairs and Institute for International Policy Studies, 1994, p. 153.

56. *Guardian*, 'Clinton backs drive to sell arms abroad', 17 November 1994.

57. William D. Hartung, *Welfare for Weapons Dealers: The Hidden Costs of the Arms Trade*, World Policy Papers, New York: World Policy Institute, 1996.

58. For an overview of the general literature on military expenditure and economic growth, see Steve Chan, 'The impact of defense spending on economic performance: a survey of evidence and problems', *Orbis* (Summer 1985): 403–34. For analyses of the UK experience in particular see J.P. Dunne and R.P. Smith, 'The economic consequences of reduced UK military expenditure', *Cambridge Journal of Economics*, 8: 297–310; Ron Smith, 'Defence spending in the United Kingdom', in Keith Hartley and Todd Sandler (eds), *The Economics of Defence Spending: An International Survey*, London and New York: Routledge, 1990, pp. 76–92; Mary Kaldor, *The Baroque Arsenal*, London: Sphere Books (Abacus), 1983; Malcolm Chalmers, *Military Spending and British Decline*, London: Pluto Press, 1985; Sir Ieuan Maddock, *Civil Exploitation of Defence Technology*, Report to the Electronics EDC, London: National Economic Development Office, February 1993; CSS (Council for Science and Society), *UK Military R&D*, Oxford: Oxford University Press.

59. Ron Smith 'Defence spending in the United Kingdom', p. 88, see note 58.

60. John Bourn, *Securing Value for Money in Defence Procurement*, RUSI Whitehall Paper Series, London: RUSI, 1994, p. 8.

61. Ron Smith, 'Military expenditure and capitalism: a reply', *Cambridge Journal of Economics*, 2 (1978): 299–304; Steve Chan, 'The impact of defense spending on economic performance, p. 417, see note 58.

62. For an overview of the general literature, see Steve Chan, 'The impact of defense spending on economic performance', see note 58.

63. *Observer*, 20 June 1982.

64. *Sunday Telegraph*, '30 UK companies part of Iraqi procurement network', 15 November 1992.

65. Richard Norton-Taylor, *Truth is a Difficult Concept*, London: Fourth Estate, 1995, p. 53.

66. Elworthy and Ingram, *International Control of the Arms Trade*, see note 31.

67. Memo by Indonesian Human Rights Campaign (TAPOL), pp. 279–88, see note 30.

68. MOD press release, 'UK and UAE sign defence co-operation accord', 28 November 1996.

69. *Jane's Defence Weekly*, 'Offsets: creating collateral benefits', 18 March 1995, pp. 53–60.

70. Joanna Spear, 'Relations with the South', in Stuart Croft (ed.), *British Security Policy: The Thatcher Years and the End of the Cold War*, London: HarperCollins Academic, 1991, p. 195.

71. Edward A. Kolodziej, *Making and Marketing Arms: The French Experience and its Implications for the International System*, Princeton, NJ: Princeton University Press, 1987, p. 102.

72. Malcolm Rifkind (secretary of state for defence), *Nato and the Post-Cold War World*, text of a speech given at Chatham House, 16 December 1993. p. 7.

73. *Guardian.* 'MOD censors Gulf War questions', 26 October 1994.

74. House of Commons Defence Committee, *The Appointment of the Head of Defence Export Services*, First Report, Session 1989–90, HC 14, London: HMSO, 1989.

75. *Guardian* 'Doubt and dismay greet BBC Arabic satellite venture', 20 June 1994.

76. Personal interview with a journalist, June 1994.

77. *Independent*, 'Secret deals in arms and bananas that condemned a man to exile', 5 January 1996.

78. Ibid.

79. *Guardian*, 'Doris and those monster morals', 20 January 1996.

80. *Independent*, 'Secret deals in arms and bananas that condemned a man to exile', see note 77.

81. *Guardian*, 'Saudi's victory stuns Howard', 6 March 1996.

82. *Guardian*, 'Major vows crackdown on foreign activists', 15 March 1996.

83. *Guardian*, 'Terrorists lose satellite haven', 22 March 1996.

84. *Guardian*, 'Saudis assured law change will stop terrorists', 3 July 1996.

85. Ibid.

86. Foreign Affairs Committee, *Public Expenditure: Pergau Hydro-Electric Project*, p. ix, para. 15, see note 30.

87. Ibid., vol. II, p. 113.

88. *Guardian*, 'Blame for Hurd over Pergau aid', 11 November 1994.

89. John Sweeney, Trading with the enemy', p. 28, see note 39.

90. *Independent*, 'Labour MP challenges response over exports', 17 Nov. 1992; Richard Norton-Taylor, *Truth is a Difficult Concept*, p. 53, see note 65.

91. Richard Norton-Taylor, *Truth is a Difficult Concept*, pp. 52–3, see note 65.

92. *Financial Times*, 'MPs hear of heavy sales to Iraq', 12 January 1993.

93. John Sweeney, *Trading with the Enemy*, p. 118, see note 39.

94. Alan Friedman, *The Spider's Web: Bush, Saddam, Thatcher and the Decade of Deceit*, London and Boston: Faber and Faber, 1993, p. 172.

95. *Independent*, 'Britain knew of Iraqi arms route', 1 May 1993; *Financial Times*, 'Government knew of arms sales to Iraq via Jordan', 18 May 1993.

96. Richard Norton-Taylor, *Truth is a Difficult Concept*, pp. 54–5, see note 65; Alan Friedman, *The Spider's Web*, pp. 171–2, see note 94.

97. John Sweeney, *Trading with the Enemy*, p. 113, see note 39.

98. Sir Richard Scott, *Report of the Inquiry into the Export of Defence Equipment and Dual-Use Goods to Iraq and Related Prosecutions*, vol. I, p. 489, para. D4.30, see note 39.

99. Richard Norton-Taylor, *Truth is a Difficult Concept*, p. 145, see note 65.

100. Paul Eavis and Oliver Sprague, 'Does Britain need to sell weapons?', in John Gittings and Ian Davies (eds), *Britain in the 21st Century: Rethinking defence and foreign policy*, Nottingham: Spokesman, 1996, p. 129.

101. *Guardian*, 'Libel payout blow to minister', 29 July 1995.

102. *Inter-Press Service International News* Europe-Armaments: 'EU Urged to help curb arms sales', 30 June 1994.

103. Sir Alan Thomas, 'Attacked from all sides', p. 44, see note 2.

7. Inefficiency in procurement

1. Ministry of Defence, *UK Defence Statistics 1996*, London: HMSO, 1996, p. 20, Table 1.10.

2. Keith Hartley and Nick Hooper, *Study of the Value of the Defence Industry to the UK Economy: A Statistical Analysis for DTI, MOD, SBAC and DMA*, London: DTI, 1995, p. 37.

3. House of Commons Defence Committee and Trade and Industry Committee, *Aspects of Defence Procurement and Industrial Policy*, First Report, Session 1995–6, HC 61, 62, London: HMSO, 1995, p. xxxix, para. 71.

4. House of Commons Defence Committee and Trade and Industry Committee, *Aspects of Defence Procurement: Minutes of Evidence, Tuesday 23 May 1995*, Session 1994–5, HC 333-iv, London: HMSO, 1995, p. 66-A1 (a).

5. House of Commons Defence Committee, *Statement on the Defence Estimates 1996*, Seventh Report, Session 1995–6, HC 215, London: HMSO, 1996, p. xvii, para. 56.

6. Keith Hartley 'Economic premise and resource availability', in G.A.S.C. Wilson (ed.), *British Security 2010: Proceedings of a Conference Held at Church House, Westminster, November 1995* [no publisher, n.d., 1996], p. 231.

7. David L.I. Kirkpatrick, 'The rising unit cost of defence equipment – the reasons and the results', *Defence and Peace Economics*, vol. 6, no. 4 (1995): 285.

8. Steven Schofield, 'The Levene reforms: an evaluation', *Defense Analysis*, vol. 11, no. 2 (1995): 157.

9. National Audit Office, *Ministry of Defence: Major Projects Report 1994*, Session 1994–5, HC 436, 1995, p. 3, para. 2.3.

10. Ibid., p. 12, fig. 5.

11. Lawrence Freedman, 'Britain and nuclear weapons', in Michael Clarke and Philip Sabin (eds), *British Defence Choices for the 21st Century*, London: Brassey's, 1993, p. 225.

12. House of Commons Defence Committee, *The Progress of the Trident Programme*, Sixth Report, Session 1992–3, HC 549, London: HMSO, 1993, p. vii, para. 7.

13. House of Commons Defence Committee, *Statement on the Defence Estimates 1996*, p. 101, table b, see note 5.

14. Ministry of Defence, *UK Defence Statistics 1996*, p. 12, table 1.3, see note 1.

15. National Audit Office, *Ministry of Defence: Major Projects Report 1994*, p. 4, fig. 1, see note 9.

16. Martyn Bittleston, 'Co-operation or competition? Defence procurement options for the 1990s, *Adelphi Papers*, no. 250, Spring 1990, London: Brassey's for the IISS, p. 63.

17. National Audit Office, *Ministry of Defence: Major Projects Report 1994* , p. 19, para. 2.33. b, see note 9.

18. Steven Schofield, 'The Levene reforms', p. 152, see note 8.

19. National Audit Office, *Ministry of Defence: Major Projects Report 1993*, HC 356, London: HMSO, 1994, p. 9, para. 3.5.

20. National Audit Office, *Ministry of Defence: Defence Procurement in the 1990s*, HC 390, London: HMSO, 1994, p. 13, para. 2.11 (ii).

21. Ibid.

22. National Audit Office, *Ministry of Defence: Major Projects Report 1993*, p. 9, para. 3.5, see note 19.

23. National Audit Office, *Ministry of Defence: Major Projects Report 1994*, p. 8, para. 2.15, see note 9; National Audit Office, *Ministry of Defence: Defence Procurement in the 1990s*, p. 12, para. 2.11(a), see note 20.

24. National Audit Office, *Ministry of Defence: Defence Procurement in the 1990s*, p. 13, para. 2.11, see note 20.

25. Todd Sandler and Keith Hartley, *The Economics of Defense*, Cambridge: Cambridge University Press, 1995, p. 195.

26. Committee of Public Accounts, *The 1989 Statement on Major Defence Projects*, Eleventh Report, Session 1990–1, HC 373, London: HMSO, 1991, p. 45, q. 4576–7.

27. Committee of Public Accounts, *Ministry of Defence: Major Projects Report 1994: Minutes of Evidence*, Session 1994–5, HC 487-I, London: HMSO, 1995, p. 19, q. 46.

28. National Audit Office, *Ministry of Defence: Major Projects Report 1994*, p. 15, para. 2.23, see note 9.

29. House of Commons Defence Committee, *Statement on the Defence Estimates 1994*, Sixth Report, Session 1993–4, HC 68, 1994, p. xvii, para. 27.

30. Committee of Public Accounts, *Ministry of Defence: Major Projects Report 1994: Minutes of Evidence*, p. 9, q. 50, see note 27.

31. National Audit Office, *Ministry of Defence: Major Projects Report 1994*, p. 15, para. 2.24, see note 9.

32. National Audit Office, *Ministry of Defence: Design and Procurement of Warships*, HC 423, London: HMSO, 1985, p. 10, para. 3.10

33. House of Commons Defence Committee, *Statement on the Defence Estimates 1996*, Minutes of evidence, p. 43, q. 1222, see note 5.

34. Ibid., p. 27, A. 4.

8. Conclusion

1. Thomas L. McNaugher, 'Weapons procurement: the futility of reform', *International Security*, vol. 12, no. 2 (Fall 1987): 63–104; Theo Farrell, 'Waste in weapons acquisition: how the Americans do it all wrong', *Contemporary Security Policy*, vol. 16, no. 2 (August 1995): 192–218; Jacques S. Gansler, *Affording Defense*, Cambridge MA, MIT Press, 1989.

2. Keith Hartley and Nick Hooper, *A Study of the Value of the Defence Industry to the UK Economy: A Statistical Analysis for DTI, MOD, SBAC and DMA*, London: DTI, 1995, p. xi.

3. House of Commons Defence Committee and Trade and Industry Committee, *Aspects of Defence Procurement and Industrial Policy: Minutes of Evidence Tuesday 23 May 1995*, Session 1994–5, HC 333-iv, London: HMSO, 1995, p. 71, para. 35.

4. Statistic derived from information provided by Labour research on company political donations to the Conservative Party.

5. National Audit Office, *Ministry of Defence: Major Projects Report 1994*, Session 1994–5, HC 436, London: HMSO, 1995, p. 5, para. 2.7.

6. National Audit Office, *Ministry of Defence: Initiatives to Manage Technical Risk on Defence Equipment Programmes*, Session 1995–6, HC 361, London: HMSO 1996, pp. 42–4.

7. House of Commons Defence Committee and Trade and Industry Committee, *Aspects of Defence Procurement and Industrial Policy*, First Report, Session 1995–6, HC 61, 62, London: HMSO, 1995, p. xviii, para. 41.

8. See for example David Omand, 'Nuclear deterrence in a changing world: the view from a UK perpsective', *RUSI Journal* (June 1996): 15–22.

9. Ibid.

10. Patrick Dunleavy, 'Policy disasters: explaining the UK's record', *Public Policy and Administration*, vol. 10, no. 2 (Summer 1995): 52–70.

11. Sue Willett, 'What are the implications of a declining defence budget?', in John Gittings and Ian Davies (eds), *Britain in the 21st Century: Rethinking defence and foreign policy*, Nottingham: Spokesman, 1996, p. 141.

12. Cited in Neil Cooper, 'Front line first: a fur coat and no knickers', *Parliamentary Brief*, vol. 4 no. 2 (November 1995): 29.

13. David Greenwood, 'Concentration of effort and complementarity', in Michael Clarke and Philip Sabin (eds), *British Defence Choices for the 21st Century*, London: Brassey's, 1993, p. 181.

14. Malcolm Chalmers, 'What do we need the armed forces for?', in John Gittings and Ian Davies (eds), *Britain in the 21st Century*, see note 11.

15. Keith Hartley, 'Economic premise and resource availability', in G.A.S.C. Wilson (ed.), *British Security 2010*, 1996, p. 224; Joint Agencies, *The Case for Aid: A Manifesto*, 1996, p. 3.

16. United Nations Development Programme, *Human Development Report 1994*, Oxford: Oxford University Press, 1994.

Index